Rachael Denhollander is a hero. She chose to speak her truth when it was painful, difficult, and certainly not the "comfortable" route to take. By doing so, she has played a significant role in making our beautiful sport safer and in protecting the livelihoods of countless child athletes. I will always stand beside her in solidarity and admiration, and I applaud her for taking the additional step of telling more of her story with this book. I know firsthand how challenging that can be, and I thank her for her courage.

DOMINIQUE MOCEANU, *New York Times* bestselling author and Olympic gold medalist

As men, we're taught not to be afraid, not to ask for help, not to be victims. And so when abuse happens to us, we feel powerless to fight it. That's my own story, but with God's help, I've learned a better way. And through *What Is a Girl Worth?*, we can all learn how to walk together toward a safer, brighter future. Do not miss this incredible true story of Rachael Denhollander, the woman who stopped an abuser. She is a living example of grace and strength in the fight against evil, and I'm standing by her side.

TERRY CREWS, actor

This is one of the most important books you'll ever read.

BETH MOORE, *New York Times* bestselling author and sexual abuse survivor

Rachael Denhollander stared down evil and changed the world. Parts of her memoir are heartbreaking, but it is ultimately uplifting, a story of faith, courage, and love. Rachael has become known internationally, but this book goes so much deeper than anything that has been said about her. It is a riveting memoir.

MARK ALESIA, reporter who first interviewed Rachael for the *Indianapolis Star*

I was utterly inspired by Rachael even before reading her memoir. But reading the story behind the story further cements my belief that this woman is a hero in every sense of the word. The courage it took to come forward and bring Larry Nassar to justice is amplified by the struggle it took to get to that point. Her willingness to put herself in harm's way to protect future generations drove her to speak out even when she thought the world might not hear her. This unflinching narrative, replete with the harrowing details of the impact of abuse and the traumatic emotional aftermath, is an act of bravery in and of itself.

JENNIFER SEY, 1986 national gymnastics champion, seven times national team member, and author of the bestseller *Chalked Up: My Life in Elite Gymnastics*

Rachael's account of her abuse shatters our certainties. A well-loved and protected child is abused by those assumed to be good. Hearing such stories makes us want to deceive ourselves. We want to look away and deny. Rachael teaches us clearly that deceit—not truth—is our enemy. The hard truth of her story brings light and hope. May we, like Rachael, have the courage to listen to the God of all truth as He teaches us through her words and her life.

DIANE LANGBERG, PHD, psychologist

No two sexual abuse cases are exactly alike, yet Rachael Denhollander's story reveals what they all have in common and the part we all can play in preventing abuse, defending the vulnerable, and pursuing justice. Sexual abuse does not take place only in dark alleys late at night. It occurs in brightly lit offices and in quiet church sanctuaries, in public spaces and in the privacy of homes. If you don't understand how this can be, please read this book. If you know too well why this is, you have even more reason to read this book. Rachael writes with moral clarity grounded in biblical truth and love. *What Is a Girl Worth?* is a must-read for anyone who cares about protecting precious lives from predators and pursuing justice for those for whom we were too late.

KAREN SWALLOW PRIOR, author of *On Reading Well: Finding the Good Life through Great Books* and *Fierce Convictions: The Extraordinary Life of Hannah More—Poet, Reformer, Abolitionist*

What Is a Girl Worth?

WHAT IS A GIRL WORTH?

My story of breaking the silence and exposing the truth
about Larry Nassar and USA Gymnastics

RACHAEL DENHOLLANDER

TYNDALE
MOMENTUM®

The nonfiction imprint of
Tyndale House Publishers, Inc.

Visit Tyndale online at www.tyndale.com.

Visit Tyndale Momentum online at www.tyndalemomentum.com.

TYNDALE, *Tyndale Momentum*, and Tyndale's quill logo are registered trademarks of Tyndale House Publishers, Inc. The Tyndale Momentum logo is a trademark of Tyndale House Publishers, Inc. Tyndale Momentum is the nonfiction imprint of Tyndale House Publishers, Inc., Carol Stream, Illinois.

What Is a Girl Worth?: My Story of Breaking the Silence and Exposing the Truth about Larry Nassar and USA Gymnastics

Designed by Dean H. Renninger

Published in association with the literary agency of United Talent Agency, LLC, 888 Seventh Avenue, 7th Floor, New York, New York 10106, USA.

Scripture quotations are taken from the New American Standard Bible,® copyright © 1960, 1962, 1963, 1968, 1971, 1972, 1973, 1975, 1977, 1995 by The Lockman Foundation. Used by permission.

The names and distinguishing details of some people in this book have been changed to protect their privacy.

For information about special discounts for bulk purchases, please contact Tyndale House Publishers at csresponse@tyndale.com, or call 1-800-323-9400.

ISBN 978-1-4964-4133-1

Printed in the United States of America

25	24	23	22	21	20	19
7	6	5	4	3	2	1

For every survivor
from every background and identity,
those who came before,
those yet to come,
and those who are no longer with us.

It is not your fault.

It is not your shame.

You are believed.

May you know how much you are worth.

Author's Note

This account is my record of the events that led me to speak out against my own abuser and expose the harm done by perpetrators, as well as the damage that follows when institutions minimize or ignore abuse. I have changed some names and identifying details to protect the privacy of individuals. While describing events, I relied not only on my memory but on my personal correspondence, media reports, court transcripts, and medical and legal records. As with any memoir, this version of my story is uniquely my own.

Prologue

August 4, 2016
10:32 a.m.

To whom it may concern . . .

I didn't expect to be writing an email that morning. With three children under five, I wanted, and needed, to spend my daytime hours savoring the simple, rich delights of my kids—and getting in a few hours of my own work whenever I could. My husband, Jacob, was a full-time graduate student and held down a job, so he was rarely home before dinner.

That morning, looking for the grocery list I'd typed up the night before, I logged into my laptop. As it happens, I had left my Facebook tab open. That's when I saw it—a trending news story posted just a few hours earlier: "A Blind Eye to Sex Abuse: How USA Gymnastics Failed to Report Cases."

There's a shocker, I thought. My husband and I had been appealing to church leaders over a similar issue involving another church they had been supporting, and the wound felt very fresh. I glanced around to make sure my five-year-old son, already a fluent reader, was nowhere nearby, and I clicked the link. What I read filled me with a grief I can't express: USA Gymnastics had been systematically burying reports of sexual misconduct in a filing cabinet—complaints about fifty-four member coaches over ten years—and some of those coaches had gone on to abuse little girls for years.[1] I wanted to cry. I knew all too well what those precious children had endured.

At the bottom of the article was this notice: "*IndyStar* will continue to investigate this topic." The reporters had provided an email address where readers could send tips. My stomach turned. At that moment I was certain of two things.

First, I was right. The United States of America Gymnastics (USAG) had been burying sexual abuse cases to save face. *If they protected their coaches*, I'd reasoned, *they absolutely would have protected* him. *They would never have listened to me.*

And second, this was the moment for which I had been waiting and watching for nearly sixteen years. Someone had blown the whistle on how USAG handled sex abuse. That meant someone had spoken up. More important, that person had been *believed*. And the article was trending. That meant the public was paying attention.

Right then and there, with my teething baby bundled on my back, I broke my steadfast rule about emailing during the day. As I bounced back and forth to keep baby Ellianna calm, I typed:

> I am emailing to report an incident. . . . I was not molested by my coach, but I was molested by Dr. Larry Nassar, the team doctor for USAG. I was fifteen years old.

I paused for a second. I knew exactly what it would mean for me and my family if the *IndyStar* team decided to pick up the story. I'd known for years what the cost would be. But it had to be done, and if it wasn't done now, it might never happen.

> I have the medical records showing my treatment. . . . They are in a file cabinet at my parents' house, which is several hours away.

I knew my evidence was scant, but I could tell by the way the *IndyStar* investigation had been done that these reporters understood the dynamics of sexual assault, what evidence looks like, and what patterns are often in place. They had seen the dark underbelly of USAG because they had believed the survivors of the coaches' abuse. Still . . . I knew what it felt like to speak up and be dismissed.

> I did not ever report Nassar to anyone, except my own coach, some years later. . . . I was told not to tell the owner of the gym . . . it would come back on me. I decided against going to the police . . . it was my word against his. . . . I was confident I would not be believed.

I looked around my kitchen. We'd barely finished breakfast, and I was writing an email that—if it did what I needed it to do—would completely upend our lives. I gave myself a mental shake, firmly pushed down the fear and nausea, and typed two final sentences:

> I have seen little hope that any light would be shed by coming forward, so I have remained quiet. If there is a possibility that is changing, I will come forward as publicly as necessary.

Then I hit Send.

1

"WHY DIDN'T YOU SAY SOMETHING SOONER?"

I have been asked that question more times than I can count. Sometimes it is motivated by a genuine desire to understand, and sometimes it's articulated like a weapon, casting doubt over whether my abuse even occurred. The truth is, I *did* say something sooner—many of us did. But as survivors of sexual assault will tell you, saying something is one thing. Being heard—and believed—is another.

Bullies and predators prey on the defenseless. They count on victims being unable to protect themselves. More important, they count on *everyone else* being too afraid to confront them. I hate injustice, but I hate silence and apathy in the face of injustice even more. Far too often, bullies' belief that no one will challenge them is both well-founded and devastating for the people they target. But it doesn't have to be this way.

I have always had a strong sense of justice and a desire to protect others. Once when I was around seven, my mom took me, my little brother, Joshua, and my little sister, Bethany, to McDonald's for a playdate with friends.

This particular restaurant had a play area with a ball pit, winding tubes, and a twisting slide guaranteed to administer a near-lethal static shock the moment you sat down and—by the time you reached the bottom—to turn even the tamest hair into a spot-on replica of Albert Einstein's.

The tunnels and ball pit were my favorite parts of the play area. So many adventures could be imagined amidst the plastic twisting labyrinth—so much "scope for imagination."[2] (Anne of Green Gables meets Ronald McDonald?)

I was hard at work scoping out the plastic tunnels for enemy invaders when I saw it. Just below me, through one of the plastic windows covered in greasy fingerprints, I noticed a boy about my age kicking my brother and sister.

A fierce wave of emotion enveloped me. As the oldest and strongest, I knew what my job was—*to protect those who couldn't protect themselves*. I had known it from the moment my mom brought my baby brother home from the hospital when I was about two and a half. It was one of those moments that seems completely unremarkable, and yet to this day, it stands out in my memory.

My baby brother was brand-new, and the most amazing tiny person I could imagine. I wanted so badly to take care of Joshua that my mom let me "help" with diaper changes, explaining every step of the process. And it was a process. In 1987, cloth diapers weren't today's fancy preformed ones with snaps, pockets, and inserts. They were the old-fashioned kind that you had to fold and pin on with enormous safety pins. I remember as if it were yesterday my mom teaching me how to do it—showing me how to fold the cloth to make the correct shape, where the diaper should fall on the baby's little belly, and how to check the legs to make sure the diaper was fitting properly. Then she did something that was forever burned in my mind. She tucked her index and middle finger under the edges where the diaper met and said, "Always remember to put your fingers between the diaper and the baby, *exactly* where you are going to push the pin through. That way, if the pin slips and someone gets hurt, it's the mom and not the baby.

"The most important thing, Rachael," she had said, "is to keep the little ones safe." And my mom did that by sacrificing herself.

Then she outfitted me with my own set of cloth diapers and pins and let me practice on my Cabbage Patch doll. Every time I changed its diaper, I did it just as she'd shown me, folding it precisely, checking my doll's position on the diaper, and inspecting the leg openings. Then I'd put my fingers between the diaper and my doll, turn the fold over to make sure my fingers were in the right spot, take a deep breath, and push the pin through. And do you know what? I never once poked my doll. Of course, every time I practiced, I felt a twinge of concern that I'd jab my finger with that pin. But I just kept reminding myself, *The most important thing is to protect the baby. That's my job.*

Five years later at McDonald's, that instinct was every bit as strong. *That's my job.*

I scrambled down the slide as fast as I could, not even trying to avoid the shock-inducing metal bolts, and ran over to the older boy. I reached my siblings in record time, and without hesitating, grabbed the bully's wrists. I pulled him away from my siblings and held my arms stiff to keep my body away from his swinging foot. He glared at me and tried to free his wrists, yelling for me to let go. I took a deep breath and quietly held on. I didn't strike back; I just felt fiercely protective and resolved. I made sure to look the boy squarely in the eyes as I spoke firmly and calmly.

"Stop. You're hurting them, and you're old enough to know better. If you try to hurt anyone again, I'll go find a grown-up."

He tried to fight back. I held on.

"Stop," I repeated. "You're old enough to know better."

Angrily he paused and then grunted a defiant "Fine."

My siblings were now out of reach, so I let go and the boy stomped away. My mom and the mother of our friends, who had looked up from their table outside the play area to see me holding the boy's wrists, made it to the door and popped their heads in.

"Is everything okay?" my mother called out.

I glanced over my shoulder at the boy, now sulking in the distance.

"We're fine," I assured her.

We went back to playing, and I was filled with relief. My siblings weren't hurt. I'd done my job. I had used what I'd been given—my age, my strength, and my words—to protect them.

I knew what to do that day because I'd been explicitly taught that you always have a right to defend yourself and others. My parents even gave me specific guidelines for what speaking up should look like and had me practice, so if I ever did need to speak up, I would know exactly what to do and say.

"You always have a right to defend yourself and others," they had said, "but never ever lash out in anger. Don't become what you are fighting. Do only what is necessary to keep everyone safe."

In other words, my motivation needed to be love—not anger, not revenge—which meant doing only what was necessary to restrain without a desire to harm the other person.

They also taught me that often kids who act out are angry and hurting, so it was important to feel compassion for them too. They told me to tell bullies the truth and remind them that they could, and *should*, be better—that they were responsible for their choices. And they told me to seek the help of an authority figure rather than angrily mete out my own form of justice.

• • •

Given these early lessons from my parents—as well as the fact that I was incredibly stubborn and argumentative if I felt I was in the right—I don't think my mom and dad were surprised when, at age eight, I announced that I wanted to become an attorney someday so I could protect families and children. I drew up my first "contract" not long afterward.

I had determined one afternoon that my mother was spending too much time on the phone helping a friend through a crisis and not enough time helping me with my math homework. I vividly remember my frustration. I knew her discussions were important, but goodness, if she expected me to do my math, she had to hold up her end of the bargain! We simply had to have some concrete, definable boundaries in this household. So in exasperation, I found a piece of paper and a pencil and sat down to fix this problem. Righteous indignation burning within me, I drew up a contract. I outlined an agreement in which she would pledge to spend a specified, limited amount of time on the phone and a required amount of time helping me with my math. In exchange, I would complete my lessons. Then I drew two lines at the bottom—a place for each of us to sign—and brought it to her. I got my point across. In the future, my math lessons were completed in a timely manner, and my parents continued to opine that law was a natural career choice for me.

I was blessed to have parents who recognized that stubbornness, properly directed, becomes perseverance and determination. As my mom would often remind me, our greatest weaknesses are also often our greatest strengths—*if* we direct them properly. So rather than attempting to squelch this part of my personality, they taught me how to channel it and use it to my advantage. Most important, they taught me to check my motivations. Was I fighting for something because I just wanted to win—even if I was technically right—or was I fighting for something because I loved God and other people? If all I wanted was to be right and win, I would ultimately be motivated by arrogance, and I would be tempted to compromise, bend or twist facts, manipulate, and maybe even ignore parts of the truth. If I were motivated solely by the desire to triumph, my gifts could become dangerous to others, and ultimately, to myself. But the safeguard against this, they told me, was to be motivated instead by love.

Love would ensure a willingness to hear and see the truth, even if it meant admitting I was wrong. Love would ensure compassion even for those who did wrong, while still enabling fierce pursuit of the truth. To that end, I was given the tools for speaking up early and often, and I was given permission to use them.

So I did.

The idea many people want to cling to—that survivors just don't know how to speak up—simply isn't true. It's a notion we need to let go of and instead do a better job understanding what really keeps victims silent.

A common thread in the societal response to abuse is the argument "I'm not saying it was her fault; I'm just saying I'd have responded differently." It feels safer to believe abuse happens only to people who "let it." But this is in fact blaming the victim, because it implies that if victims had just responded differently, they could have stopped the abuse. This myth needs to be abandoned, and we need to make an effort to better understand why survivors don't speak up during, or even after, abuse.

The truth is, I had the tools I needed, and I knew how to use them from an early age. Yet when the time came, they were not enough to help me be heard and be believed.

2

"I'M NOT ALLOWED OUT of the house very often," I whispered timidly, shrinking back against the office chair. "And it is distressing to be in public."

"Don't. You. Dare!" my mom threatened, clearly trying not to burst out laughing.

We were at the pulmonologist's office. I was around twelve. I had severe, persistent asthma, and the clinic we went to required a yearly checkup, not only with my doctor, but also with a social worker and a child psychologist. And because it was part of a teaching school, sometimes a resident or two would accompany the physician and caseworker. Homeschooling was still relatively rare in the 1990s, so when my medical team learned I was taught at home, they usually had a lot of questions. That is why I had a rather wicked desire to play up all the homeschool stereotypes, just to see what they'd do.

"You're going to get us both reported!" my mom said with a grin. We were still laughing when the psychologist and resident opened the exam room door and asked what was so funny. I didn't tell, although I knew that, unfortunately, they sometimes had good reasons to ask questions.

I actually loved that medical clinic. My pulmonologist was great, and his nurse, Margaret, had been my favorite since I was very young. Shortly after this visit, she transferred to a research department, but she would come up to visit me anytime I was in, and I would jokingly offer to let her conduct experiments on me if it meant we got to visit her more.

I also loved being homeschooled, and not just because of the fodder it provided for inside jokes. The opportunities it afforded were priceless. My parents believed in the value of diligence and a good work ethic, so in addition to classwork, I held a wide variety of jobs. By the time I turned eleven, I was babysitting, and I was already nannying part-time before I was in my teens. Sometimes that meant school had to be done in the evenings, on weekends, or during the early morning so I could complete my assignments before I was picked up to nanny, but it also meant learning time- and money-management skills early and well.

My mom read aloud to us every day, and my dad often joined in as well, offering renditions of *The Hobbit* and The Lord of the Rings complete with a goose bumps–inciting Gollum voice. When I was in junior high, I enrolled in a speech and debate class through a local homeschool co-op, where I discovered a new love. I didn't care much for informational speaking, but persuasive speaking and debate were a different ball game. I learned how to listen for and respond to questions, how to cross-examine an opponent, how to compile and use evidence, and how to use information to build a case. I loved the intellectual rigor required.

My parents were intentional about engaging me and my siblings in the community and cultivating hearts of service, and our flexible school schedule allowed us to participate in a wide variety of ministries. They wanted us to learn to love and communicate with people of all ages and backgrounds—not as special projects, but as part of daily life.

Once when I was around ten, my friends and I put on a family fun festival to raise money for a nonprofit that helped care for women in crisis situations. It was the brainchild of my friends' parents, and we had games, prizes, and a store full of almost entirely useless homemade crafts that people purchased purely out of the goodness of their hearts in order to benefit the ministry. My friends and I had spent hours assembling trinkets to sell—the more gaudy and garish, the better.

Sarah, Michelle, and I had known each other since a fateful day in my backyard, when Chelle and I solemnly asked each other the most important question two five-year-olds can ask: "Do you want to be friends?" We agreed, and her older sister, Sarah, naturally became part of our tribe. Katie joined our trio a bit later, and Jessie sometime after that.

We found ample outlets for expressing and enjoying ourselves over the years. There were the progressive sleepovers, where we would skip from house to house on successive nights. Those led to all sorts of adventures—sack races in two feet of fresh Michigan snow, late-night scavenger hunts at the grocery store, and midnight conversations galore.

●　●　●

Along for all these adventures were my parents, teaching me and my siblings to love in ways I didn't yet fully understand. They often told us that if we could learn to get along with, love, and help one another through life's hurdles and conflicts, we'd be able to get along with just about anyone. And they were right. We had all the normal sibling spats, but we learned early the art of compromise, working together, and saying "I'm sorry"—skills necessitated in part by the fact that we lived in a small house.

My parents showed us that love was the foundation for everything, and they modeled what it looked like lived out. Love didn't thrive on authority; it thrived on sacrifice. Love sought to communicate and understand. Love was humble, admitting wrongs and seeking to repair the damage. Love protected.

Behind everything was love for Jesus Christ. My parents had an uncanny ability to weave truths from the Bible into almost every situation. In fact, I came to understand my own sin and need for forgiveness through a most unusual vehicle—toilet paper.

I was the ripe old age of three and fascinated with the inner cardboard roll that the toilet paper was wound around. There were so many imaginative possibilities when one possessed a few of those multipurpose cardboard tubes. Then one fateful day, there was no empty toilet paper roll to be found, and I *had* to have one for the current adventure I'd concocted in my stubborn little head. So I slipped into the bathroom—quietly, for I knew what I was about to do was strictly forbidden—and tiptoed up to the full toilet paper roll. With the door closed, I furtively began unwinding the toilet paper so I could get at that magic cardboard tube underneath. Significantly into my endeavor, I realized I was leaving a rather obvious trail of my illegal activities strewn all over the tile floor. Undaunted, I paused in my efforts and began concealing my recent activity by stuffing all the emptied toilet paper straight into the toilet. I briefly questioned whether it would all flush, and that is where my mother found me—hurriedly shoving paper into the toilet.

My mother, who was very skilled at drawing parallels, calmly asked me what I'd done. I knew the word for it—sin. I'd chosen to rebel against what I'd been told. Sitting on our plaid couch with the morning sun pouring in, my mom connected the dots. I wasn't the only one who had disobeyed; Adam and Eve had too. Just as they had tried to hide their sin unsuccessfully, my efforts to hide my sin had been futile, and no amount of good things I might otherwise do would undo the sin already committed. I understood. The pieces fell into place, and even at my young age, I realized how desperately I needed a Savior. Right then and there, I repented of my sin, turned to Christ for forgiveness and salvation, and in doing so, became a pastor's worst nightmare—a stubborn three-year-old insistent upon being baptized.

I'd been forgiven of my sins, and I knew exactly what was supposed to happen next. I was supposed to publicly declare it, openly identify with Christ, and tell people what He'd done. So that Sunday, I eagerly rushed up to our pastor and explained what had happened and what I was ready to do. Somehow, however, the issue seemed less clear-cut to him. He hemmed and hawed, and eventually told my parents he didn't baptize children until they were at least eight. I was devastated. And I was frustrated.

"He is keeping me from obeying Jesus!" I protested. "Doesn't he believe I've really been saved?"

I appealed to him again the following Sunday. And the next. And the next. He remained resolute, and my desperation to be obedient grew. Finally, my dad realized I wouldn't be able to rest until I had done what I knew I was supposed to do. So on a hot summer's day, he pulled our little blue wading pool into the middle of the backyard, tucked the green garden hose into it, and filled it. He told me he knew I wanted to obey Jesus and would baptize me right there so I could publicly declare my faith. I remember climbing into the cold water and kneeling down. I gave my testimony and recited my favorite Bible verse, then I covered my mouth and nose with my hands, and my dad baptized me. I still remember the relief and joy that washed over my soul as tangibly as the cold water swept over my skin. I had been obedient. When I eventually reached the magic age that my pastor had designated for "real" baptism, I joyfully participated, knowing full well it was only a continuation of what I'd already expressed and begun many years before.

The pattern of sacrificial love that was displayed by Christ on the cross was the one my parents followed. Their love wasn't obsessed with authority for power's sake. Instead, it sacrificed daily for us, even in little ways, like taking the time to listen to the concerns of a young child or petulant teen. They taught us that their authority was limited and would only be exercised for the right reasons and in the right way. This meant that they would discuss their decisions with us, hear and respect our input, and work with us to find a way forward. It didn't mean that obedience wasn't necessary or that we were allowed to argue them into changing their minds. Rather, it meant that we could approach them and be heard. We could trust their decisions, even those we didn't like or agree with, because we trusted *them*.

But while I learned that love listened and heard, I also learned that love acted and protected. One day when I was around seven, my siblings and I had been bickering with each other, whining over every little thing, and flat-out refusing to obey my mom when she asked us to do anything. Near the end of the day, she'd had it and took refuge in the only place that occasionally allows a mother to lock a door and keep it that way—the bathroom. My siblings and I, realizing we'd been left to our own devices, immediately stopped fighting and became partners in crime, enjoying our independence to the fullest. In defiant, exuberant glee, we jumped as high and as hard as we could on the beds in the room I shared with my sister, sending stuffed animals and baby dolls catapulting about with every bounce, knowing full well that Mom was long past the point of stopping us. Of course, we all harbored a slight suspicion that in the end the revelry was not going to be worth it, but since we had already crossed the line from which there was no going back, we intended to enjoy ourselves to the fullest until Dad got home.

Not much later, we heard him arrive and call out to my mom, who was still in the bathroom. We instantly grew quiet. Dolls stopped flying around the room, and we soberly slid off the beds with an uncomfortable feeling that judgment was coming. Moments later, he exited the bathroom and called for me, his grave, deep tone a harbinger that the fun was definitely over and the reckoning about to begin. I came to him, expecting to hear about how we'd fought or jumped on the beds and to be disciplined for our behavior. Instead, Dad shifted the focus.

"Did you know your mother was crying in the bathroom?" he demanded.

I hadn't known it was *quite* that bad, though it did explain her non-presence for the last thirty minutes. I quietly shook my head.

"That's my wife." His voice was filled with unmistakable resolve and seriousness. I felt the weight settling squarely on my shoulders.

"That's my wife," he repeated. "Your behavior today hurt my wife, and you need to know this: I love her, and I will protect her."

To this day, I don't remember what official consequence was meted out for our infractions, but I do remember this: My mom was protected. And she was protected because my dad *loved*.

I also learned that love sought to communicate and to understand, because I was the recipient of that display of love too. One warm summer's day, my mother happened to look out her bedroom window just in time to see me take a flying leap onto the smaller frame of my five-year-old brother. I wasn't often an aggressive child, but I was angry that summer. I had severe allergies and had begun receiving weekly allergy shots. My treatment wasn't going well. My doctor was a grim, stern man. Tall, thin, and bald, he looked eerily like Captain Jean-Luc Picard from *Star Trek*, but without the disarming smile or kind voice. He genuinely cared about his patients, but it came out in blunt, brusque, no-nonsense mannerisms that did little to make me feel cared for or more receptive to painful weekly injections. It didn't help that he had to compound the serum himself to get the correct dosages, which resulted in a grim process of trial and error, sparking severe and sometimes painful reactions.

I didn't realize how angry I was; I just knew I had no choices, no voice, and no option to stop the treatment. But my mom understood. First, she rescued my brother and made sure he was fine. Then she brought me inside. I knew

I was in for it. But instead of swift discipline or anger, my mom got down at my eye level and gave me a hug.

"I know you are angry right now," she said. "You don't have a lot of choices, and we're having to do things that hurt. I know it's really hard for you."

She talked with me about everything—how sick I was and how frustrated and angry I felt at being forced to do something that was painful.

"I can't let you hurt people," she told me, "but I want to help you work through this and find ways to express what you're feeling while keeping everyone else safe." And then she cried with me. Love sought to understand and communicate. Instead of lashing out in frustration at what I'd done, my mom had sought to reach me with love—without sacrificing the truth or leaving others unprotected.

My parents were equally quick to ask forgiveness when they had been wrong. Taking responsibility for the choices we each made, being humble enough to admit those choices, and asking forgiveness was nonnegotiable in our family. It was one of the aspects of our family life that I appreciated the most, because I'd seen what it looked like when that didn't happen.

●　●　●

When I was little, I watched a family we were close to fall apart as the result of abuse. The dad had massive anger issues, and when something didn't go his way, he exploded on his gentle wife and young children—never physically, but his verbal, emotional, and psychological abuse left wounds on their souls every bit as painful as fists on flesh. He always had reasons—they had done something to cause it, he'd say. And he'd often acknowledge that he should have responded differently, but his apologies were always followed with a "but *you* . . ."

The day everything came to a head was my first experience holding a weeping abuse victim. The woman was in her thirties; I was nine. I will never forget standing on my tiptoes, reaching up to hold her, trying to keep my balance while she wept, and wanting to throw up because my grief at the damage that had been done to her made me physically ill. Many times throughout the process of working with their friend to get her help, my parents talked with us kids about what we were seeing. Because of my parents, we'd already learned to love and appreciate the light; now they wanted us to be able to recognize the darkness as well.

"This is what abusers do," they explained. "Everything centers on them. Even when they apologize, they keep the focus on themselves—how they've been wronged or what they think they've done well—to try to shift the focus away from the pain they've caused. They don't truly take responsibility for anything." Abusers pass the blame to others, they told me. But that's not what love does. Love cares first about the harm done to the other person. Unlike abuse, love does not excuse or minimize wrongdoing.

My parents said, "When you've hurt someone and need to apologize, you say, 'I'm sorry for *blank*,' and then you stop. You put a period there. You don't say anything else to justify, minimize, or excuse what you've done. You are always responsible for your choices, no matter what someone else did." Then they modeled this kind of love for me daily.

I learned the hallmarks of abusers when I was nine. Because of severe asthma and allergies, I also learned early on that even the best-intentioned doctors embark on treatment plans that can be uncomfortable. But it would be years before I realized how cleverly patterns of abuse could masquerade as sincerity, or how kindly they might be packaged.

3

"YOU'RE GOING TO BE DISAPPOINTED," my dad said soberly.

"What?" I nearly shrieked. "Did they lose? What do you mean?"

"I mean you're going to be disappointed," he repeated, his voice crackling over the phone.

"Oh no . . . ," I moaned. "How could they lose? They were so far ahead last night! You've got to tell me what happened!"

"Nope," came Dad's cheerful voice. "You've got to wait until we watch it together tonight."

"You're infuriating!"

It was the summer of 1996. The Olympic Games were in Atlanta, and the women's gymnastics team finals had aired the night before. I'd been obsessively following the sport for a while. The gymnasts, their coaches, the scoring system, international competitors . . . it was all incredible to me. I knew each gymnast's floor music, my favorite sequences in their routines, which gymnasts were tall like me, and which ones appeared likely to break records in the Games. I'd watched every competition right up until the previous night, when the women competed in the team finals. Like the rest of the country, I'd been waiting months for what promised to be an unbelievable competition. There was only one problem. Those team finals? They aired late at night—really late—and my parents made me go to bed before then.

Let that sink in for a moment.

It was the biggest event in gymnastics, our team was set to become the first-ever US women's team to win a gold medal, and my parents made me go to bed.

They'd promised to record it for me so I could see every routine. We'd watch it together the next day, they said. Great idea. Except when I woke up that morning and jumped out of bed yelling, "Did they win? What happened? Did they win?" all I got back was, "We'll all watch it together," which was essentially code for "and we won't tell you *anything* until we do!"

Even worse, "together" meant "with your dad." After work. At night. Which meant I had to wait *all day* to find out what had happened.

No matter how much I cajoled, my mom refused to say one word about how the previous night's finals had gone.

"You *need* to tell me!" I told my mom in an almost-irritated whine.

"Of course not!" she responded, clearly enjoying every moment. "You wanted the full experience of watching it unfold, so I can't tell you anything! You have to discover it for yourself when we watch it tonight!"

"Ahh!" I yelled. Then a moment of brilliance hit. I waited until Mom left the kitchen, then dashed over to the recycling bin stashed near the hutch and began rifling through the newspapers. My dad got a morning paper every day. It would be in there. The results were always printed in the next day's paper.

Ha! I thought triumphantly, careful not to make any noise. Truth was, I hated suspense and I hated not knowing things. I was that kid who used a dictionary to look up every word my parents told me they'd explain when I was older. I was self-sufficient. I could find the answers. I'd just take a peek at the results and not tell them I knew, so they could enjoy what they *thought* was my surprise that night. *Where is that stupid paper?*

"Oh, we hid the morning paper," Mom yelled from the living room, "so don't bother trying that."

My parents were basically sadists.

Finally, that night, I got to revel in what the rest of the country—everyone who didn't have parents who enforced reasonable bedtimes—had enjoyed the night before. I shrieked at every beautifully executed tumbling pass, bar set, and beam routine, in awe of the absolute perfection flipping across our TV screen. The incredible diligence and hard work of these young women was paying off right before my eyes as they nailed one routine after another. And like the rest of the world, I gasped in shock when Dominique Moceanu fell on both of her vault landings in the second to last routine of the competition, threatening to unseat the US team from the gold-medal spot at the very last minute. I couldn't imagine how she must have felt, knowing she was so capable, had worked so hard, and cared so much. Only Kerri Strug was left— the last vault of the night. I knew how the scoring system worked; one stuck vault would basically clinch it for the team. I leaned forward, every muscle tense as she bolted down the runway, then launched herself up and over the horse, and then . . . Kerri failed to land her vault too. As she limped back to the starting place to attempt her second vault, it was clear her foot was injured.

"No no no no no!" I wailed, covering my face. "They're going to lose. They're so close, and they're going to lose!" I groaned. This must have been what my dad meant. Still, there was a slight glimmer of hope. There was one vault left. And like the rest of the world, I screamed with excitement when Kerri stuck that last vault, only to pause as she dropped to the mat, clearly in overwhelming pain.

I watched as the coaches and a doctor rushed to her side. "I got her, I got her, I got her," I could hear a male voice say.

The emotion of the moment was palpable. These little girls with perfect bodies had done what no other US women's gymnastics team had ever done. They'd paid a high price, including the injury of a teammate, and still they had persisted. It was incredible.

And it reminded me of how much I loved that sport. I'd taken a gymnastics class once when I was little, and I had been in awe of it ever since. I didn't remember much—except how bad the foam pit smelled and how much I'd wanted to continue but couldn't. It was just too expensive.

I was eleven and a half now, years too late to be a serious gymnast, but I still wanted back in the gym. Everything about it amazed me. I loved the combination of mental and physical acuity the sport required, the level of perfection and amount of repetition needed to make every move flawless and beautiful. I marveled at the gymnasts' physical strength and flexibility, as well as their diligence and determination. I loved that you couldn't do this sport halfway or pick it up casually. I was a perfectionist, and I wanted a sport that demanded this from me.

After watching the team bring home gold, I began asking to enroll in classes again. And asking, and asking, and asking. My mom called a few places, but the gym fees, even for entry-level classes, were pretty steep, and they escalated quickly from there.

Finally one day as we were discussing it again, I blurted out, "I'll help pay for it."

"What?" my mom asked, a bit shocked.

"I'll help pay for it," I repeated.

She paused. "You really want it that badly?"

"Yes." I took a deep breath. "Yes, I do."

I had been babysitting for a while, and I was used to chipping in for the extras. I was already helping Mom clean my piano teacher's house in exchange for lessons—a gracious move on my teacher's part that made studying music possible for me and my siblings—so the idea of working for my gym time made perfect sense to me. All I was asking for was a chance.

"Okay," my mom answered. "If it means that much to you, we'll find a way to make it work."

•   •   •

A few weeks later I found myself standing inside a little store space tucked into a shopping mall. The minuscule lobby was crammed with plastic chairs, and I watched as a girl twisted out of her front handspring vault.

The renovated store that housed the gym was so small that it allowed for only half a tumbling floor, a shortened vault runway, one set of uneven parallel bars, and a couple of balance beams. A few mats and the required equipment for men's gymnastics rounded out the tightly packed little arena. It was a small operation—just a handful of girls on the competitive team and a few recreational classes.

Next door, workers at Claire's Boutique were peddling scented lotions and sparkly hair clips, while gymnasts with bleeding hands and utilitarian ponytails were flipping through the air one space over. You could smell the chalk dust in the air. I loved it.

My mom connected immediately with the receptionist, remarking as we left how much she appreciated that everything in the gym could be seen and heard by the parents. Neither of us had any idea yet of the dark underbelly of the sport I loved, but my mom was chock-full of common sense. Knowing what was going on with her children had always been a priority for her, and she wasn't afraid to be the one parent who stuck around to observe, even when other parents mocked her for it. "It doesn't matter what other people say or think," she'd tell me. "Your physical and mental health are worth my being the oddball!"

When we left the gym that day, I was enrolled in level 1 classes, possessed my first leotard (cotton, with a dusty-blue plaid pattern), and was so excited that I had butterflies in my stomach. The five days I had to wait until my first class felt like an eternity.

A week later, I walked out of that gym again, exhausted but elated. My coach was the gym's owner, a former gold medalist from Eastern Europe. He did most of the coaching—from training the amazing girl I'd seen flipping across the half-sized floor a week ago to working with entry-level gymnasts like me.

Speaking of which . . . I looked ridiculous and I knew it. Almost twelve, I was five feet six, long torsoed, and gangly—nothing like the pint-size athletes whom I was practicing alongside, with their compact muscles and perfect physiques. Still, I knew what I wanted and that if I worked hard at it, that would be enough. In fact, doing it for the simple joy it brought me was enough.

I left that first one-hour practice ecstatic, not just because I was finally there, but because I had a glimpse of what I needed to do. My coach was old school, and I have yet to meet another coach who conditions his athletes the way he trained us. As a level 1 recreational gymnast, my first practice included sprints, sixty push-ups, sixty sit-ups, laughable attempts at pull-ups and chin-ups, frog jumps, relevés (rising onto my toes like a ballerina), extensive stretching, and instruction on basic gymnastics technique. I knew if I were ever to make it to the competitive level, it would require a tireless work ethic, and the routine from that first practice gave me a template to work from.

That night I stretched for two hours and repeated the entire conditioning routine. There wasn't much I could do in the way of practicing at home, but I could become as strong and flexible as possible, thereby maximizing my time in the gym. Every night after lights-out, I stretched and conditioned for at least an hour, and within two weeks I could correctly do each split and pump out the required conditioning sets with relatively correct technique and form. It wasn't much, but it was a start.

All that fall, winter, spring, and summer, I practiced at the little gym in the shopping mall and supplemented my training at home. I sat in the splits to do schoolwork, conditioned for an hour before bed, turned pirouettes on our kitchen floor, and did half of my science reading upside down in a half handstand against the laundry room door. I used the couch to stretch into oversplits more often than I sat on it, and the rough wooden plank running alongside the newly planted trees in our backyard became a makeshift beam.

Nine months after I first walked into that little gym, my coach said the words I'd been waiting to hear: "I'd like to talk about Rachael joining the competitive team."

For a twelve-year-old gymnast who didn't "fit the profile," this was as good as it got. I wasn't bound for college gymnastics, much less anything like the Olympics. Many coaches wouldn't have given me the time of day, but mine gave me a chance. I'd finally get to be a USA Gymnastics member. I'd get the pin, the membership card, and a real competition leotard. This was what I'd worked so hard for, and I was thrilled.

•　•　•

"What do you think?" my mom asked.

We'd been at an informational meeting, finding out what it would look like to become part of the competitive program—fees for the gym, competition, and apparel, as well as costs for "incidentals" like grips and extra practice leotards; the number of days and hours required for practice; the fund-raising requirements. It all added up to more than my family could afford, and more than I could pay for on my own. My mom had other concerns as well. She knew body image issues ran rampant and that injuries were commonplace. But I wanted it. I wanted it so badly.

"I've got that part-time nannying position," I suggested. "I'm using some of that money to help pay for the biology class, but the rest could go toward my gym fees."

She thought about it for a minute, then offered, "I suppose we could see if there's any extra work we could do at the gym to help offset the fees."

My pulse quickened. *Yes! It's going to happen!*

"But what if you get injured?" Mom asked, bringing me back down to earth. "Your dad and I want you to be able to do what you love, but honey, nothing is worth your health and safety. If we do this, you have to be prepared for the possibility of an injury that makes it unwise to keep going."

My parents weren't ones to shy away from discussing the hard topics, so that night we discussed every eventuality before making a decision: the safeguards we would put in place to make sure I wasn't falling prey to body image issues; how we would keep communication open so I could come to my parents with any concerns; how I would deal with the pressure of attaining a "gymnast's body" and the desire to please my coach; my willingness to give up the sport if doing so was in my best physical, mental, or emotional interest; what boundaries there should be for coaches when spotting or stretching me; how I would maintain privacy in the locker room; and what sorts of topics a coach should never discuss with me as an athlete. We talked about it all.

In the end, we decided to go for it, but with my mom's admonition ringing in my ears: "If your dad and I see anything that gives us a reason to be concerned for your health or safety, you'll be out faster than you can imagine." She knew pulling me from the sport would be hard and I wouldn't like it. "But I'm willing to risk your anger toward me, if it means keeping you safe."

With that in mind, we signed the paperwork, put down the first installment of fees, and bought my first set of dowel grips (the special handgrips with a wooden rod near the fingertips that help you hold on to the uneven bars—LIKE THE OLYMPIANS WEAR! And, yes, at that point in my life, I thought about them in all caps).

Truth be told, I was terrified as I walked into that first team practice.

The gym had just recently moved into what had been a mechanic's garage, upgraded with a (nearly) full-size tumbling floor, an extended vault runway, a second set of old uneven bars, and a team locker room. Actually, that last feature was a tiny room with one wall covered in wooden cubbyholes, but it was still *the team locker room.*

There were nine of us on that tiny team, ranging from aspiring level 5s like me to our solitary level 9 gymnast. I was almost the oldest and by far the least accomplished, a fact I felt rather self-conscious about.

My nervousness quickly dissipated, though, as the more experienced girls walked me through self-directed warm-ups and the hour of conditioning that started each three-hour practice. They answered all the questions that accompanied a raging perfectionist terrified of making a mistake and kindly told self-deprecating stories of *their* first days on the team. As a result, I didn't feel quite so stupid when my legs turned to Jell-O halfway through the hour of muscle training (though that was nothing compared to the soreness I experienced for the next two weeks).

Slowly, team life became a routine. My hands blistered, ripped, and callused, and then blistered, ripped, and callused again as my muscles grew accustomed to the intense conditioning routine. Every day, I did my schoolwork, nannied, and went to the gym, and once a week—to help cover the cost of my coveted gym time—I, and often my siblings, helped my mom clean the whole facility.

As the days progressed, I felt more a part of the tightly knit little team that exceeded my expectations. There were no ego fights, no competitions between gymnasts, no nasty remarks, and no poking fun at those who couldn't back tumble to save their souls (and yes, that would be me). Instead, everybody on the team helped one another, offering kind corrections and hugs when discouragement hit. We rejoiced at each other's successes and helped each other along, and our coach helped facilitate it all. He was soft-spoken, mild-mannered, reserved, and calm. His "very well," spoken with a gradually thinning Eastern European accent, was the highest compliment we could get for a routine well-done.

The gym had no bells and whistles, and I loved that. We did our best with what we had, even though that meant in the winter we'd usually arrive to find an icicle hanging from the bathroom faucet because we ran the heat only when we were in the gym. We bonded over shrieks of "I'm so cold I'm going to die!" as we ran shivering into the locker room before the heat kicked on, and idly wondered together if the water in the toilet would ever freeze solid like the dripping faucet and what would happen if it did. Fortunately, a gym our size heated up quickly. Within a few minutes, the ice would melt, we'd take off our sweatpants, and practice would start. In the summer, we had the opposite problem—no air-conditioning. We were blessed to have garage doors that fully opened, allowing a breeze to enter the front of the gym, but with nine of us working out for three hours in ninety-degree weather, breeze or no breeze, that locker room was ripe.

We were admonished almost daily by our coach to eat well and hydrate better, something I now know few coaches do. The other girls drank Gatorade, but—much to everyone else's disgust—I preferred iced V8 for a quick calorie boost during practice. Bottom line, life fell into a rhythm, and it was good.

To monitor our progress at the end of that summer, our coach put us through a variety of strength and flexibility tests, including rope climbs—a feat whereby a gymnast would extend her legs in a perfect L shape and climb up and down a massively long rope using only her arm strength and without touching the ground between climbs.

"Come on, almost there! You can make one more!" we called as one of our teammates scaled the ceiling-high rope—hands-only—for the third time in a row. Gasping, pausing, and reaching again, she finally made it to the top and whacked the metal beam the rope hung from, its cold metallic *thunk* echoing to us below, signaling her success.

As she started back down, my coach's calm voice called out, "Careful . . . careful." Then, with just a tinge of caution coming through, "Watch your hands."

When she made it to the ground without a rope burn, he joyfully exclaimed, "Where did *that* come from?" Then he pointed to her wiry arms, gesturing to show his shock that her tiny frame had managed the climb so well.

"They're like Jell-O," she gasped back.

He grabbed her wrists and gently shook the exhaustion from her arms.

"Do mine! Do mine!" another teammate jumped in, sticking her arms out. He laughed and obligingly wiggled her arms too.

We actually loved testing days. It was fun to see the progress—see what we could *really* do. We cheered each other on—joined by our coach—poking good-natured fun at one another when our arms or legs finally gave out at the end of each test. Practice was serious, and we were expected to be self-motivated and diligent, but it was also fun and safe.

I didn't know yet how unusual that was until two weeks later, when we had a guest gymnast train with us from another gym. She was young, around eleven years old. We were practicing tumbling passes, half of us at one corner, half at the other. My teammate and I had already taken our turns and were waiting for the rest of the team to make it across again. We held our breath as the new gymnast prepared to go. She had braces on both her wrists and another on one knee, and we knew she was fighting pain in her back and hamstrings too. Her mom had mentioned it to our coach before we started, insisting, "She's used to working through it."

She went again, throwing herself into a full twisting layout with incredible effort, and my teammate and I gasped.

"She's going to get seriously hurt," my teammate whispered to me. "This is not okay."

And it wasn't.

The guest gymnast was dangerously low, resulting in her slamming into the carpet with each landing, ankles and knees hyperextended to absorb the impact resulting from the incorrect angle. Worse, her head was much too close to the ground.

"She could break her neck," my teammate said, shaking her head.

Even *I* could tell her layout was nowhere near tight enough to be practicing a twist when she was healthy, much less when she was injured.

"Who's got her training like this?" I asked my teammate in disbelief. "Can't they see how dangerous it is for her?"

"She's one of John's girls," my teammate answered, resigned.

"Oh."

We both knew what that meant.

"One of John's girls" meant she was an athlete at Twistars, one of the most prominent gyms in the state. It was run by a man named John Geddert, and his reputation in the gymnastics community preceded him. His girls were often injured, much of the time seriously. Back, knee, and hamstring injuries plagued almost all of them, even at the lowest levels. Teammates and parents who'd been in the gymnastics world for years said that he pushed them to perform skills they weren't ready for, or even healthy enough to do, many times resulting in even worse injuries. He screamed. He berated. Some girls and parents at our gym had seen him throw things. It was whispered that sometimes this included his own gymnasts. And this behavior occurred not just during practices—he did it at meets, too, right in front of the parents, the USAG judges, and other coaches.

But no one stopped him.

Because John got results.

John's gymnasts were just a means to an end. If one athlete was injured, there was another one ready to take her place. Once after a meet, our team went out to dinner and talked soberly about how afraid John's girls were to eat, even after a competition. Teammates of mine who had gone out with some of John's upper-level gymnasts whispered that bits of salad were often the only things on their plates, despite competing all day. They all knew they'd be weighed at the next practice, and they knew John was always watching.[3]

If this guest gymnast was John's athlete, there was nothing my teammates or our coach could do.

That was the year I read the book *Little Girls in Pretty Boxes* by *San Francisco Chronicle* sportswriter Joan Ryan. It was a damning indictment of the world of competitive gymnastics and figure skating, laying bare the physical, emotional, and even sexual abuse that the author alleged was almost a hallmark of these sports. Little girls, she argued, were worth nothing more than the medals they could win, so they were starved, abused, and used to keep their bodies and skills perfect—like "pretty boxes." That was what the public wanted to see. With each chapter I read, I could feel a war within my soul. I knew some of the characterizations of coaches in the sport were true, because I'd seen them. But the day I finished that book, I closed it, sat down on the scratchy Berber carpet in our basement, and shook my head. My stomach was churning and my mind racing.

This can't be true, I thought. *This cannot all be true. The author has to have exaggerated. She must have picked the worst examples and left out all the good ones.*

A gnawing feeling in the pit of my stomach kept tugging at me as I intentionally pushed down the thought that reality might actually be this ugly. I turned the book over and over in my hands.

Nothing she's saying is a secret, I thought. *If she's telling the truth, all the evidence is right here. It's not hard to find. She found it. If she's telling the truth, everyone at USAG knows this stuff is going on.*

I took a deep breath and shook my head as if to shake the doubts and concerns away. "It can't be true," I repeated aloud. "Because if it *is* true and it *is* this bad, then everyone knows. If they knew, they'd stop it, right? Surely no one really believes medals are worth more than little girls."

I repeated it again and again, comforting myself with that thought. *This can't be true, because if it was, someone would stop it. Someone would speak up for these girls.*

Someone would stop *it.*

Someone *would stop it.*

Right?

4

"YES!" **ERIN SHRIEKED,** fist pumping in the air. "You did it! You did it!" She yelled loud enough for the entire gym to hear, as she swept a gymnast up in a bear hug. "I am so proud of you!"

It was the middle of summer, and Erin had taken over coaching for the term to allow the owner to visit his family overseas. She was, by far, the most energetic coach any of us had ever had, pouring herself into shaping our tiny team, and each person on it, with an unmatched sense of purpose. She expected a lot out of us, but she coupled her instruction with an intense enthusiasm that energized the entire gym.

"Stand here," she told me one day as she pointed to a line on the floor. She was trying to get me to understand the angle I needed to achieve to be able to properly extend my back handspring. I obligingly stood where she asked; then she came and stood in front of me, just inches away.

"When we're done, you should be able to do this," she explained, and without a word, whipped backward into a back handspring, her perfectly pointed feet flashing by my face. Because she was at the correct angle, I felt only the wind rushing by, and not a solid blow to the jaw. "See how I didn't kick you?"

I nodded vigorously, though I'd just seen my life literally flash before my eyes. "If you tried that right now, you'd kill me!" she explained, smiling. "When I say shoulders back, I mean it!"

Erin wasn't able to fix my back pass that year, though the problem was squarely on my end, not hers. What she did accomplish, however, was much more important. She taught me how a healthy coach invests in the next generation. We weren't just skills and scores to Erin. We were people, with hearts, minds, bodies, and souls to be shaped. She cared about us, about developing who we were, and about who we would be when we left the gym.

"What you learn here will follow you through life," she said.

And she was right. She taught us lessons, both in words and by example, that left us better people when the summer was over—the value of investing in the individual, not just in the people who would get us noticed; the joy of hard work and a job well done; and most important, the powerful truth that love is the greatest motivator one will ever have. We all flourished that summer because our hearts, minds, bodies, and souls were safe. We worked even harder on our skills and our attitudes because we were valued. And we learned to cultivate diligence, perseverance, focus, and a strong work ethic in ways we'd never been taught before.

Abusive coaches may have gotten the attention, but they left behind shells of little girls with bodies and emotions so broken that some would never fully heal. Erin never became a famous coach, but she and our gym owner did more good in that tiny gym in Kalamazoo, Michigan, than those coaches would ever do in their state-of-the-art complexes lined with trophies purchased with the literal blood, sweat, and tears of little girls.

• • •

Thanks to our coach's intense and thorough conditioning and technique training, our gym had a very low injury rate. But even that wasn't enough to save me. That summer the pain in my wrists and back got really bad. Simply put, I wasn't made for gymnastics. My long torso, inflexible shoulders, and late start in the sport all worked against me, and my body was simply worn out from the constant pounding. When it got to the point that I started waking up in the morning with one leg numb and pain radiating from my sciatic nerve, my mom wasted no time in getting me to the doctor.

The day I sat on the crinkly white paper in the office of one of the most prominent sports medicine clinics in the area was one of the most frustrating days of my gymnastics career. The doctor marched in not unkindly, but very businesslike, clearly having other things he needed to do.

He introduced himself, shook my mom's and my hands, and then looked at me and asked, "So what's going on here?"

I explained my back and wrist pain, pointing to the area where my thumbs would often go numb and demonstrating the positions that increased the pain.

"And your back?" he prompted. "What sorts of things bother that?"

I described the movements and then added, "But just sitting, walking, doing normal stuff can really be a problem."

"Hmm." He glanced down at my chart and the brief medical history noted in the manila folder. "Well, the tendons and muscles are probably inflamed, causing pressure on the nerves, which results in pain and numbness." Then he looked up and said, "Icing would be a good idea."

I blinked. *Icing? He says this like it's a new idea. Did he hear that part about me being a gymnast? We subsist on sports tape and ice.*

He reread the notes and examined my wrists a bit more. I waited with anticipation for some much-needed clarity and direction. Finally he nodded. I steeled myself. *This is it . . .*

"I think the tendons are really overworked," he announced confidently, closing the manila folder.

"Well . . . yes," I agreed, striving to maintain a cordial tone. "Gymnastics takes a lot of work. What I'm really wondering is if you have any ideas for helping it get better or not get injured so easily."

Surely there's got to be something, I was thinking. *Physical therapy, guidance on what to do or not do. Stretches or exercises. Something I can try to change in practice.*

"Well, you'll just have to rest everything," he said as if he couldn't understand why we were even having this conversation.

"Okay. What do you mean by that?" I inquired tentatively.

"I mean you need to take some time off."

"Like, completely?" I asked. "Can't you give me some guidance on what I can and can't do safely?"

He reiterated the need for complete rest.

I tried again. "Well, gymnastics doesn't really work that way. Usually we at least keep up with the training we can do while an injury heals. Can you give me some help with that?"

He remained firm.

"Just take some time off," he said nonchalantly.

I tried not to show my frustration. "Okay, how long do you anticipate this taking?"

"Mmm . . . I'd start with two months."

"Two months?" I almost yelped. "I can't just take two months off!" I was trying to keep my cool, but I was quickly losing that battle.

"Sorry." He shrugged. "That's the only option."

I opened my mouth again, then shut it without a word. There was no point. I was clearly not going to get anywhere here.

Mom and I checked out and walked to the minivan.

"This is stupid!" I let my frustration vent. "We haven't even *tried* anything yet, and he just tells me to take two months off?"

Mom was at a loss. She knew how frustrated I was but had no other ideas either.

"I'm really sorry, honey," she empathized. "I don't know what else to do, though. It would be foolish to keep up with this, given how much pain you're in. Nothing is worth long-term damage."

I stared, frustrated, at the gray-carpeted floor of our van. Later that day, I asked my mom to enroll me in ballet. I could at least spend those two months honing my dance skills so that when I did return to the gym, I'd have achieved something that was potentially applicable going forward. Still, it felt like time was crawling during those eight long weeks. I went to ballet one hour per week and left feeling completely unchallenged. My wrists and back improved to a point, but they certainly were not back to normal. By the end of the two months, I'd had it. I had to at least try again.

On my first day back, I rushed into the team locker room, set my gym bag down in my cubby, and took a deep breath. The familiar smell of chalk dust, leather grips, and yes, sweaty leotards filled my nostrils. This was right. This was where I was supposed to be.

Starting up after two full months off, however, was a whole different level of frustration. *Just do the best you can do*, I kept repeating to myself. There was nothing I could do about those lost two months, so there was no sense in wasting mental and emotional energy on them. *All you can control is what you are given today.*

For the next few weeks, I replayed this mantra over and over, trying to ignore the sinking feeling in the pit of my stomach. With each practice, my wrists and back got worse. It was as if the two months off had accomplished essentially nothing. My thumbs were already starting to get numb again, and I was waking up in the mornings to the familiar electric buzz down one of my legs. I fought hopelessness. *What now?* We'd already been to the best sports medicine practice in the area, and I knew exactly what I'd be told if we went back.

"What am I supposed to do? I can't just keep taking two months off in perpetuity!" I huffed in exasperation after one practice. I was standing with my mom near the waist-high wall separating the parents' viewing area from the carpeted blue floor. "There are no good options anymore!"

While I finished my sets and sat in oversplits for the last few minutes of practice, my mom started talking with the receptionist about the problem. I walked up at the tail end of the conversation.

"It can be really hard finding a doctor who knows the sport well enough to be helpful," the receptionist said empathetically. With both her daughters competing as higher-level gymnasts, she had far more experience navigating this world, and moms often sought out her input when working through concerns with their own daughters. She looked back and forth between my mom and me. "Have you thought about taking her to see Larry?"

My mind flashed back to 1996. *I got her, I got her, I got her.* I remembered the doctor rushing to take care of Kerri Strug after her iconic vault—the man standing behind the athlete barrier, reaching his hand out, watching intensely, coming to her aid. *I got her, I got her, I got her.* That was Larry Nassar. The Olympic team doctor. The elite medical coordinator for USAG.

In the gymnastics world, Larry wrote the book, literally, on sports therapy. His book on conditioning was considered the best, and gymnasts who failed to follow his counsel did so at their own peril.

I had once heard about a gymnast from a neighboring gym who had broken her neck. When she went to Larry for rehab, he expressed shock at her lack of muscle development and asked, "Don't your coaches have my book?"

When she told him they did, but they didn't really follow it, he spoke words that, when I heard about them, gutted me. "If your coaches had followed my protocol, your injury would have been completely avoidable." A gymnast's life had changed forever in a catastrophic injury that would have been preventable if Larry had just been listened to.

"He's the best of the best." The receptionist's voice snapped me back to reality. "He finds things no one else does and can treat them in ways no one else is able to do."

I nodded. Everyone knew that, but I was just a level 5 gymnast. How exactly would that even work? My mom had the same question.

"Does he even see kids at this level?" she asked.

"Oh, Larry will see anyone!" she assured us. "He works out of Michigan State's sports medicine clinic, and that's open to the public, so you just have to call to get an appointment."

I shrugged and slung my bright-blue gym bag over my shoulder. "Anything is worth a try, I guess."

Still, I found it hard to believe that a physician of Dr. Nassar's caliber would really have time for a gymnast in my situation. Plus, it was an hour and a half drive to get there—three hours round-trip. I wasn't quite sure how that would work either. Mom, however, was a little more enthused.

"Thank you!" she said emphatically. "I'll call tomorrow!"

• • •

"Well," my mom said, with just a hint of excitement in her voice, "we've got an appointment!"

It was faster than I'd expected. Faster than we'd both expected. Most specialists take a long time to get in to, and Larry . . . he was the doctor for the Olympians. Mom and I had both steeled ourselves for a long wait, but much to our surprise, my appointment was just a few weeks out. February 2, not even two months after my fifteenth birthday.

I shook my head in disbelief. "Okay!" For the first time, I felt the faintest twinge of hope.

"Yep," Mom agreed. "We don't need to do anything now except wait. Also, the clinic receptionist said we should bring a pair of loose shorts for you to wear. The exams are pretty thorough, I guess, and you need to be able to move easily."

I nodded. That made sense to me. Gymnastics was a physical sport. All I knew was that it was now just a matter of a few short weeks before I'd finally get some help.

Later that week, Mom and I were out walking around the block together, as was our habit whenever there was much to discuss. This time, the topic was gymnastics, my injuries, and what to keep in mind as we moved forward.

"It's not just about whether you can keep doing gymnastics, you know," Mom said. "It may still be the case that you'll need to quit. What I don't want is for you to end up with a long-term injury that could have gotten better had you stopped earlier."

"I know," I acquiesced, though I didn't want to admit it. "I know having to stop might be the answer, but I want to do what we can before making that decision. And you're right, the most important part is getting better. I think seeing Larry is the best shot we have at that."

My mom nodded and took a couple of deep breaths as we picked up the pace. "There is another option we could consider if we need to," she said, a note of hesitation in her voice. "I was talking to Mrs. Hart, and she asked how you were doing. I told her how poorly that visit to the sports medicine clinic went, and she had a suggestion."

"What was it?" I asked, swinging my arms in rhythm to our steps.

"Well . . . you know she's had a lot of pain in her back and with her tailbone, and she told me the only help she's found has been with a therapist who treats all the bones and muscles in that area, but . . ." Mom paused again and then spoke a little cautiously. "The therapist does it by accessing everything internally. She said it's a relatively new type of treatment, but it's worked wonders for her. She suggested trying her therapist if we can't find help for you somewhere else."

I let the pause hang in the air as I processed what she was saying. When we rounded the corner toward home, Mom said, "Go around again?"

"Yeah, might as well," I answered slowly, still thinking. "I mean, I'm open to trying her therapist if necessary, I guess. It's not a particularly comfortable idea, but it's better than a long-term injury, right?"

Mom nodded in agreement. "Sometimes there are things you have to do medically that aren't the most comfortable but are necessary for your health." Then she reminded me that her friend Stacy was a physical therapist. "I'm pretty sure there's a female therapist in her office who does this therapy, too, and we could always consider that."

That would definitely be preferable, I thought. "Okay, good to know. I think it's better to start with Larry, though. He knows the sport. I mean, this *is* his area of expertise. I don't think it gets any better than Larry."

A few weeks later, my mom, my siblings, and I all piled into the minivan to go see "the best of the best." It was, like everything else, a total family sacrifice to make it to this appointment. Three hours round-trip in the car and at least another full hour at the office—a major disruption to everyone's day and routine. But for a chance to see the doctor who took care of the Olympians, it was worth it. After all, who else got an opportunity like this?

Walking into the office felt surreal. A few other athletes dotted the chairs in the small waiting room. Some were obviously gymnasts, and I could tell just by their body type and muscle structure that they were much better than me. I felt awkward and out of place. The receptionist smiled and took my mom's insurance card. Then she handed me a clipboard full of papers.

"We especially need this top one," she said, gesturing to a form filled with lists of symptoms to check off and a diagram of the female body, front and back, where I was instructed to put an *x* everywhere I had pain.

I sat down in an office chair, soaking in the photographs of the Michigan State University women's gymnastics team that covered the wall in front of me. Larry was their doctor too. *This is everyone's top choice for a doctor*, I marveled. *Seriously. Cannot believe I'm here.*

Turning my focus back to the forms, I marked both wrists and the sciatic region in my lower back and began working my way through the list of symptoms. *Tingling?* Check. *Buzzing?* Check. *Numbness?* Check again.

"Do we have high cholesterol in our family?" I whispered to my mom when I got to the family history section of the form. Between the two of us, we filled it all out. As I handed it back to the receptionist, the door to the exam rooms opened, and I watched a gymnast wearing a knee brace hobble out. She was with a congenial-looking man who held the door for her.

"You got that all right? Okay, kiddo, get better." He lifted his hand in a wave and rushed off down the hall. It was Larry. I was surprised he'd walked this girl right to the door. Most doctors just send you off on your own, *maybe* pointing you in the right direction as they speed away. But Larry had walked out with this gymnast to make sure she was all right, even though he was clearly insanely busy. I figured she must have been coming here for a while, given how casually and familiarly he interacted with her.

Not long after, I found myself walking through that same door, trying not to squeal with excitement at the photos lining the hall: the Magnificent Seven from the 1996 Olympics. They were the greatest gymnastics team in US history, and Larry had photographs of many of them, some even bearing an inscription and personal tribute to Larry. I tried not to gawk as we moved through the hall to an empty exam room.

The nurse opened the door, and we stepped inside. I noticed a doctor's table in the right-hand corner, diagonal from the counter, sink, and cabinets. The counter was longer than normal, with just a jar of cream tucked along the back wall and a soap dispenser nearby. One solitary chair was near the head of the exam table, and the doctor's stool was pushed back near the sink.

The nurse told me to go ahead and change into my loose shorts. "He'll be right with you," she said as she walked out.

"Did you see the pictures of the Magnificent Seven?" I whispered to my mom, quickly slipping on the baggy, cotton knit shorts I'd brought.

She nodded and took a seat in the chair by the exam table. We didn't have long to wait.

"Hey," a kind voice drawled as the door opened. And in walked Larry, polo shirt tucked into gray pleated pants, cell phone clipped to his belt, and glasses perched on the end of his nose. He moved quickly, extending his hand to me first and then to my mom. His voice was cheerful. "Looks like you've got a lot we need to deal with, kiddo!" he said, pulling out the chart.

I nodded and smiled shyly. He laughed with me. As he glanced down at the chart, he noticed my ankle boots lined up by my mom's chair.

"Cute boots!" he exclaimed. "I love those! Okay, let's see what we've got going on here."

And the evaluation began. He tested my flexibility and core strength, putting me through a battery of movements and tests. He positioned me however he needed me to be for the next test, talking away while he worked, making swift notes in the chart he carried. The sports med doctor in Kalamazoo hadn't done a fraction of the evaluation Larry did. With each test my confidence grew. He clearly knew what he was doing.

"Go like this," he instructed me, tucking his thumbs into curled fists, bent elbows at his sides, curled hands in front. "Now tip them down."

I did exactly as he asked.

"Does that hurt?" he asked.

I grimaced and nodded.

"Yeah, I knew it would," he said with a chuckle. He then took one of my hands and began explaining the structures, naming the tendons that were sore and showing where they connected and ran up my arm.

"De Quervain's tenosynovitis," he said. "Don't worry, kiddo. We'll get it fixed up."

By the end of the evaluation, I'd learned several key things. First, my shoulder flexibility was awful, causing me to hyperextend my wrists with each tumbling movement and putting massive pressure on my lower back. Second, the muscles in my back didn't fire in the right order, so my lower back was carrying way more weight than it should. And third, my hips were improperly rotated.

Larry gave me a battery of stretches and exercises for my wrists and showed me which wrist braces to order for tumbling. Then he walked me through exercises to retrain the muscles in my back and stretches for my shoulders. As for the improper hip rotation—he could fix that now, he told me. He pulled a model of a pelvis from a drawer.

"See this?" he said, extending it to Mom. "So this side of her pelvis is rotated," he explained. "What I need to do is adjust it. I'm going to grab the pelvic bone and pull it back into place, okay?" He pushed his glasses up on his nose, raised his eyebrows, and nodded at her as if asking a question.

"Okay," Mom answered.

Then Larry pulled me to the middle of the room, just a few feet from my mom, and slid my feet about twelve inches apart. He knelt down and placed one hand firmly on my lower back, looked down at the floor as if concentrating, and wrapped his second hand around the inside of my leg, under the shorts.

"Okay, I'm going to apply some pressure now," he reminded me. Suddenly, his hand went inside my shorts. Inside my underwear. Inside *me*. *Wait—what?* I glanced down at him. He was biting his lip a bit as if concentrating—no sign of anything being off. My mom sat there right in front of me, watching him adjust my hip. He pushed his fingers farther in and pulled hard. It hurt.

"There!" he announced. "Got it!" He smiled up at me.

Inside my head was a running dialogue. *He said he needed to rotate the pelvic bone. That therapist Mom and I talked about . . . he works on the bones and muscles internally, too. This must be that technique,* I thought. *So I guess Larry really is the last-ditch effort. If he's doing that internal technique already, there's not much else to try.*

"All right, kiddo, hop up here and lie down on your stomach," he instructed, patting the table.

"I'd like to do some soft tissue work—myofascial release," he said, looking at my mom. "She's carrying a ton of tension in her lower back, and that's going to cause a lot of extra strain and inflammation.

"Yeah, yeah . . . like that," he said, continuing to position me and get things ready as he talked.

He lowered my shorts a bit, tucking a towel into them to keep them down, chatting away with me and my mom as he did.

"I saw your chemistry book," he began. "What section are you in? Just gonna use some massage cream here," he added nonchalantly, using a tongue depressor to wipe a large scoop on the inside of my upper thigh. Then he grabbed some with his right hand and began massaging my lower back, kneading the sore muscles with his fist, open palm, and then using his forearm for firm, gliding strokes across the full back. He closed his eyes in concentration. That didn't bother me; I'd seen physical therapists do this many times when treating soft tissues so they could focus on what they were feeling in the muscle fibers. But then his left hand slid up again, scooping a bit of massage cream as he went. Up my shorts. Inside my underwear. Two fingers inside me. Casually massaging. I glanced at my mom sitting inches away from me. She smiled reassuringly and answered Larry's most recent question about my chemistry unit.

I glanced up at Larry. Eyes closed while chatting away with my mom. *This must be that therapy Mom and I talked about before*, I reasoned. I didn't want to say anything at all. This was awkward enough, and if he knew how self-conscious I felt, it would be more awkward yet. The last thing I wanted to do was draw any more attention to myself. *Mom knows about that internal therapy*, I reasoned. *She'd say something if it was weird.* Larry was standing right between her and me. *She could easily ask him a question if something didn't look right to her. This must be that therapy.*

I thought back to all the pictures on the wall. *USAG trusts Larry with their very best gymnasts, and so does MSU.* I thought about Larry's confident, brazen movements. *This is clearly something he does regularly. I'm not a test case. This is normal treatment for him.* Other patients would have certainly described this treatment to adults before. There was no way that other adults at MSU and USAG hadn't heard of this. And surely if there was any question about what he was doing, someone would have checked into it.

If there was something wrong, someone would have stopped him.

Wouldn't they?

5

"ALL RIGHT, KIDDO, I think you're good for today," Larry said as he reposi-tioned my shorts. He turned and walked to the sink, washing the massage cream off his hands while chatting with my mom.

"We can get her fixed up," he chirped cheerfully, tossing the paper towels into a small wastebasket before turning his attention back to me. "I'm going to give you a list of stretches and exercises, and I'd like to see you regularly for a while to monitor your progress. I think we should add some physical therapy in between appointments to work on stabilizing your back and pelvis. I can work with your therapists to direct them on what's best. Hang on just a minute and I'll get what you need."

As he exited the exam room, my mom turned to me and asked, "Well, what do you think?"

I thought about it carefully. He was thorough. He pinpointed issues no one else had found. He could tell me exactly what to do to work on the prob-lem, and what I could and couldn't do in the gym. He was putting in tons of time to coordinate care with a physical therapist and put together a plan specific to me. *And we know internal pelvic floor therapy is practiced by a lot of other therapists*, I reminded myself.

After the last go-around with the doctor in Kalamazoo, honestly, Larry's approach was amazing. Unlike the white-coated doctor who could hardly be bothered to look up from my chart, Larry paid attention. He asked questions to find out exactly what was causing my pain and what skills I was working on. He seemed genuinely interested in me—who I was, not just as a patient, but as a person. He engaged with my mom about the simple things in life—school, family, church. Instead of being treated by a physician who couldn't be bothered to offer even one practical suggestion, I was receiving a tailor-made plan designed to address every aspect of my current injuries and prevent them from happening again. The doctor trusted with our Olympians was willing to put time into a no-name level 5 gymnast just because I needed it.

"I think he's really good!" I said, almost in disbelief. "What do you think?"

My mom was a pretty hands-on parent. She wasn't afraid to ask questions and push for answers, and a doctor who didn't explain things or who treated questions like a nuisance was a huge turnoff for her. But Larry—he seemed to do everything right. Better than any doctor I'd ever seen. He even brought out a skeleton to explain what was happening with my spine and told me all the names of the muscles, bones, and tendons involved in my back and wrist pain. He also explained the physics of what was happening to my wrists and back when I performed certain skills and why the exercises and stretches he gave me would help.

"He seems very good," she agreed. "I appreciate his thoroughness and his willingness to talk about what's going on. It's definitely a lot more help than we've gotten anywhere else."

Just then the door opened, and Larry walked back in as he riffled through a stack of papers. "These are the exercises and stretches we talked about for you to do at home and in the gym, okay?" He walked me through the pages, then handed me a second set. "This is for your coach if he needs more detail about what's going on." Then he pulled out a few more sheets that included his medical diagnosis and some handwritten notes about what types of activities I should avoid. "Take this packet with you to physical therapy. It has the more technical info for your therapist. My number is on there. They can call me anytime if they need to discuss your treatment plan or progression." He smiled and turned to my mom. "Oh, and she might be a little sore after the hip adjustment, so an Advil is totally fine if needed."

I flinched a little. That just seemed so . . . private. My mom smiled back. "Yep, we can do that!"

"All right," Larry said, "I'll walk you to the front. Let's see you back here every few weeks, okay?" I looked at my mom, nodded, and smiled. "Go ahead and get about six appointments on the books so we have the time set aside, and we'll see where we go from there."

He put his hand on my shoulder and gently guided me out. We walked back down the hall, past the photos of the Olympians and toward my siblings, who were still patiently doing their schoolwork in the waiting room. Larry held the door open for me, and as we left, he enthusiastically greeted his next patient, a girl a bit younger than me. "Heyyyy! Good to see you! How's the knee? Come on back, kiddo. Let's get you fixed up."

Fixed up. That sounded good.

I returned to the gym the next day with a purpose and determination—wrist braces on order, the new taping method Larry had shown me for my wrists in place, and for the first time, a sense of direction. I followed his instructions religiously, avoiding the things I'd been told to avoid, but pouring out effort wherever I could. I added the new stretches and physical therapy he suggested to my conditioning routine, and my coach worked with me to find options to replace the things I couldn't do. I was fortunate to have a coach who actually wanted me to get better and didn't balk at the limitations and revisions that needed to be put into place to get me there, so I threw myself into the options I had and hoped they would be enough.

•   •   •

The physical therapy tool—a long, white foam column, a bit longer than my spine—was on the floor, and I was lying on it. Or at least, I was supposed to be. This handy-dandy little contraption had a multitude of uses, one of which was training spine alignment. The idea was to lie down on it so that the column ran the length of my spine. "Keep your feet on the floor and your hands on your stomach," my therapist explained.

"The goal is to keep balanced on this. Just lift one foot a few inches off the floor and then switch and do the other one. If there's a misalignment, it will show."

I raised one foot as instructed. *No problem.* I mean, I trained four days a week on a four-inch beam. I was used to self-correcting and pulling things back in line—how hard could this be?

"Great, let's try the other one," the therapist said. I obligingly put the first foot down and began to raise the other one. That's when I found out what she meant about a misalignment becoming obvious. Out slid the stiff foam roller, down went the barely raised foot, and up flew the other one, trying to compensate for what felt like a massive shift in weight. My hands shot out and pressed down against the floor, and I rolled off the side.

"Holy smokes!" I started giggling, and the therapist laughed with me. She'd seen this a time or two before.

"Let's try again," she said. We did. With the same result. No matter what I did, I could not stay on the roller when I raised my right foot.

"So we're going to practice this," my therapist said. She explained that repeating these simple steps would help train my muscles to fire properly and keep my spine better aligned. We added the foam roller to the growing list of therapy tools to take home and work with.

"Let's check your hips now," she said. She had me stand in front of her while she used her thumbs to find the back of my pelvic bones. She checked front and back, noting one side's rotation and height difference.

"Yeah, you're rotated and off center again."

Yep, just like Larry said, I thought.

"I'm going to teach you how to self-correct this, okay?" She took a moment to explain the concept of counterpressure and how it can be used to help pull the pelvis back into place. She showed me how to check for improper alignment and then use something firm, like a doorsill or couch, to push against and self-correct the misalignment. My clothes stayed on the whole time.

I wonder why Larry does it the other way? I thought briefly, as I didn't have much time to ponder the question. My therapist was dragging out a couple of big Swiss exercise balls and measuring me to see which size I needed. I loved

Swiss ball exercises. The challenge was so fun, and let's face it—who *doesn't* love to play with a giant bouncy ball big enough to sit on?

I left with yet more exercises to add to the regimen and more papers to take back to Larry. We hadn't really done much for my wrists yet, even though by now I'd seen him a few times. He seemed focused on my back, and that internal treatment he'd done the first time had become a regular thing. *That's probably the more pressing issue*, I thought. *I'm sure we'll get to the wrists when the back problems are under control.*

• • •

"All right, round-off warm-up," my coach called softly across the floor, his *r* rolling just a little with his accent. It was a few days before Easter, and I was trying to get the most from every practice before state finals. We were cross tumbling—groups of us stood in two different corners and performed our passes alternatingly across the floor to the opposite corner, like the lines on an *X*. I'd just finished my series of front handspring step-outs and was beginning drills for back tumbling. I winced a little at the first pass. The bone in the back of my shins had been bothering me for a while, with an occasional sharp pain on impact, but getting my back and wrists better was by far the first priority, so I hadn't thought much about the shin pain. I just gritted my way through it.

"Rachael, through your shoulders. Your shoulders!" my coach called out. The "block" part of the round-off, where the hands are *supposed* to come into contact with the floor and push off quickly (the way a rubber ball bounces on impact), wasn't my strong suit. Let's be honest: back tumbling in general was not my thing. I did handstand hops on the vault runway to drill that part of the skill while I waited for my next turn, listening to the rhythmic pounding of my teammates as they sprinted and flipped across the floor. I was next.

"Shoulders!" my coach reminded me.

I nodded and began to sprint. One, two, three, hurdle. I stretched, focusing on the block, and twisted ever so slightly on the way down, feeling that twinge in the back of my shin as I landed.

Pop.

I felt that.

I heard that.

I'd landed with the left side of my foot slightly rolled under. Something wasn't right. I felt an odd mix of deep pain and numbness. I shook it while I waited in line again, trying to get the feeling to return and the buzzing to stop. At my next turn, I started into the sprint and stopped two steps in. It felt like I didn't have complete control over my foot. I shook my head.

"Something's not right," I told my coach. "I landed sideways on it," I explained, pointing down.

"Yeah, I saw that." He suggested I stop tumbling for a bit and just work on snap-down drills and bars. I nodded, frustrated with yet another potential problem. I stretched into a handstand, arching my back to rest my feet on the wall—mimicking the last portion of a back handspring—then snapping down to my feet. Over and over I repeated the snap-down drill, but nausea from the pain became so bad that I eventually moved to bars. That didn't go any better. The least bit of pressure on my foot made me feel dizzy and sick to my stomach. I finally went back to my coach.

"I think I might throw up," I admitted.

"Let me see it," he said, gesturing toward my foot.

I put my foot up on the giant marshmallow mat and he gently took it, running his fingers over a spot on the side that had popped. There was clearly a swollen area and a bruise. "Girrrrl . . ." He paused. "Did you break your foot now?"

I shrugged. I didn't know what to think. He shook his head.

"I think you better go home and see how it goes. You might need an X-ray."

I exhaled in frustration, but also with a sense of relief. Deep down, I knew I couldn't keep working out on my foot, and I was grateful he made the decision for me.

"I'll talk to your mom," he assured me. "You go ahead and get ready to go. Call me tomorrow and let me know what the doctor says, okay?"

I listened as my coach talked with my mom. "Keep it iced and let her get some sleep tonight, but if the pain keeps her awake, take her to urgent care first thing in the morning."

The pain intensified overnight. By the time we arrived at urgent care, we were all pretty sure what the X-ray would show. We were shocked when the doctor walked in and announced, "Yeah, you have some bone fractures in that ankle."

Ankle? I blinked. *I'm not here for my ankle.*

"I'm not here for my ankle," I repeated out loud. "It's my foot."

"No, no," the doctor insisted. "The break is in your ankle."

I took a deep breath in frustration. "No," I repeated. I pointed one more time to the spot on my foot. "It's my foot. I hurt my *foot*." I pointed emphatically. "Right here. The fifth metatarsal." *God bless my biology teacher*, I added internally. "I landed on it tumbling last night."

"Oh . . . ," the doctor responded. "Hmmm. I'll check again."

I was trying to be gracious, but I'd been up half the night in excruciating pain and being told I didn't know the difference between my foot and my ankle wasn't endearing anyone to me at that moment.

The doctor came back in and slapped a set of X-rays up against the light. "Yep, it's broken. Your foot, I mean. I didn't notice the foot because when I first looked at the X-ray, I saw the bone chips in your ankle, and they aren't healed." He pointed out three small places that looked like little wisps in between my ankle bones. "But, yeah, you've broken your foot. Fortunately, the bone isn't displaced, so we'll cast it and then refer you to an orthopedist here."

Perfect, I thought, grimacing.

As the doctor left to get the supplies for casting, I looked at my mom despairingly.

She echoed my frustration. "You know what? I'm going to call Larry. Maybe there's a chance he can get you in, and we can get things checked out more thoroughly."

I felt a slight sense of hope. Larry would at least know what I could do, even with a cast.

And once again, Larry came through. No sooner had my mom called than we had an appointment. He was going to take care of me.

• • •

"Oh, man!" Larry said, giving me a hug and rubbing my shoulder. "I'm so sorry. What'd you go and do that for?" he joked, pointing at my blue cast. Blue was my gym's team color. *If all else fails, at least represent*, I'd figured.

"Let's look at the X-rays." He slapped them up on the light box and peered at them.

"The first doctor thought it was my ankle," I said in exasperation. "He didn't even see the break in the foot."

"You mean this stress fracture here?" He gestured to a spot on the fibula bone. "That's nowhere near your foot!"

I blinked. "No, he didn't say anything about stress fractures. I have stress fractures?"

"Yeah, yeah, right here. Has your shin been bothering you at all?" He walked over and picked up my good leg. "We should probably check the other leg. If you've got it on one side, you may have it on both. About right here," he said, pressing his finger gently into a spot.

"Yeah!" I grimaced and yelped. "That's the spot."

Larry laughed and apologized. "We need to get another set of X-rays on this leg," he announced.

"The other doctor didn't say anything about that, though," I protested. "He just mentioned my ankle."

Larry chuckled and waved his hand. "These are hard to catch. Most doctors don't know to look for them."

"But what did he mean about my ankle?" I asked. "He kept saying I'd come in for my ankle, and it took forever to convince him it was my foot."

Larry pushed his glasses up a bit and pointed again at the X-ray. "He meant these. You have some bone chips here. This is really common. It happens when gymnasts land short on tumbling passes. But when the shards are that tiny, you don't see them until the ankle starts to heal. The fact that he could see them should have let him know that wasn't the recent injury."

I took a deep, frustrated breath. "So how long do you have to wait to see them? I mean, to be able to diagnose?"

"Oh, they'll show up within a few weeks . . . if you know what you're looking for," he said. "But not that fast, and these are pretty old. They're almost healed."

By now I was really irked. What Larry didn't know was that before seeing him, I'd been to an orthopedist twice to check that ankle. I saw that doctor first, after landing short and having a lot of pain. I went back six weeks later to have him recheck it because it was still really bothering me. He'd even ordered X-rays. After examining them, the doctor told me there was nothing wrong.

I started mentally counting off the doctors I'd seen who had completely missed problems or been unable to help. *Ugh. It's good we finally switched to seeing just Larry.*

Larry sent me off for a second set of X-rays at his office, which confirmed a second stress fracture in the right fibula.

When I came back to the exam room, Larry was waiting. "As long as you're here, how's your back?" he asked. "I'd imagine pretty sore after coming down sideways and being on crutches?"

I nodded.

"Okay, well, since you're here already, we might as well do what we can to get you fixed up. Physical therapy will have to wait a bit, but I can take care of some of it now even with the cast."

He motioned to the table and helped me up, grabbing the massage cream on the way. "Poor kid, everything hurts!" he said with a compassionate smile. I took a deep breath and remembered my frustration in the urgent care. *I'm so glad he was willing to fit me in*, I thought, as I felt him roll my shorts down.

The treatment was awkward, and I didn't like it. But finally someone was paying attention and willing to help. I glanced up at my mom sitting in the chair. I could barely see her behind Larry. She smiled, and so did I. We'd finally gotten help.

● ● ●

A few weeks later, I was back in the gym—on crutches and with a cast, but at least I was back. Enough healing had taken place that Larry wasn't worried about the bone moving out if I jolted my foot accidentally, so he'd okayed it. I couldn't do skills, but I could condition and stretch and run through some of my physical therapy. Getting a leotard over the cast was a comic routine in itself, but I was so ready to be back in one, I couldn't have cared less.

For the next few months, I conditioned during every practice, first with the cast and then in a walking boot, waiting . . . *waiting* for the bone to heal. I didn't love the cast, but I did love the muscle that came with lugging around an extra ten pounds on every chin-up and leg lift. I'd been pretty strong before, but by June, I discovered I could arm wrestle most guys my age and win, and that was worth something. Having six-pack abs outlined by my leotard was also pretty awesome, and I knew that the more fit I stayed, the easier it would be to pick the sport back up when Larry gave the signal.

Through it all, Larry was there. I went to him instead of an orthopedist for regular checks. He kept in touch with my physical therapist so I could begin rehabbing my leg and foot as soon as the cast came off. And every time I'd come in, he'd ask how my back was doing. Being on crutches was pulling everything out of alignment again. I wasn't there to see him for my back, but he knew it hurt, so he'd offer to treat it every visit anyway.

"Hop on up, kiddo," he'd say, and I would. A few times his hand slipped forward inside my shorts.

It must have slipped.

Is it possible to slip like that?

Of course it was a slip. What else would it be?

Once when my mom and I came out from the exam area, the hallway and office area were dark. Everyone had gone home. I was surprised Larry would be left entirely alone with a patient and shocked at how late it was. I had no idea we'd been in there that long.

"Who should we call tomorrow to make sure this gets claimed on insurance?" my mom asked. "We weren't supposed to be here for her back, so I'll need to let someone know."

Larry waved his hand as if brushing her concern aside. "Oh, don't worry about it. She needed the help. This one's on the house. Just get better, okay, Rach?" He gave us both hugs, and we left. He was such a contrast to the doctors who couldn't even look up from their paperwork or listen when I explained which body part was in pain. I hobbled past the photos of the Magnificent Seven, their signatures barely visible in the dark. *No wonder USAG and MSU want to keep him around!*

• • •

"So . . . that was weird," my teammate Ashley whispered.

We were sitting in the back of my mom's minivan, driving home from

Lansing. Now that my walking boot was off, I was back at the gym, though I was still limited in what I could do as I continued rehab and physical therapy. Larry, of course, was overseeing it all.

Ashley had been having significant back trouble, and her mom hadn't been able to take her to see him, so we were carpooling to our appointments with him. "Is that how he treats your back too?" she asked.

I considered what Ashley was telling me about what had just happened. Mom had brought Ashley and me back to the same exam room. She wanted to make sure someone was with Ashley and could let her mom know about the path going forward. Larry came in with hugs all around, making small talk and asking questions about our school and gym. Then he got down to business. He did a thorough evaluation of Ashley's back and then put together a comprehensive plan—it was Larry, after all. He told her he'd like to do some soft-tissue work to help ease up the muscles and get everything back in alignment.

"Would you like them to step out, or are you okay with them in the room?" he asked. I appreciated that he'd given her the choice to protect her privacy.

"Naw, we're teammates. We all see everything anyway," she laughed.

Larry returned the laugh. "No secrets in the locker room!" he chuckled.

He had her hop up on the table and lie on her stomach, just like I did. I saw him drape her hips with a towel, lower her shorts and shirt a bit, and begin to massage her back with his right hand and forearm, just like he did mine. Then I noticed that he slid his left hand casually under the towel as he talked, joking and laughing with her as he kneaded the tender muscles with his visible hand.

I'd hardly even noticed the hand under the towel. *Wow. If I didn't know what he was doing, I'd never even guess it. I didn't realize how discreet he's able to be.*

In fact, until Ashley confirmed it with her question, I hadn't even been sure that Larry was doing the same thing to her that he did to me, despite experiencing this internal treatment myself many times by now. I was relieved to discover that it was all but imperceptible. After all, we want doctors to protect our privacy, don't we? The ability to perform such a sensitive treatment without revealing anything or drawing attention to it seemed responsive to the need to keep private procedures private.

"Yeah, it *is* a little awkward." I paused. "He always treats my back that way too, though. Like, every time."

His movements were so rehearsed, it was obvious to me that it was a normal method of treatment for him. The fact that Ashley and I were experiencing the same thing—with each other in the room, no less—confirmed it.

"Well . . . I mean, it's Larry, right? So . . ." Her voice trailed off. I murmured in assent as we traveled down the freeway. Ashley was right. It was *Larry*. He treated girls all day, every day. Even the Olympians. It had to be normal.

Ashley and I didn't talk much the rest of the way home.

• • •

Weeks later, my mom informed me we needed to switch the date of my next appointment due to a mechanical problem with one of our vehicles.

"Oh, that's fine," I replied casually. "We probably would have had to switch anyway. My period's due around then." I kept sweeping the floor without a second thought.

"Why would that matter?" my mom's puzzled voice broke in.

I laughed. *Awkward!* I thought. *Umm, do I really have to explain it?* "Well . . . I mean, he can't really treat me if I have it then!" I said with a little laugh, giving her a wry look that, in my mind, should have made it clear.

"Why can't he treat you?" my mom said with a touch more urgency. "Rachael, is he . . . is he doing something internal?"

I paused and set down the broom, confused. "Yeah?"

Why is this news to her? We've been going for months. I didn't get it.

"Rachael, I didn't know that."

Shock and confusion, mingled with a fear I didn't understand, crashed down. I forced a laugh. *Don't make this more awkward than it already is*, I told myself sternly. I didn't want a fuss. It was embarrassing enough without drawing extra attention to it. My mom had always been so good at communicating with my siblings and me about our bodies and sexuality, but still . . . it was *private*.

"I mean, how'd you think he was rotating my pelvis?" I asked with a forced nonchalance.

"Externally," my mom replied firmly. "I didn't realize he was doing anything internal." She paused and took a deep breath. "Well," she asked with a steady voice, "what do you think about it?"

I thought for a minute before answering. Larry was the doctor USAG trusted with their Olympians. Larry was the doctor MSU trusted with their own gymnasts. Larry treated girls every single day and had been for years. I knew he did this all the time, multiple times a day even. And I knew from our family friend that physical therapists could be specially trained to do internal pelvic floor manipulation. I measured my words carefully and honestly.

"I mean, it's awkward . . . but medical stuff can be sometimes, can't it?"

"Yeah . . . ," my mom replied, clearly not convinced.

"And we *do* know that therapists practice internal pelvic floor therapy. We already even talked about my possibly needing it, right? And that it might not be exactly fun, but could be necessary?" I pressed.

"Yeah, we did." Mom sighed. "We did. I'd just planned to take you to a female therapist if it turned out you really did need anything done internally."

I shrugged and started sweeping again. The brown hutch sitting in our dining room was breeding dust bunnies, I was sure of it. I dragged a particularly large one out from the left corner. "I guess I thought since Larry could do all of it and had the gymnastics expertise, we'd decided to stay there?" I said.

Mom nodded, but she wasn't done yet. She didn't give up so easily, and I soon discovered I'd be answering questions at about a rate of one per dust bunny captured.

Had I ever felt like it was unprofessional?

Did it make me more uncomfortable than a normal medical exam?

Had he ever done anything that didn't seem truly medical?

"No."

"No."

"No."

And I believed my answers. Only a dirty mind would sexualize a medical exam. The fact that sometimes I had to work at not "reading into" what was happening was on *me*.

Finally Mom relented. "All right. But if you are ever the least bit uncomfortable or feel like something isn't quite right, tell me right away. We can always switch to another therapist. There are several PTs in the area who do internal therapy."

I nodded in agreement. "I will." And I meant it, because I knew she did too. If anything was really wrong, I'd tell her. But if anything was really wrong, surely Larry wouldn't be seeing girls every day.

6

"AND HOW'S YOUR WIFE, now that your baby is almost here?"

Larry bowed his head and shook it in disbelief. "Oh, man. She's great, Rach. I mean, she's pretty uncomfortable, of course, but we are so ready for this little girl." He paused. "I just can't wait." His tone was joyful, full of deep emotion and awe.

It was late summer of 2001, more than a year and a half after I'd first walked into the MSU clinic. Larry's firstborn, a baby girl, was due in a matter of weeks, and he was almost giddy whenever he talked about her. I'd met his wife, Stephanie, just recently. Cute and quite petite, she was all baby, so I could understand why they were both eager for this little girl's arrival.

"Being a dad is going to be just incredible." He shook his head again, sighed, and then transitioned to work mode. "All right, kiddo, hop on up. Let's see where we're at." He ran me through the battery of strength and flexibility exercises, yelping in pain and shaking his fingers when I inadvertently pinched them between my spine and the exam table during a test for abdominal strength. "Geez, no problems with your core!" he said with a laugh.

"Now turn over and let's work on those back muscles." He grabbed the massage cream, applied it, and began to work. Left hand inserted, right hand massaging my back, he made small talk with my mom. "What are the other two kids doing for science right now?" he asked.

Before she could answer, he interrupted himself. "Man, I love those boots!" he said, glancing down at my black button-up ankle boots sitting next to Mom's chair. I doubted he really cared about my footwear, but he knew I liked them, so complimenting them was a nice gesture.

"Science is so important," he said, picking up his conversation with my mom. He always chatted with her about all the little things, including the homework lessons my siblings often worked on in the exam waiting room during my appointments. He had even flipped through my science book earlier that year, exclaiming in pleasant surprise at the college-level cellular and molecular biology units.

He fell silent for a moment as he concentrated. "Wow, you're really tight here." I lay still as he worked on a sore spot on my lower back, left hand always massaging internally. His voice trailed off, and he closed his eyes. Then he casually pulled his hand out and moved closer to my shoulders, standing in between my mom and me. Without a pause he unhooked my bra through my shirt.

He must need to work on my upper back, I reasoned, though he had never done so before. His breathing became faster, and I glanced up. Eyes still closed, he seemed totally lost in thought. I put my head back down but looked up again in surprise a few minutes later when he came around to the other side of the table.

He's never done that before, I thought. *He always stands on the other side between Mom and me.* Wordlessly, he put his hands on my hips and rotated me to my side, facing him, away from my mom. *Why . . . ? What's . . . ? That's totally new . . .*

I glanced over at him. *Something is wrong.* Fear swept over me. I didn't know why or how I could tell, but something was very, very wrong. I glanced at Larry again. Eyes closed, he was breathing heavily, almost panting. His face was visibly flushed. And his pants . . . I noticed a visible bulge in the front of his pants. *That's not . . . that's not possible!*

His right hand reached over my hip and he kept massaging my back. His left hand stayed in the front, bracing me as he pushed with his right on the sore muscles from behind. He began working his way up my torso, one hand on my back, one hand in front. My mind raced. He was going to go up my shirt. *He wouldn't. Of course he wouldn't.* But at the same time, I knew that's exactly what he was going to do. Time compressed as my mind raced with questions, second-guessing my own instincts because it was *Larry*.

Without a pause, without missing a beat, he kept working and his hand went up. Confusion and fear swirled around me. I was screaming for him to stop, but not a sound was coming out. Panic set in, and for a brief moment the room went dark and I blacked out. Dizzy and disoriented, I eventually felt him turn me back over and rehook my bra.

"I think that does it. Go ahead and sit up!" he chirped cheerfully.

What just happened?

He guided me to a sitting position. I still felt so light-headed and confused I thought I might pass out. So much shock was rushing through my mind and body, I couldn't say a word, and even if I could, what would I say?

What just happened?

Who is *this?* This Olympic doctor? The one who'd taken care of me? The husband of the cute pregnant woman I'd just recently met? The father of a soon-to-be born daughter? *Who is this?* I was sixteen. He was nearing forty.

I sat on the crinkly paper absentmindedly responding when appropriate as he gave instructions to my mom for further physical therapy. Everything I knew about Larry, everything he'd said and done swirled around me.

I could not reconcile the man I knew with the man who had just been touching me in places and in ways I was *sure* he shouldn't. I went through the motions of ending the appointment and checking out. I did everything I could to appear normal. I didn't want him to know how ashamed and afraid I'd been. I now realize that at some level I understood that, though I'd failed at keeping him from my body, I could keep him from my mind. I could protect my thoughts and emotions. I could shut him out of those.

Who else has he done this to?

I could protect myself by not drawing extra attention to the shame. I smiled and thanked him, and we left.

As I lay in bed that night, my mind raced. *Am I reading too much into this? Could there have been a reason?* Larry had done it on purpose. It was calculated. I knew this. And I knew what that meant. The Larry I thought I knew was not the real Larry. *How is that possible?* Even thinking someone was a sexual abuser was an incredibly serious accusation.

How arrogant can you be to think he'd find you attractive? I didn't know then that sexual abuse isn't about external sex appeal. It is about control. Anyone can be a target. Even teens in the totally awkward stage of their adolescent years. But what if it was really just the oversexualized, overly dramatic thinking of my teenage mind? If I was wrong, I would ruin not just Larry, but myself, too.

But I wasn't wrong.

All night long I fought with myself, shaking my head as if I could clear away the arguing voices the way a small child vehemently shakes pennies from a piggy bank. I squeezed my hands into fists, my fingernails digging into my palms, the sharp pinch giving me something to focus on and use to orient myself.

I knew what the truth was, but it didn't bring clarity. It upended everything I thought I knew. Every perception I'd had. Every interaction. Every word. Every comment. The truth didn't bring calm. It brought confusion, disorientation, anger. *Who is this man?* The person who had calculatingly abused me that afternoon and the person everyone knew, *whom I knew*—how did those two sides fit together? And what should I do?

While I knew something had happened to me that was wrong, I didn't know yet that the penetration and everything I'd written off as "pelvic floor therapy" had been anything *but* legitimate. I was, however, certain that no one would care about a teenage girl getting groped. Anyone could look around and know that. The sexual harassment and objectification of women, the dirty jokes, the "locker room talk," and the sexually aggressive behavior of men were constantly downplayed.

What I also knew was that my abuse was likely to be viewed by many as a compliment rather than a crime. And that was *if* anyone even believed me. Sadly, I'd been down that road before—in, of all places, the church I grew up in.

• • •

I still remember it like it was yesterday. The church was small, just a few hundred people, and everyone knew everyone. My mom played flute and sang on occasion. I earned a reputation early on for loving children, and I frequently cuddled babies for tired moms after the service or played with their toddlers in the nursery during business meetings. Our family was part of a tight-knit small group Bible study that was a highlight of every week, and my parents had been close friends with many of the people there long before I was born. I'd been born alongside their children, and we had grown up together. That church was part of our family, and we were part of it.

But something changed when I was seven. I stopped heading straight from Sunday school to the church mailbox—a small set of cubbies, each with a family's name inscribed—to check for notes and newsletters. I didn't walk the hallways anymore, using my finger to trace the lines between the giant bricks covered in thick cream paint. And I wandered the bright-green lawn with the other kids a lot less. I spent a lot more time hiding in the girls' bathroom, shaking and wishing someone would ask what was wrong but knowing I wouldn't know what to say if they did.

I had been abused and was still being preyed upon by a college student at the church. He'd managed to do it while sitting me on his lap during a church Bible study. No one knew except me, and I wasn't sure what I knew, except that I felt terrified and physically ill. I wasn't about to describe what made me feel that way, either. So I hung out in the washroom, the one place he couldn't find me. Then one week, he didn't come back. I figured he'd finished college and moved. But somehow, even after he was gone, things didn't go back to normal. The Bible study we were part of eventually ended. The adults I loved and trusted suddenly seemed icy and distant. Some of our closest friends left to start a new church. The ones who remained weren't close to us anymore. More than a year later, we left too. The reasons were vague and unclear. I was devastated at the loss and frustrated that I couldn't understand or just be told what had happened.

Years later, when I was about twelve, unable to shake the vivid memories from that time, I told my mom what he'd done. She paused for a long moment and then said a broken "I'm so sorry." We talked about it. I asked questions, and I finally got the answers I wanted. But I didn't like them.

It turned out that my abuser had been asked to leave because several female college students had complained about his behavior. But alarms had been raised much earlier about his behavior toward me and another little girl in the church. A missionary couple and a group of adults who were sexual assault counselors saw the warning signs—grooming and targeting, inordinate amounts of targeted attention, and physical overfamiliarity. They spoke up, not realizing anything had already happened. My parents responded immediately by taking steps to protect me. Truth be told, they were uncomfortable with some of his behaviors too and had already put up some boundaries. But they hadn't cut off contact yet, second-guessing their instincts, knowing how serious it was to even entertain the idea that someone might be a predator. Because of adults who spoke up and parents who responded immediately, I'd been saved from worse abuse, and for that I will always be profoundly grateful.

But I also learned the other side of the story. Many of our friends, a number of them lay leaders and prominent people in the church, didn't see my parents' actions as protective. Because I hadn't verbalized any abuse, my parents' response was viewed as an accusation made with no proof, and the expertise of the sexual assault counselors was discounted by many because they used materials by psychologists and licensed therapists. The fact that these psychologists were Christian didn't really matter. The materials were "outside Scripture," so they couldn't be trusted.

Some of the people who raised an alarm, my mom included, were themselves survivors of abuse. At times, skeptics wielded this against them like a weapon: "Survivors always oversexualize everything," they said, "imposing their experiences on everything around them," so they couldn't be trusted either.

And it wasn't just me. The issue of sexual assault and how it should be handled had been a stick in the church's proverbial craw for a very long time. Animosity over what methods were and weren't appropriate and biblical to use in the church's sexual abuse counseling ministry had pitted members against one another for years. My mom explained that, in the same building where survivors wept and prayed with counselors, other church members passed out cassette tapes attacking the materials and experts the counselors relied upon, branding them as unbiblical and ungodly. Certain small groups didn't want members of the counseling ministry in their Bible studies. And all the while this man was preying upon me, and the animosity was reaching a fever pitch.

As so often happens, misguided theology and a refusal to interact with experts on this issue led the church to miss—and then cover up—sexual abuse within its own walls. And it hadn't affected only me. Other serious and credible allegations of this form of abuse had been buried. For a small church of only a few hundred people, sexual abuse had become a predominant, well-kept secret. Each time an abuser was found or a scandal uncovered, the response was the same. Quietly dismiss the abuser. Hush it up. Tell no one. My parents knew many of the details only because they were savvy enough to know the methods of dismissal didn't add up, and they were close enough to key leaders in the church to demand answers.

The information my mom gave me after I told her what had happened brought clarity to questions that had swirled in my mind for years and explained icy behaviors I couldn't previously understand. It also left me with a lesson I've never forgotten and had in fact taken into the exam room with Larry: *If you can't prove it, don't speak up. Because it will cost you everything.*

As I lay in bed the night after Larry abused me, I remembered the time I'd found out why we'd lost our church and had begun to recognize how too many churches treat sexual abuse. The unwillingness to believe. The refusal to engage with experts. The denigration of those who do. Hushed secrecy to preserve the pristine image of "the gospel," when justice would demonstrate the love of Christ much better. And I knew the situation outside the church wasn't any different. If our own friends hadn't been willing to believe my parents' concerns about a college student, the general public would *never* believe the word of a no-name sixteen-year-old gymnast against a world-renowned Olympic doctor. As much as my church wanted to avoid negative press and preserve its reputation, a Big Ten university like Michigan State and an Olympic governing body like USAG would want to avoid it even more. And they would have the power to bury whatever I reported. My mom and I knew from the earlier abuse we'd suffered that when abusers feel empowered and uncatchable, they typically tend to escalate their activities. Trying and failing would have serious consequences for far more people than just me.

I thought about telling my mom. I knew she'd believe me. But I was too afraid to put words to it. Words would make it so much more real. And the confusion that swirled around me in that moment still hadn't left. I wasn't even sure how to think clearly. Besides, there was nothing she could do. Her voice added to mine would be no more powerful against the institutions and people surrounding Larry.

There was nothing I could do.

• • •

A few days later, I realized I had another problem. I was supposed to keep seeing Larry for treatment. If I stopped, I would have to explain why, which felt impossible. So I determined I would simply tell Larry my back felt better. He could treat my wrists, and we'd leave it at that.

At the next visit, it seemed like nothing had changed, at least for him—same engaging demeanor, same small talk, same eye contact with my mom and me. When I told him my back was doing better, he seemed glad and didn't miss a beat, focusing on my wrists instead. Only one thing was really new. Larry had finally become what he'd been waiting for. He was a dad.

"Come here, come here!" Larry insisted, almost in a whisper, his voice full of excitement. "Come on!" He motioned for me to stand by the door and slipped away for a moment, returning with a soft, tiny bundle. "I know you really wanted to see her, and I've just got to show her off!" His face beamed with pride as he brought his newborn daughter to me. His wife had come for a visit earlier, and when Larry noticed I had come in, he called her cell and asked her to come back to the office so I could see the baby.

"Do you want to hold her?" he asked, already knowing the answer. He knew how much I loved children. He placed the baby in my arms and whispered, "She's amazing."

His firstborn had a tiny button nose, butterfly eyelids closed in sleep, and dark hair just like Larry's. A delicate hand peeked out of her swaddled blanket. "She looks just like you," I whispered.

That was the last time I saw Larry. He just never asked me to schedule another appointment. My wrists weren't better. Perhaps there really was nothing more to be done at that point. Perhaps he'd lost interest. Or he had simply gotten what he wanted. In any case, it was over.

For the next year, I tried to put it out of my mind. Whenever memories resurfaced, I gave myself a firm mental shake. There was nothing I could do, I reasoned, so there was no point in thinking about it. Whenever I felt anger or fear, I chastised myself, repeating the same lies I'd heard society tell every sexual assault victim: *Stop being overdramatic. It wasn't that big of a deal. You're reading into it and making something worse than it was.*

Why . . . *why* couldn't I just get over it?

• • •

As the months went by, I found myself continually growing more agitated. My threshold for the general leering that women deal with on a regular basis was slim to none. I knew now that thoughts could be turned into actions without warning, and I constantly felt unsafe and exposed. Nightmares came without warning, and memories of my first abuser resurfaced with a vengeance. My mind replayed everything Larry had done to gain my trust—simple compliments, innocent touches, light conversation, interest in who I was.

How do I trust that anyone is sincere? I wondered.

The most basic acts of human relationships had been misused. My own trust had been weaponized. My request for help had been exploited. Perhaps the only way to prevent being abused again was simply to shut these things down. Don't trust. Ever. Period.

My mom was noticing a shift too. Crowded places, men standing behind me, simple trips to shopping malls or fast-food places were becoming a problem. What would start out as a fun mom-daughter date would swiftly and without warning devolve into an attitude shift that left me flustered and snappish. She knew something wasn't right.

After one particularly disastrous trip to Subway, where the normally even-keeled version of me morphed into a backbiting, agitated version that couldn't provide a civil answer to the simplest question, my mom was sure something had to have happened that she didn't know about. Being the astute woman she is, she didn't hash it out then and there; instead, she maintained her cool and waited for a better time to dig a little deeper.

"So, can I ask you what was going on at Subway?" she asked nonchalantly over the sound of running water. It was a day or two later. We were washing dishes together, and she was handling the rinsing while I washed. I was a relatively captive audience, and she knew it.

"Yeah, I'm sorry," I sighed. "I know I got crabby. I was just really hungry." I washed the glass tumbler in my hand a little more enthusiastically than was probably necessary. Truth be told, I didn't even understand my own responses. In the rare instances when I did let myself realize why I was agitated or fearful, a quick shake and admonition to "stop being so dramatic" would quickly shove it down.

"Are you sure that's all?" she asked, taking the glass from me and running it under the hot water. "I've noticed a pattern. It's not just when you're hungry. Is there a reason having someone stand behind you is making you so agitated?"

I put another cup into the sink and feigned innocence. "Does it?"

"Honey . . ." Mom paused. "Has something happened that I don't know about?" In the silence that followed, she took the cup I offered her and rinsed it.

"I don't know." *Okay, yeah, that's a lie.*

"What's going on?" Mom persisted gently. I knew her well enough to know I wasn't getting away with it any longer. I focused on the handful of silverware I was scrubbing and told her how Larry had groped my breast. She kept her voice calm as more bubbles met their demise under the running water.

"That makes me very, very angry. I am so sorry." Her voice was filled with grief, anger, and regret.

She believed me. I knew she would. She knew what it was like not to be believed.

"I don't even know where to start," she said.

I knew she'd be honest with me.

"I am so sorry, honey. How could I have missed that? I was right there in the room."

And I knew she'd blame herself. The grief in her voice was obvious.

"It wasn't your fault," I assured her. "He knew exactly what he was doing and turned me away so you couldn't see. There's no way you could have seen, and I didn't say anything." *It was my fault*, I finished silently.

"I wouldn't expect you to be able to," she countered. "This is not your fault." Her mind-reading skills were typically spot-on. We washed and rinsed in silence a bit more. "Your dad really needs to know. How are you most comfortable handling that?"

I thought for a minute. "I'd rather have you tell him. I'm not really comfortable talking about it very much."

"I thought so," she acknowledged. "I'll let you know after I talk to him so you don't have to wonder."

I lifted the stack of plates into the soapy water, trying not to splash anything into the yellow washing gloves I always wore. The plates clattered gently, and the running water made soft swishing sounds across the glasses still being rinsed.

"I am so sorry," Mom said again.

We finished the dishes in silence. There wasn't much more to be said.

. . .

A few days later, we laced on our tennis shoes after dinner and went for a walk.

"Can I ask you something about Larry?" Mom asked, as we rounded the first corner.

I nodded.

"Do you think it's possible that anything was wrong with the pelvic floor treatment?" she asked.

My heart sank. That was the one question I didn't want to face. It was also the question that whispered in the back of my mind no matter how often I tried to drown it out. I shook myself mentally. *Reason it out. Don't over-dramatize and read into everything!* I sternly warned myself.

"I've wondered that," I admitted, "but I don't think so. I mean, we know it's a legitimate form of treatment. We know physical therapists here practice it. We know Larry does treatments no one else does. If he's doing pelvic floor treatment as often as he obviously is, there's no way he isn't certified. Someone would have stopped him a long time ago. I mean . . ." I flashed back to the appointment with Ashley. "We know he's doing this all the time, multiple times a day."

I could sense she wasn't satisfied. "I'm just wondering because . . . as I look back on it, some things seem a little off." She listed a few things. He hadn't worn gloves. He hadn't asked her permission or really explained what he was doing. I nodded and took a few deep breaths. I didn't really have an answer, but I also wasn't ready to let myself go there. I didn't *know* I wasn't ready. In my mind, the answers I gave just made sense.

She paused again. "When he touched your breasts, it was the second-to-last visit, wasn't it?"

I nodded.

"I thought so, because I saw an erection. I'm so sorry, honey." She searched for words. "I thought I must have been mistaken . . ." Her voice trailed off. "There was one other appointment where I thought I saw it. I just . . . didn't think it was possible. It was *Larry*."

I understood. I also knew most people wouldn't.

"Okay, I have one more question." She paused. "Have you thought about needing to go to the police?" My heart sank again. There were actually two questions I didn't want to deal with, and of course she'd found both of them.

"I don't know what to do," I said in calm desperation. Our feet crunched the sticks littering the sidewalk as we passed under the large maple trees lining the block nearest our house.

"Around again?" Mom asked.

"Yeah," I acquiesced, still thinking about her question. "I don't know what to do, Mom. The police almost never charge small crimes like this. The likelihood that anything would be done is next to nothing. But he'd know that I know and that he didn't get caught."

Mom nodded. "Have you thought about the fact that he's probably going to do this again, and probably has done it lots before?"

I sighed, my heart aching. This weighed on me more than anything. "Yeah, and it scares the daylights out of me. But Mom, if he's doing this a lot, chances are someone has already spoken up, maybe lots of people. But he's still doing it, which means no one has listened. And they won't listen to me."

My mom let out an exhausted sigh. "I don't know how we would get anyone to believe us." I was grateful she didn't sugarcoat the reality.

"MSU and USAG will have a lot of reasons to want to bury this," I added, completing her thought. "I can't fight both organizations. I wouldn't even know how to generate the kind of pressure needed to force them to take me seriously."

It felt like an insurmountable hurdle. How does one person overcome two massive institutions and the international fame and beloved status of an abuser?

"What if we went to the press?" my mom asked.

I had thought about that. It *might* work. It was 2002, and the *Boston Globe*'s Spotlight investigation into the Catholic Church sex abuse scandal was still sending shock waves through the world.

"That might be the only way to create enough pressure to get someone to listen. If we could reach other victims . . . get it out of his control and out of the control of the organizations. *But how would we even do that?*"

And here again, we both knew we were stuck.

"I mean, could we drive down to the local news station and tell them the story?" Mom wondered.

I shook my head. "Journalists don't just do stories like that. You have to have some sort of proof, and my word won't be enough." I paused. "And if anyone ever does find out what he's doing, it will be a national news story because of who he is. I honestly don't know if I can handle my abuse being a national news story, and even if we tried to protect my identity, there's a good chance my name would come out."

I knew that was a real possibility. Deep down, I knew I would take that chance if I had to, but I needed an actual way forward first, and I just didn't see it. No media outlet would pick up a story without something to back it up, and the likelihood of being believed in the first place . . . that was slim to none.

"But what if he does it again?" Mom asked once more.

I felt despair settle in. "He probably will, but I have no idea how to stop him. One anonymous voice will never be enough."

Mom was quiet. We both knew the reality. There was nothing that could be done.

7

"HOORAY, HOORAY, HOORAY FOR ME!" sang the tiny gymnast, her blonde pigtails bouncing up and down as she danced in a circle waving her arms. I had just complimented this tiny person on keeping her tummy tucked in when she did a cast, pushing her body away from the single-rail bar and returning to it again, and she was now doing her own personalized victory dance, congratulating herself on a job well done. I burst out laughing and scooped her up.

"You did great, baby girl. I'm so proud of your hard work!" I looked around at the diminutive gymnasts clad in sparkly leotards of various colors, and smiled. Along the far wall, Leigh was practicing her kick handstands, but she was so young, no matter how "hollow" she tried to be, her rotund little belly popped out adorably. She smiled at me from in between her upside-down pigtails, her dimpled little cheeks showing how much toddler still remained in the newly minted four-year-old. On the small balance beam, Greta was practicing her relevé walks, cheeks sucked in, her mouth forming a perfect little *o* in concentration. In various stations around me, half a dozen little girls—my "baby gymnasts"—were practicing their skills or sitting crisscross applesauce on a giant yellow rubber circle, bouncing their little legs up and down with boundless energy. My heart felt full. I had made the perfect transition.

About six months earlier, Jackie, the head coach at my new gym, had talked with me about options. She had been coaching me since my Kalamazoo gym had merged with one in another city a few years before. "You know, Rach, I'm here for whatever you want, and I'm always happy to work with you. But if you do decide to stop training, I can help you transition to coaching. It's a great way to stay involved in the sport, and you could have a huge impact on little girls."

I knew she was being sincere. We both knew I was never going to go anywhere in the sport, and if I did return to competing, it wouldn't be impressive. But she'd poured into me anyway, working within my limits, suggesting novel and creative skills I could put into routines to make what I *could* do unique and even keep my training fun. While her personality was very different from that of Erin, my former coach, her philosophy was much the same, and it showed. She cared about every girl individually and what the sport could teach them, rather than what the girls could earn her. She was calm, reasonable, and kindly firm. We knew we could approach her with concerns and be heard and cared for, but we definitely couldn't run her over. She didn't do a victory dance as Erin had when we finally nailed a skill, but her sincere "I am so happy for you!" meant just as much.

We talked about it for a few weeks, and then I made the decision after I considered my other commitments and priorities. I had recently finished high school and realized that full-time college work wasn't compatible with competitive training. My chances of competing again were slim to none, and even if I did, I probably would gain nothing—other than more injuries. But what I could learn from Jackie about working with kids, helping them overcome fears, and teaching them life skills through the sport—*that* had lasting value.

I jumped at the chance to learn under her, and it was everything I'd hoped for. Not long afterward, I started coaching a few classes of my own.

Life revolved around schoolwork and the gym, but now it took on a new form. I still studied while doing the splits and conditioned to maintain my physical fitness, and every once in a while, when the classes were over, I'd flip around just for fun. But mostly I coached. In addition to helping with the competitive teams, I coached the team-oriented programs for little girls, classes designed for the kids who showed promise in the sport.

"You'll see it in their eyes," the gym owner told me. "There's a sharpness there. The kids who love it and have 'got it'—their eyes light up. If you aren't sure whether a child is ready for a team program, look for the sparkle in their eyes."

He was right. It takes more than physical ability to excel in gymnastics. Kids who are ready for more are also mentally and emotionally distinct. They have an intellectual sharpness that enables them to understand instructions and apply corrections even at a very young age. They are capable of grasping cause and effect, the impact their work has on their ability to progress. They have a fire and a drive to learn, and an emotional maturity that enables them to focus and handle more rigorous training. These kids tend to be precocious and witty, and that leads to a great deal of fun for a coach.

As my class of eight girls—all around six years old—gathered one day, Jade and Jillian sat down next to each other a few feet away from me. I was sitting in a pike position and had just given them a new set of leg lifts to perform as part of our conditioning.

Jade and Jillian were aware enough to follow instructions, but somehow entirely oblivious to the reality that I could follow every word of their conversation.

"Why do you think coaches don't wear leotards?" Jade asked Jillian.

Jillian shrugged. "I don't know. It would probably be easier not to. But we have to wear them, so coaches *definitely* probably should."

"Well, coaches are *really* big," Jade observed, "and leotards aren't. I think maybe they don't make leotards big enough for her." She nodded in my direction as she brought her legs up to touch her nose.

Jillian pondered this as she counted but shook her head and announced in a statement that ended the conversation for the moment: "Naw, I think they can make big ones. I think she just doesn't wear a leotard because she'd be *embarrassed*."

Other times, my precocious and precious little people were more direct in expressing their thoughts, like the time one of my babies, an adorable five-year-old girl whose favorite leotard was purple with sparkles, looked up at me when I came over to help stretch out her splits and asked, "Are you wearing lipstick today?"

"Nope," I cheerfully responded. "I didn't have time to put any on before I came here. I would have been late!"

"Hmph," she replied in a cheerful tone. Then, without missing a beat, she declared, "Well, you *should*. You look a *whole* lot better with it!"

I burst out laughing. Life was never dull with the baby gymnasts around.

I was also learning about the incredible power a coach had. Gymnastics is an intensely physical sport that is dependent on correct technique, not just to progress in skill, but to stay safe. This meant that even at the lowest levels, coaches had to have a significant amount of physical contact with children: repositioning them to emphasize correct body shape and placement, and spotting so that everyone stayed safe even while gymnasts trained in the most basic skills. Granted, this came with some risk to a coach—like the time I was spotting an athlete on the uneven bars, and she straddled when she should have piked and broke my nose with her knee. I never told her because I knew she'd feel terrible!

But coaches' opportunities to misuse their access to children's bodies created far more risk. Sometimes coaches could endanger gymnasts physically—overstretching athletes or pushing them beyond what was safe and desired—and sometimes verbally and emotionally, via demeaning or threatening words that tied the children's value to their status in the athletic world. I also saw the risk for sexual abuse. Girls not only had to *accept* being touched by a coach, but their safety was dependent on it, and they knew it.

Beyond that, I saw the close bonds kids developed with their coaches. By the time children were competing at the lowest levels, they were typically in the gym at least four nights every week, and often this started when they were only eight or nine years old. The gymnasts' coaches were with them through it all—from the grief, frustration, and pain of injuries to the excitement and joy of every milestone and progression reached. This, coupled with intense amounts of time together and the constant need to be in close physical contact, created the perfect environment for a great deal of harm.

Most athletes—conditioned from a very young age to trust their coaches and respond to them as authority figures—would be unlikely to recognize verbal, emotional, and yes, even physical and sexual abuse. Worse, many gyms operated in a way that cut parents off from their children, providing very little viewing space, making it hard to see and impossible to hear what was going on in the gym.

Gymnasts who went to meets were often not allowed to travel or stay with their parents on the road—including very young girls at beginning levels of competition. Even the most vigilant parent eventually gets used to the gym routine and simply can't stay to watch practice every day of the week. Perhaps most disturbing, the same dynamics that lead a gymnast to trust her coach—intense time and significant experiences together, justifiable close physical contact, and a dependence on the coach for growth and safety—often cause parents to develop a deep trust and care for the coach. In many cases, this leads to a good working relationship. But it can also lead parents to brush off or entirely miss warning signs of a predator, leaving their children unprotected and with nowhere to turn if something goes wrong.

I remembered practicing at a new gym once while on vacation with my family and feeling shocked when the head coach, at the end of practice, gleefully gave a young gymnast her "birthday spankings," his hands repeatedly and playfully smacking her little bottom. Not ten feet away, the row of moms waiting to pick up their daughters watched and laughed. "He does this with all of them at their birthdays. It's so cute!" I heard one say. I didn't know if that coach was a predator, but I realized with horror that this coach had just used play to normalize touching a young girl's private areas, and he'd done it so successfully that the parents thought it was cute.

Shutting a parent out of the gym wasn't the only way to get away with abuse. Letting them in on everything and then normalizing questionable or dangerous behavior often worked just as well. A community could definitely be manipulated into silence through fear, the way I'd heard that the coach at Twistars terrified both the gymnasts and parents into absolute compliance. But sometimes an even more effective barrier to the truth is a community dedicated to an abuser because of what feels like a caring and good relationship.

I was grateful not to see any of these dynamics in either my old or new gym, but I knew those dangers were out there and very real. I felt that coaching was my way of doing what I could to positively impact a child, and I was determined to use the power that came with coaching to help grow these little girls into safe, strong, confident, valued women.

More than anything, I wanted my gymnasts to understand that their value didn't come from what they *did*, but rather who they *were*. Gymnastics might feel like their whole life now, but I knew their days in the gym would end, and if their value was tied up in a sport, they were likely to struggle at many things in life. They were more likely not to know when to say no to the sport or a coach, even if their own health or safety was at risk. And if athletic success defined their value, they would also be far more likely to suffer from anxiety, depression, or struggles with body image and self-worth. How I spoke to them and how I treated them would teach them what they were worth. And those lessons, I knew, would follow them forever.

As I modified my own approach to help ensure these outcomes, I started altering the way I corrected them. If a gymnast was fooling around and not focusing, I didn't correct her failure to achieve a skill; instead, I reminded her that her ability to learn depended on how well she used her time. If an athlete mastered a skill, I didn't praise her for nailing it but told her how proud I was of her focus and how excited she should be to see her hard work pay off. At the end of that practice, I might turn to her teammate who was working just as hard but not as successfully. I'd remind that girl how proud I was of her diligence, telling her, "You've kept working at it even though it's taking a long time, and that's really hard to do. You did very well today." The sweetest moments in coaching often were not the days a gymnastics skill was achieved, but the days a life skill was.

●　　●　　●

By the time the 2003–2004 competition season rolled around, I'd been coaching my own precompetitive teams for a while. I loved my work and the sport. I had grown in my skills as a coach and as a person. The one thing I felt I'd made no progress in was "getting over" what Larry had done. I still had nightmares, I was no less fearful in close quarters with men than I had been a year ago, and getting medical care, while necessary, felt impossible.

I hated that it affected my daily life, my work, everything I loved. I chastised myself repeatedly for not moving past it, but felt it was impossible to discern who was safe and who was only pretending to be safe. And that competition season, my apprehension followed me to the gym in ways I had hoped it never would.

I'd just finished a private lesson with a little girl I'd been working with since that spring. Around seven years old, she was as sweet and quiet as they come, but fiercely determined. It was a fantastic combination. There was only one problem. Her feet turned significantly inward, making gymnastics difficult and potentially unsafe as she progressed. We'd been doing stretches and exercises with her ankles and knees, hoping to help correct the issue, but over the past year it hadn't gotten any better.

Though Jackie was in the middle of a training session, she stopped for a minute to discuss the situation once she saw I'd finished working with the girl for that day. "I'm concerned that some of her pigeon toe might be structural, coming from her hips. I think she needs to see a specialist," Jackie said, keeping her eyes on her gymnasts as we talked.

I nodded. That made sense.

After starting to walk toward her team, Jackie paused and said, "So I've told her mom I'd like her to see Larry to get her hips checked out. They've got an appointment set up, and we'll go from there."

Wait, what?

She kept moving. "Okay, girls, grab a drink and head to beam."

I stood, frozen. *Larry. For her hips.* I felt sick. If she was going to him for her hips, he'd have easy access to everything. I knew there was no way I could let that happen. That was *my* baby. *My* little gymnast. *No one* was going to touch her. I was going to have to tell someone and just hope I'd be believed. Options raced through my mind as I started setting up for my next class.

Who do I tell? What do I tell them? I shook my head as I put a wedge up against the wall for handstands. *There is no way anyone is going to believe this.* I felt hopeless, and I felt desperate. I dropped the toddler bars down a notch—my next girls were pretty tiny. *You've got to try. It doesn't matter what happens; you have to try.* That was *my* gymnast. She was under *my* protection. *I* was responsible.

I went home that night feeling sick but determined to come up with a plan.

"I've got to tell someone, Mom," I said desperately. She agreed. We both knew what had to be done. We mulled over how to handle it. Did we go together? Have Mom call someone? Who should we talk to? How would we even explain what happened?

I took a deep breath and stepped back to think it through calmly. What were my options? My immediate concern was stopping my little girl from seeing Larry. Just telling the police wouldn't accomplish this. I had to talk to someone directly related to her. *Her mom?* I decided against this. She was determined that her daughter was going to be successful, and from experience I knew she wasn't inclined to listen to a younger coach. And if I did tell her, she'd go straight to Jackie or the gym owner for confirmation anyway, which they wouldn't be able to give if I didn't tell them first. I had a better chance of being listened to if someone in authority backed me up. Otherwise I'd get nowhere.

Should I start with the gym owner? I ran my hands through my ponytail; they were a bit chalky from coaching that day. The gym owner was good friends with Larry. In fact, he'd recently been treating her for an injury she'd sustained after other doctors had botched recovery. And the gym had been sending girls to Larry for a while. They had a good working relationship with him. The owner *might* believe me, but I didn't think it was likely. *If someone else comes with me, though . . . if someone else she trusts believes me, she just might believe too.*

Jackie. It had to be Jackie. She was the head coach and well respected by the gymnastics community. She also had a good relationship with the gym owner and the little girl's mom. If she so much as told them she was concerned, there was a much higher chance they would listen. There was also another dynamic I considered very important—her boyfriend, Mike. Jackie was in a stable, long-term relationship with a police officer. I knew he worked with assault victims in his job. If anyone would understand trauma and why victims don't speak up, or how cunning an abuser can be, it would be Mike. I didn't know if Jackie would understand these dynamics, but Mike should, and I *knew* she'd talk to him. He could help her understand.

I traced the rose-colored pattern on my bedspread. The thought of putting what I had experienced into words filled me with shame and fear. The reality that those words would be transmitted to a man was even worse. But it was also my best chance, and I had to do what was most likely to succeed, no matter what. I knew something else—police officers often don't get behind sexual assault investigations. Yet I also knew that if someone in blue at least vouched for me—if Mike so much as told an investigating officer that I was credible—my chances of getting police to take my claims seriously would go up exponentially.

Maybe, just maybe, I could now report what had happened. This was not just a last-ditch effort to save my little girl. This was a test. Would someone in the gymnastics community believe me enough to act? Could I convince a police officer I personally knew that I was telling the truth? If I couldn't do that, there was no hope that someone who didn't know me would believe me. But if they did believe me . . . maybe now I could report Larry. Maybe now I could stop him. I knew they both would want to do the right thing, but it would be my word against Larry's—my perceptions of what he'd done against Larry's reputation. If I couldn't get someone who wanted to do the right thing to understand who and what Larry was, and to believe that when I said I'd been abused, I really did know what had happened, then I'd never get anyone to *really* believe me.

When I went to work the next day, I was determined to talk with Jackie immediately. Classes would start in just a few minutes, so I needed to handle it right away. I picked my way over the mat-strewn floor toward the balance beams, my stomach churning as I went. Jackie was engaged in conversation with another coach, Megan, as they worked through that day's practice schedule for the compulsory team.

"Hey, Jackie, I've got something I need to talk to you about privately," I said when there was a lull in conversation.

I glanced at Megan. "Do you want me to leave?" she asked kindly, taking the hint.

"No, you're fine," Jackie interjected. "What's up, Rach?"

I took a deep breath. *Okay.* I calmed myself. *I guess I'm telling two people today.* "I need to talk to you about sending Sophie to see Larry. I . . . I don't think you should do that."

Jackie looked at me patiently.

I'm not doing this well. I bit my lip and tried again. "Larry . . . Larry does things. He's really good at hiding what he's doing while pretending to do exams and treatments. He does things that aren't . . . kosher." I pleaded silently for her to understand what I meant before I had to say it more explicitly.

"What do you mean?" she asked calmly.

You have to say it explicitly. I felt the heat rush to my face. I refused to cry. I was *not* going to throw up. I traced the mat seam with my finger.

"Larry sexually abuses his patients under the guise of medical treatment. He abused me."

Megan stared in silence.

"Well . . . I mean, how do you know? There have to be medical reasons for what he's doing?" Jackie said.

Oh, this is not going well. I understood her confusion; I had felt it, too. I'd *lived* it.

"There have to be medical reasons," Jackie repeated.

I felt like crying. *You've got to try again.*

"There was no medical reason for him to unhook my bra and massage my bare breast."

No one spoke.

"And there's other stuff that I don't think is right either." *Not. Going. To. Cry.* I had thought through what details to share the night before. I wasn't sure yet about the pelvic floor treatment. I had growing concerns that the abuse might be worse than I had understood, but I couldn't prove it yet. So I told her about it and the warning signs that it wasn't right, but I focused extra emphasis on that last visit. A breast massage should obviously be crossing the line for anyone.

It was the first time I'd spoken those words out loud to anyone except my mom. I wouldn't even write them. For the past two years, I'd fought letting those memories resurface, and now I had to describe them. I took a deep breath. She had to understand how good Larry was at hiding this.

"He had an erection while he was doing it," I told her. "My mom was right there in the room, and he was able to hide the abuse from her. He knows what he's doing. No one should be seeing him." I stopped. There was nothing else to say.

"Well . . . okay. I'm glad you told me. I'll have to think about this a little bit." She stood up from the mat and moved to start the next practice.

Right. I think about it too. I fought back tears and took a deep breath. I had to go coach now too. *Get it together.* I'd done the best I could do. Now I had to wait. *Maybe she and Mike will believe me. Maybe I can report this now. Maybe we can stop him.* But I felt less than confident.

• • •

"Jackie called me," Mom said as I climbed into the minivan after my class at the community college.

"Oh?" I felt a tiny bit of hope rise. "What did she say?"

"She said you'd told her something that she felt she needed to talk to me about."

Okay. That's good. She took it seriously enough to ask more questions. I knew she'd care. That's why I picked her to tell. Autumn colors graced the trees and flashed outside our window as we drove down a road lined with sugar maples.

"And?" I pressed.

Mom relayed the rest of the conversation. "She asked me not to take this the wrong way, but how was that possible if I was in the room?"

I winced. It was a fair question and I knew it, but it still stung. *I ask myself how I could have let this happen with someone in the room every time,* I thought, guilt rushing over me. *How could I not know? Why didn't I fight back?* I shook my head to get the thoughts out. It didn't matter. What mattered was the ultimate decision. Was I believed?

"I told her about seeing Larry's erection. I was really blunt; I felt like I had to be," Mom apologized. "She asked if I was sure, and I told her any married or sexually active woman knows what it looks like. There isn't any mistake. I told her about his face being flushed, the rapid breathing, all the signs he was aroused. I told her about the penetration, too, and why we thought it was problematic." She paused. Both of us hated this, and I knew Mom still felt that horrible guilt, even though I never thought it was her fault.

"And?" I pressed again, as we sat at a red light.

"And that was basically it," Mom sighed, starting to drive again. "I told her everything I knew, that you'd told me about what he did, and that we just hadn't known what to do. And that was it."

"Do you think she believes us?" I asked.

Mom sighed. "I think she's trying to figure it out, honey, and I understand that." We both did. The difficulty in getting anyone to believe such abuse was possible was the hurdle we hadn't been sure how to get over all along.

• • •

Several days later I walked into the gym, thinking through the plyometrics drills I wanted to run with my girls that night. I walked through the empty parent viewing area toward the office, glancing into the gym with lights just starting to come on as I went. I still hadn't heard anything from Jackie since she had spoken with my mom, but I was sure that, at a minimum, Sophie would be sent to a different doctor. My mind was focused on the lesson plans for that night, so I wasn't prepared when Jackie popped out of the office and came toward me.

"Hey, I wanted to follow up on our conversation the other day," she said, speaking quickly. "I talked to Mike." *I'd expected that.* "He used every channel he could to see if anyone has raised a complaint about Larry before. We looked everywhere. We can't find any evidence anyone else has ever raised the slightest concern about him."

I felt my heart sinking. *Of course not. Don't you know how many victims most predators have before anyone speaks up? That should be expected.*

"So I've decided to still have Sophie see Larry." I felt shock sweep across me. I opened my mouth, unsure what to even say. Jackie quickly held up her hands, gesturing for me to pause. "*But* I told her mom to make sure she understood everything Larry was doing. Like, ask a lot of questions and everything."

But . . . but I told you he abused me with my mom in the room. I told you he was really good at hiding it. My mom told you. My mind raced. What now? Should I go directly to Sophie's mom? I knew that risked a lot—undercutting the authority chain in that way—but I had to try. I snapped back to the present. Jackie was still talking.

"She's actually already had her appointment."

No. Oh no.

"He referred her to another specialist anyway."

Nothing. There was nothing I could do. It was already done. I felt absolute defeat. *Is there any chance someone else in the gym would believe me? Could I try again?*

"I really don't think you should say anything else," Jackie cautioned. "The gym owners are really close with him, especially after how much he's helped their gymnasts and even treated their own injuries. It could really go badly for you if it gets around to them."

I felt like I couldn't breathe.

"Okay. Well, I just wanted to follow up with you on that." And with that, she walked into the gym, flipping through her attendance book as she went.

I walked into the office feeling numb, replaying our conversation in my mind. *"We can't find any evidence anyone else has ever raised the slightest concern about him."* Jackie and Mike found that reassuring. I didn't. I knew that meant one thing, and one thing only: Whoever else was speaking up about Larry was getting shut down too. One voice was never going to be enough. Never.

I knew Jackie. And I knew Mike. I knew they really cared. I knew they wanted to do the right thing. And that made it so much worse. Jackie hadn't said they didn't believe me, but you don't send a child to someone you've been told is an abuser *if you really believe that person abuses*. You don't tell someone *not* to warn others. You help them do the warning *if you really believe someone is dangerous*. I hadn't saved Sophie. If I couldn't get a coach and a police officer who knew me to believe me enough to stop sending children to Larry, no one would ever listen.

8

"IT'S *YOU*!"

I blinked. I had *no idea* who this guy was. It was autumn of 2003, not long after I'd spoken to Jackie about Larry. I had finished my paralegal certificate a year earlier and was waiting for law school to begin, so I had taken a part-time job working for my state representative at the Michigan State Capitol on the days I wasn't coaching. I'd been considering some form of public policy work as a future career, so I'd jumped at the chance to work for a legislator whom I respected and who sat on several important budget and education committees.

"It's *you*!" the man said again. "You're the kid from a couple of years ago!"

I extended my hand to shake his. "I'm Rachael," I offered, a note of confusion in my voice.

"Hey," he called over my shoulder to my boss. "It's her! It's that kid I told you about a few years ago!"

I raised my eyebrows in amusement. I still had no idea where I'd apparently met this man before.

"Seriously? That was Rachael? I didn't know that!" My boss burst out laughing as the man turned to me.

"It's me—Mark," he explained. "You were at that camp. I testified before your committee, and you tore me to shreds. You were awful!"

A light was slowly dawning. "You mean the Student Statesmanship Institute?" I asked. The SSI was a Christian camp for high schoolers interested in government and leadership that I'd attended since 2000. After being broken into caucuses and committees, we were assigned real pieces of legislation to study and debate. Then we'd hold mock committee meetings and a mock legislature, and current legislators or their staff would play the roles of lobbyists.

"Yeah, that's it! They needed someone to role-play as a lobbyist, and Jack sent me," he continued. "Told me it was easy and not to worry about it. I had the info packet and everything, but you were insane! You had all this extra data and evidence that wasn't even in the packet, and you hammered me with questions and wouldn't let it go!" He laughed and shook his head.

I still couldn't place him.

"The actual representative chairing your committee basically offered you a job at the end of it."

Oh, now I remembered. I thought back to 2000, the first year I'd attended the camp. Despite loving debate, I was actually very quiet and shy. That was also the year I started being treated by Larry. I constantly felt unsafe but didn't know why, which only compounded my quiet and reserved demeanor. It was so noticeable the camp director thought I might not make it through the week.

I grinned at Mark. "Oooh, I remember that year. It *was* kinda bad, wasn't it?" The look on his face said it all. Not only did I not leave camp early that year, but by the end of the week, I had earned the nickname "Pit Bull"—in part because of *that* committee hearing.

"You're like this ferocious dog!" explained the counselor who gave me the nickname. "You look all sweet and innocent, and people *think* they're safe. But when you get hold of something, you sink your teeth into it, and you just won't let go! Straight for the throat with everything you've got," the counselor said with a laugh, "and you just won't give it up! It's incredibly effective."

The nickname had stuck with me ever since, including my last year at camp, when I'd given the closing argument at the camp's inaugural mock trial program. The judge for our team, a former federal judge and professor at a prominent law school in Lansing, had told me it was one of the best closings he'd heard in his entire career, and he suggested that I strongly consider law school. SSI had sparked my interest in public policy and debate. It had solidified my desire for law school. It had even been responsible for many of the political connections I had made to that point. But I hadn't anticipated it following me *quite* so closely into my work!

"Sorry," I said.

He laughed. "I came back here and told Jack about you. I said he ought to hire you!"

Wow. That's encouraging to hear, I thought.

"Well, welcome to the office . . . three years later." He smiled and then disappeared into a cubicle.

I loved working at the capitol. Of course, being back in Lansing several days a week also brought back a lot of memories—memories I didn't like. The ubiquitous MSU Spartans colors reminded me of more than football now. No matter how hard I tried, I just couldn't shake what had happened with Larry. It followed me everywhere—from the copy room, where close quarters with the staffer who was training me made focusing on the key code I was supposed to memorize very difficult; to my desk, whenever coworkers would reach across me for a piece of paper or come up behind my chair to ask a question. It made me agitated throughout the hour-and-a-half-long carpool to and from Lansing whenever a male coworker would sit behind me. It didn't matter that I was, in fact, confident the people I drove and worked with had integrity. No matter how much "sense" I tried to talk into myself, Larry had always been behind me during my medical appointments, and my mind and body remembered that as being dangerous. As a result, I intuitively responded with fear whenever someone stood behind me or too close to me. I hated it. It frustrated me. It made me angry. Not at Larry, but at myself. I was being overly dramatic. I was weak. The only way I knew how to cope was to try shutting the memories out and just "not let them bother me." I did everything I could to bury those thoughts. And when I couldn't, I blamed myself.

I remember driving home with my carpool one gray, rainy day when the cohosts of a radio talk show began discussing the sexual assault allegations against Michael Jackson.

"Crazy, huh?" one of them squawked incredulously. "I mean, how does a parent not pick up on something like that?"

I watched the raindrops slip across the windshield and kept my hands folded loosely in my lap. *Don't look tense.* I bit my lip and breathed slowly, counting the raindrops. I understood all too well how parents could miss the warning signs. *It's not so simple when you are living it*, I lamented silently.

I knew the guilt my own parents carried. I knew it wasn't their fault, and I'd told them as much, but I knew they still carried it.

"I mean, Michael was calling the kid on the phone!" the host continued.

I flashed back to my first abuser's face—the college student at church. *I got phone calls too.* I remembered my mom refusing to let him talk to me. I remembered hiding in the women's bathroom so he wouldn't find me.

"Seems like a pretty clear warning sign. Yet the kid apparently never said anything either!" the cohost sighed.

They think the child is partly to blame. I'm partly to blame. It was my fault. Both times. My fault.

Mark reached to turn the volume down and looked over at me. "Does this bother you?" he asked suddenly. I jumped ever so slightly and forced myself to make eye contact.

"No. No, it's fine," I responded as nonchalantly as I could. I was honestly grateful he'd asked, but now I felt even more fearful. I hadn't masked my emotions well enough to hide my discomfort. I'd left myself vulnerable. Exposed. The one thing Larry never had access to was my mind, and I was determined to protect it. I needed to appear calm, cool, and professional. Anything else reeked of vulnerability, and I was determined never to put myself in that position again.

● ● ●

That fall, my mom and I began doing a little more research into pelvic floor therapy. Both of us had a lingering sense of uneasiness about the "procedure" Larry had done with me, and we wanted to find out more about it. When I read up on the proper techniques, I was stunned to find nothing that resembled what he had done. Most of the time, I shut out the possibility of what *might* have been happening, but every once in a while, the questions would seep back in. *Was there more going on than I realized? Was there a reason I had felt so uneasy the whole time I saw him?* And yet the idea that I could have missed something so terrible—could have *allowed* something so violating—was unimaginable.

I continued to research the procedure in a desperate attempt to convince myself that what Larry had done was legitimate. Then I would stop again. Not because I wasn't finding answers, but because I wasn't getting the answers I wanted.

"Do you want me to ask Sue?" Mom finally asked. Sue was the owner of the physical therapy practice I'd been going to. She'd treated my back herself several times. One of the therapists she worked with specialized in pelvic floor treatment. I considered it for a moment.

"What if we just asked?" Mom pressed gently. "Just talked to her in general terms to find out what's normal?" I hated the idea. I hated the thought of even discussing it. But I also desperately wanted answers.

"Maybe you can ask while I'm working on my wrist?" I suggested. She readily agreed. I hadn't described to anyone exactly *how* Larry had done his supposed treatment, but there were some general things Mom knew. He never wore gloves. He didn't explain the procedure. And neither of us had ever given consent. So the next day, while I sat at a table with minuscule electrodes attached to my wrist, Mom slipped out of the room to find Sue.

"Can I talk to you privately for a minute?" I heard her ask. I couldn't make out the rest. It was probably for the best.

I didn't ask my mom about it when we got in the car. I didn't want to bring it up; I didn't want to seem like I cared. I was fine. It was fine. But Mom offered. "So I did talk to Sue and Kathy."

"What'd you tell them?" I asked softly, watching out the window as we drove.

"I told them that you'd been getting pelvic floor treatment and that we were beginning to have questions about whether it was all okay." Mom paused. "Honey, she said it doesn't sound right. She said not to take you back there."

The lack of gloves, no explanation, and definitely no informed consent—especially given that I was a minor at the time of treatment—didn't pass the smell test for either therapist. It wasn't conclusive—I hadn't described anything, nor did we ask what normal techniques would be—but I felt my heart sink. *How do I try to heal from something when I don't even know what that "something" really is, when it "started," or how far it went?* I wanted answers so badly, but I was afraid of where the ones I was getting were pointing me.

• • •

"You've gotta deal with this, honey," my mom told me gently but emphatically a few months later. "You can't keep burying it. It will destroy you." Dad was worried about me too. Mom told me about his anger, grief, and guilt, as well as his love and support, but at my request, he and I never talked about it directly.

She knew how much anger and pain was seething inside me, and we'd been talking about it off and on. Whenever she suggested I see a counselor, I would absolutely refuse. I was not going to talk about it, and I hung on to any shred of control and choice I had. *No one will ever know.* (I don't recommend survivors follow my stubborn example!)

Since I wouldn't see a counselor, Mom searched for other options that would enable me to begin processing my feelings. "What about journaling?" she asked me. "No one will see it—just you."

I hated that idea too, simply because it would mean admitting that the abuse had happened and that I wasn't fine. I was clinging desperately to the charade of a girl who had it together. That kind of girl was strong. That kind of girl wasn't vulnerable. That kind of girl couldn't be hurt by someone. I fished for excuses.

"How? I have no space to do anything!"

It was true. We lived in a small house—not much more than one thousand square feet—and I shared a modest-sized bedroom with my sister. I loved her, but there wasn't a shred of privacy to give me the space to really process or grieve anything.

"We will do whatever we need to do," Mom said matter-of-factly. "What if we moved your bedroom down to the basement for a while and made that *your* space?"

At first, the idea seemed ridiculous. The basement, which encompassed the same footprint as the main level of our house, was already home to a lot—the bookshelves and desks where we all did school, the laundry room, our storage areas, my dad's workshop, the upright grand piano my sister practiced on, and a second bathroom. *But*, I reasoned, *the half with the bathroom is finished, and I can shut the door at the top of the stairs to be alone.* That *was* more privacy than I had upstairs. As much as my psyche resented my mother's implication that I needed help, deep down I knew she was right. I also knew if I didn't give a little ground, she'd never give up.

"Fine," I answered flatly. "But I don't know what you think I'm going to do down there." I was angry. Frustrated. Defiant. I was determined to keep the walls up and the memories out, but Mom was one of those wonderfully dreadful people who always knew when something was brewing. And she was persistent. She wasn't pushy in an unhealthy way. She knew how and when to give us time and space to work through things on our own. But she also wasn't about to wring her hands and avoid communication or attempts to help just because it would be hard or we might not like it. "I love you too much not to deal with real issues" was her mantra.

"Just try journaling," she suggested. "Write down what you are thinking and feeling. Write down your prayers. Start putting words to everything so it isn't all bottled up anymore."

A few days later, Mom and Dad picked up an air mattress for me and helped me move some of my belongings downstairs. I spent the next few months taking advantage of the solitude to wrestle with myself, with God, and with everyone else.

The plan was simple. I was going to calmly step back, reason my way through this, and reach the right conclusions, and then I'd be fine. I knew what I needed to do. I couldn't choose what had happened, but I *could* choose how I responded. I knew what choices I needed to make, and I wanted—more than anything—to make them. I wanted to be done with the fear and shame. I wanted to be done with the grief. I wanted to feel whole again.

One night, I journaled the choices I could make—the choices I *wanted* to make:

I choose to give it up.

I choose to let go.

I choose to live with the consequences of what Nassar did.

I knew that pretending those consequences weren't there wasn't working. I had to admit the damage and face it—not bury it anymore.

I choose to not need an apology from him.

I choose to not hope he remembers sorrowfully what he did.

My healing couldn't be dependent on Larry. I had to face, admit, and hold fast to the truth, no matter what he chose to do. I couldn't make choices for him, but I could make choices for me.

I choose to trust God's justice instead of wanting to deal with Larry myself.

I knew I'd take the first chance I got to stop Larry from hurting others, but I also knew I could no longer live obsessing about getting justice. The chances of ever seeing it were slim to none. If my healing was conditional on getting a verdict or jail time, I would never be able to heal.

I choose to leave it in God's hands instead of wishing I could make Larry see what he took.

I couldn't make Larry comprehend the damage he'd done. I couldn't make him feel grief about it. But the truth wasn't dependent on what Larry thought or felt, and I had to remember that.

I choose to forgive.

I choose to want Larry's repentance and salvation because
it is what he needs, not what I want.

I closed the folder I'd stashed my loose-leaf journal in.

I felt better.

I'd handled it.

I was fine. Two days later, I realized . . . it wasn't that easy.

Letting the memories out, even a little, unleashed a torrent of anger and self-protection. All the lies I'd fought to bury for years screamed in my head more loudly than I thought possible. *Your fault! You didn't fight back! Who is so stupid they don't even know what's happening? You didn't protect yourself because you didn't care enough! Your fault!*

I was angry. Did God care? Did *anyone* care? I viewed my parents' concern as too biased to be reliable. Of course *they* cared—just as every parent thinks their newborn is the most beautiful baby ever. I was indescribably thankful my parents were on my side, but I couldn't let myself trust their assessment.

I angrily scrawled another journal entry.

Is value lost when something is stolen from it?

I thought back to a week during my high school Sunday school class when we'd had a substitute teacher. He'd chosen to teach on the story of David and Bathsheba, a narrative in which the ancient Israelite king David summons a young woman he sees bathing on her rooftop and then sleeps with her. The story gets even darker when David has her husband killed to cover up the resulting pregnancy.

"So what do y'all think about Bathsheba?" the teacher asked casually. "Does she bear any responsibility for this?"

I flinched. *Oh no . . . please don't go there.* I silently pleaded.

Just then, a female classmate spoke up, pointing out that David, as the king, held Bathsheba's life in his hands, and therefore, she *couldn't* have said no.

Thank you, I sighed, amazed she'd had the courage to say something. I wouldn't have touched that one with a ten-foot pole. Not at that point, anyway. I was too afraid I'd break down if I tried. But my relief quickly dissipated when one of the only guys in the class whom I respected jumped into the discussion.

"I don't think that's right," he offered calmly. "She could have chosen death. This wasn't abuse."

Anger welled up inside me, and I held my breath to keep it from bursting forth. *This wasn't abuse? He held her life in his hands but it's* her *fault?* There was no way I was going to speak up. I wouldn't be able to without someone figuring out why it mattered so much. But the anger quickly gave way to grief as the discussion continued to swirl around me.

"Mm-hmm." The teacher nodded casually.

He agrees. I wanted to get up and leave. This wasn't just about me. I knew there was at least one rape victim sitting in that class too, and statistically, many more survivors. *What if* she *couldn't fight back either? Does* she *know it's not her fault? What have we just communicated to these girls?* I knew they would feel guilt for their abuse—and the sting of those words, untrue though they were, could be devastating—especially if they lacked the family support that I was fortunate enough to have.

I glanced over at my male friend. I knew his interpretation was wrong. That wasn't even how the Bible told the story. Later on—in the part the teacher hadn't bothered to address and apparently no one remembered—David is confronted with the evil he's done in the form of an allegory. In the story, David is portrayed as a self-centered, powerful, rich man who stole and killed an innocent lamb (Bathsheba). Far from being assigned blame, she is referred to tenderly as an innocent who has been violated.

I knew from past experience that false ideas about abuse had a stronghold in the church, where wrong ideas often had a veneer of piety put over them and were adhered to both out of ignorance and firm conviction.

If they see Bathsheba that way, they would see me that way too—better off dead than violated.

Church wasn't safe. Nowhere was safe.

I slept down in the basement for months, journaling my anger, my confusion, my guilt. By the time spring rolled around, things were a bit better. Getting my thoughts down on paper had at least helped identify *some* of the damage. I was feeling a little less tense and fearful. I didn't have any answers yet, and I hadn't really moved beyond the questions, but at least I was asking them, after refusing to for so long. *It's going to be better now, right?*

Wrong.

•　•　•

I thought I was over it, I wrote that April, propped up on my air mattress. I'd just returned home from a week in Oklahoma, where my law school had held its orientation. The school I'd selected was the same one from which I had pursued my paralegal certificate. Its modified distance-learning format was designed to allow students to accelerate their education and combine professional experience with academic learning. Those opportunities—coupled with the lower tuition—meant that if everything went as planned, I'd finish my coursework before I turned twenty-four, pass the bar, and graduate debt-free, with a good résumé to boot. I would do most of the coursework from home, but periodically, I'd meet my class at a conference center for exam prep and modular courses like trial and appellate advocacy.

I'd been looking forward to our orientation for months. Classes were typically very small in alternative programs like this, and from what I'd been told—and based on my own experience in the paralegal program—the groups were often tight-knit, forming deep, lifelong friendships.

I'd arrived to find that, out of my class of about fifty students, I was one of only four women, and the only one under forty. That didn't bother me. I was used to multigenerational learning and interaction, and I'd been blessed to have many close male friends growing up—something I'd deeply valued despite, and in part *because* of, what I'd been through. But by the end of the first day, I knew I had a problem—specifically, one of the older male students. Whenever I turned around, he was there—everywhere I went, as close as he could get. His blatant leering went unabated, and he rarely focused on my face. His hands gestured far too close when he was speaking. He liked what he saw, and he made it clear without ever speaking a word. I tried to ignore him, to place myself within other groups, to find different tables and study areas, but it just didn't matter. By the third day, I could barely pick at my food during mealtimes, leading a fellow classmate to kindly ask if I'd ever struggled with anorexia during my days as a gymnast.

I felt unsafe everywhere. I fought to hide it but realized I wasn't fully succeeding one day when I stepped into the elevator to head up to my room. A male classmate about my age had gotten on too. As we started our ascent, he turned and asked me, "Do I scare you?"

I froze. *What had I done? How did he know to ask?* I made myself look up and smile. "No," I laughed—lightheartedly, I hoped. "I'm just a quiet person." The last part was true; I was naturally more reserved. But the first part was a total lie, and I knew it. Everything felt unsafe right now, and close quarters, like elevators, only made it worse. I exited at my floor and bid what I *hoped* was a cheerful good-bye, then berated myself all the way down the long hallway. I'd clearly let something slip—some emotion, thought, or instinctive reflex—and I hadn't even known it. But it left me vulnerable. Fears and emotions were too easily exploited and manipulated, and I wasn't about to provide one more chance for that to happen.

Where else have I failed to protect myself? I asked over and over, searching my memory for any time I might have let the mask drop. *No one will ever, ever know*, I promised myself again. I closed the door to my room and locked it, resolved to just as firmly shut out any hint of vulnerability.

I made it through the rest of the week, but the simplest things were so much more difficult than they should have been. Starting law school felt like trying to drink from a fire hose of information, and the constant feeling of being unsafe made focusing difficult. Study hours were long, and sleep was no longer restful. I had gone into the week excited and eager, but bad memories now cast a shadow over everything. It wasn't supposed to be this way, and I was angry at myself for not being able to "get it together."

Even the simple ritual of taking a class photo caused far more stress than the progress exam at the end of the week. I stood on the stage with the three other women where the photographer motioned us to wait while he lined up the rest of the class. After that, the photographer could evaluate the best place to pop us in. I took one look at the rows of suited-up men jostling and laughing, and I could feel the panic rising. *Too close. Too close. Too close.* My mind raced. What if someone took advantage of "inadvertent" jostling? I'd passed off some of Larry's contact as accidental before and paid dearly for my innocence. How would I know if an accidental touch as we all squeezed to get into place really was an accident? If I reacted and it *was* just an accident, I'd have to explain my over-the-top response. Or someone might even guess what no one was supposed to know. But if someone did something "accidentally" and I *didn't* react, I'd have failed to protect myself—again.

There were just too many. Too many men. I couldn't trust anything. Not accidents. Not innocent contact. Not casual compliments. All of it had been wielded like weapons by both of my abusers before. Nothing was safe.

When the photographer motioned to me, I walked over to the spot where he told me to stand, pulling back from the men around me as far as I could without being obvious. *Stop it*, I angrily told myself. I focused on looking relaxed and happy. *No one will know.* I stepped back in between shots to regroup as much as I could. *This was my fault. I hadn't stopped the abuse, and that was my fault. And I couldn't stop the damage. That was my fault too.*

Now safely on my air mattress at home, I pulled myself back to the present and glanced down at my journal. I'd ended up with a rough poem, scrawling my thoughts as I remembered how the week had gone. I hated the words. But they were there. Just like the abuse. Just like the damage. It was all there. And I hadn't been able to stop it. I closed the cheerful Anne Geddes–style folder, buried my face in my pillow, and tried to shake the last lines from my head.

Just when I think it is over, think it is done,
I find myself shivering again, in the warmth of the sun.

9

TWO WEEKS AFTER I realized it wasn't "done," I had no words left to journal. I didn't know what to say or ask for anymore. The rawness of my pain and despair was so great, I could no longer find words to express it.

So that May, I began writing out passages of the Bible and songs—letting someone else express the depths of hopelessness and grief when I no longer could. The book of Psalms, in particular, enabled me to ride the waves of pain I couldn't seem to escape:

Save me, O God,
For the waters have threatened my life.
I have sunk in deep mire, and there is no foothold;
I have come into deep waters, and a flood overflows me.
I am weary with my crying. . . .
What I did not steal, I then have to restore.
PSALM 69:1-4

I sat in the chilly basement, wrapped in an old, handmade quilt my dad had been given back in his college days. It was the heaviest blanket we owned, and the encompassing weight of it comforted me. I toyed with a bit of the blue yarn that adorned each corner of the quilt squares and wondered, *Is restoring what was lost even possible?*

The reality of living with abuse was more frustrating than I could express. Rarely did society recognize the incredible damage of abuse, and I'd absorbed its minimizing message every day, blaming myself for the fear, the nightmares, and the anxiety. I'd been willing, to a point, to *admit* the abuse, but I still tried to bury the damage from it, believing that it was my failure that allowed me to be so damaged. *Why do I have to be so overdramatic?* I'd ask myself.

The best response I could manage at this point was to give myself a mental shake and a firm command to *stop it* whenever I felt fear or a flashback creeping up. I didn't realize it then, but I was also trying to protect myself. If the damage was a result of my failure to respond properly, then it was something I could control—*if* I just did it right. The last thing I wanted was to lose control again. Blaming myself for not being "over it" gave me some assurance, however small, that I was in control and could fix things—*if* I just did it right. The problem was, I clearly *wasn't* getting it right, because I wasn't better yet. The "magic words" of forgiveness I'd journaled months before hadn't fixed the nightmares, flashbacks, and fear.

I kept trying to calm the internal Mount Vesuvius that had erupted in my head at the most inopportune times—like during the class photo. What Larry had done had taken everything I needed for normal interaction and flipped it upside down. Small talk, innocent and friendly touch, kindness, trust, the appearance of being "on my side" and "working together" for solutions, charity work, and care for others—everything that would normally assure me someone was a good person, everything that was at the heart of healthy human connection, had been twisted, manipulated, and outright weaponized against me. Everything that would ordinarily lay the foundation for any sort of friendship—or even casual acquaintance—had been wielded to facilitate violations at the deepest level.

Questions raged inside. At what point should I have realized there was a problem? Abusers don't just flip a switch. It wasn't as if Larry decided to abuse me right before the actual act. It had been long calculated. I had been prepped for it. When should I have stopped trusting him? What should have tipped me off? When he complimented my shoes? *But people give little compliments to each other all the time*, I reasoned. When he gave me a quick hug? *How many other guy friends or dad figures have given me brief hugs? They aren't all abusers.* When he made small talk about my science homework or asked about my siblings? When should I have known? How could I have stopped him before he violated me? The simplest things were now unsafe because I knew that even they could be wielded like a weapon. And if I didn't see it—if I trusted someone—I could be hurt in unfathomable ways all over again.

I had no answers, and the questions were exhausting.

● ● ●

I eventually moved back upstairs to my bedroom—I couldn't hide out in the basement forever—and tried to get on with life. I coached my teams and classes, spent time with friends, and grew closer to many of my law school classmates. In short, I poured myself into my life, which I felt incredibly blessed to have. But I also continued to bury the tears that threatened to spring up whenever bad memories surfaced.

My senses were particularly on high alert during medical treatment. For instance, I needed exploratory surgery because the wrist Larry was supposed to heal never got better. Unfortunately, the only surgeons available were male, and the best was near Larry's age with dark hair just like his. The thought of being under anesthesia while a male doctor operated on me was unfathomable, and I would have given anything to have been able to cancel that surgery. But then I'd have to admit I wasn't fine, and that meant being vulnerable. And anyway, what options did I have? So I kept the mask on and had the surgery.

I also needed more images taken of my back, and when I sat up from the X-ray table, garbed in the hated open-backed hospital gown, I discovered that a male technician had walked into the room while my back was turned. I realized instead of alerting me to his presence, he had been standing there the entire time while the female tech who was taking the images had been behind the curtain. He wasn't helping. He'd just come in . . . to watch. And because he waited until I was positioned on the X-ray table, back turned to the door, I had no idea how long he'd been there, enjoying the view. But his relaxed stance as he leaned against the wall and his pointed smile let me know it had been too long. Nothing, nothing was safe.

I continued my studies in legal research and writing, tort law, contract law, and criminal law, fighting panic attacks every time I came across a sex-related case or crime. Wrapping myself up in blankets became a helpful practice, but I knew I wouldn't be able to do that when my class reconvened for a review course before comprehensive exams. *What if I can't hide it*, I wondered, *and someone figures it out?*

That summer I returned to the government camp in Lansing that had sparked my interest in law and policy, only now I'd been given free rein to create and teach the appellate advocacy track. I loved it—except for the time a fellow chaperone made a casual reference to sexual abuse. I must have flinched, because he immediately turned to me and said, "You stepped back defensively when I said that." I shrugged. I had, but just barely. I hadn't even realized it.

"My sister is a survivor," he said calmly. "I know the signs."

I didn't answer. Clearly, I needed to do a better job of hiding everything.

Nightmares left only to spring up again without warning. Sometimes it was one predator. Sometimes it was the other. Sometimes it was some innocuous person from the past or present, subtly underscoring the question I now always lived with: *Who am I trusting that I shouldn't trust? Who else isn't really safe?*

* * *

I also wrestled with my faith—over and over and over again. I remember my questions coming to a head one day in the spring of 2007 as I was attempting to study for one of my law classes. I was sitting on our couch, sunlight pouring in through the huge picture window that graced the front of our living room. *Does God care? If He does, why didn't He do something? Why didn't He say more in all the pages of the Bible?* My mind drifted back to what had happened when I was seven. If abuse and injustice were as bad as I felt like they were, why did Christians get this so wrong? Or was I wrong? Maybe I didn't need to heal. Maybe I just needed to get my act together.

How do You see me? I'd written in a prayer just a few weeks before. I felt despair, and I felt anger. I squeezed the dotted throw pillow I'd been curled up against and clenched my teeth, silently venting my frustration. The house was empty, but I still felt the need to remain reserved and quiet.

I methodically thought through everything I believed. I knew myself well enough to know I'd done plenty that needed forgiveness. Even though I wasn't *anything* like Larry, I still believed that my forgiveness had to be found in Christ's sacrifice on the cross. Logically, anything good that I did wouldn't change the bad, any more than Larry's charity work could nullify one ounce of the damage he'd caused me. I couldn't "work" my way out of mistakes I'd made. If God was really perfect—which I believed Him to be—He'd be wrong to act as if bad things weren't really bad or could be erased by doing nice things. I knew that God hates sin.

But I noticed that fellow Christians pretty much talked only about our need to understand the wrong things *we'd* done. No one talked about God's supposed hatred for the wrongs done *against* us. Whenever anyone at church talked about injustice in the world, it was almost always to emphasize how wrong it was to be angry, bitter, or unforgiving, as if *not* being those things was the cure for pain—that they mattered *more* than what any abuser might have done.

I rested my forehead in my hands. I didn't think bitterness was right, much less healthy. *But not being bitter isn't fixing the nightmares*, I thought. For my own well-being, I did want to forgive Larry. But I didn't want my forgiveness to be used as an excuse to act as if something terrible wasn't really that bad. Prominent teachers had implied, "You haven't really forgiven and trusted until you can be thankful for the evil done to you." *Is that really what forgiveness means?* It wasn't right, but I'd heard it from authority figures so often that I felt completely alone in my grief.

"Trust God to bring something beautiful from it," others taught. I knew all the verses about God bringing beauty from ashes, but I also knew that idea was used far too often like a Band-Aid on a gaping wound. "But look at all the good that's come from it!" people said, as if the good that resulted made the evil somehow less evil.

That morning in our living room, I felt tears and anger welling up at the thought. The only thing of which I was certain was that everyone minimized the evil and damage from abuse; I didn't need them using platitudes as a way of telling me it wasn't a big deal.

I closed my eyes. The war that raged continually inside me was exhausting. I wanted it to end. I wanted answers, but they never seemed to come.

What are my alternatives? My eyes flew open. *What if God were removed from the picture?*

I shook my head. I'd mentally been down that path many times, and it didn't fix the problem. If truth's parameters were established by people alone, I had no way to define evil, or even justice for that matter. Something from C. S. Lewis's writings rang in my mind: "A man does not call a line crooked unless he has some idea of a straight line."[4] Removing God didn't fix the problem of evil. It actually made it worse. A weak God who couldn't stop evil was of no use either. What hope is there in a moral lawgiver who is impotent to ensure that the law is followed or justice done? I sighed in frustration. The alternatives—removing or changing the idea of God—didn't help resolve my questions. Not really. Not if I was intellectually honest.

I picked up the notebook and pen I'd left lying nearby, which I turned to whenever memories made studying impossible. At those times, I would draw or write as I thought things through. This morning I flashed back to the previous summer. My family had gone camping with three other families I'd grown up with, a group one of the moms had nicknamed "The Tribe." Often on those trips we would sit together and talk through struggles we'd had or things we were currently working through. I'd never shared my abuse with anyone, but there were always plenty of other things to discuss. That day had been particularly hot, and we'd all congregated in my parents' screened-in dining tent, a little mesh square filled with camping chairs and a picnic table. The light breeze brought a bit of relief as the shadows of maple leaves flickered on every surface.

"Sometimes," one dad had shared, "I haven't liked the answers God's given me. Or I haven't gotten answers at all."

I understood what that was like.

"But, you know," he continued, "I keep going back to the time when Jesus asked Peter if he wanted to walk away—stop following Him. Peter asked, 'Where else would I go, Lord?' I gotta ask myself that, too, when things feel darkest."

As I sat on the couch, I knew his answer was mine. It was all I had left. Over the past few years I'd explored every other option. Removing God from the picture, changing how Scripture defined Him, considering other faith traditions—none of them fixed my problems or answered my questions. I'd explored science and information theory, history, and philosophical concepts. I'd considered principles of evidence and grappled with the critiques of the Christian faith. No matter where I looked, I was confronted with things I couldn't explain without God. And specifically, without the gospel. Every other faith tradition relied on some form of good works to absolve people from guilt or reach "heaven" or some higher order. But justice didn't work that way. Doing good didn't erase the bad. Not for Larry. Not for me. And while it felt good to say all the ideas were right, that didn't work either. Each faith tradition made specific truth claims that didn't fit with other faiths. They couldn't all be true. I needed real answers. Not just what felt nice. And the more I tried, the more convinced I became that, while I couldn't explain everything, I had more real answers through my faith than I had without it. *Where else would I go, Lord?*

I drew two circles in my notebook, noting my inability to draw anything perfectly round. *What do I know is true and real?* I asked myself. I filled in the first circle with the answers I had so far—what I *knew* to be true.

There is right and wrong.

I believed those two things existed—not just in people's minds, but really and truly existed. People could look at evil, like the Holocaust, murder, or sexual assault, and know it was wrong. We didn't have to question it or base our conclusions on what someone else thought. No one looked at photos of Auschwitz, turned to a friend, and said, "I think this might be morally acceptable; what's your opinion?" I shook my head. No. We knew that at least some standard of right and wrong existed—no matter what anyone said, and no matter what a culture might have condoned for a time.

Truth, right and wrong—they do exist.

Then I wrote down the next conclusion that naturally flowed from that.

There is a God who defines good and evil.

There was no way around that. Either truth was, in some form, dependent on human ideas, which meant that good and evil were subject to opinion, or the definition of good and evil came from someone higher than human beings. Yes, people often disagreed about where those lines were drawn and how we knew them, and there had to be room for those discussions. Even so, we all knew that certain things were good, and others were evil, no matter what anyone said. Behind all the infighting, there was still some absolute standard that didn't come from human opinion—which meant it came from something higher. There had to be a God.

I glanced out at the giant maple tree just across the street, watching its branches sway gently in the spring breeze. In the midafternoon sun, the green of the new leaves was as vibrant as I'd ever seen. I looked at the two things I had written. *And there is nowhere else to go. If there is no God, and no real good and evil, I can't even call what Larry did to me wrong. Not really. Not if "right and wrong" are only constructs of human opinion.*

I picked up my pen again.

This God is the God of the Bible.

I didn't have room to write all the reasons I was confident that if a god did exist, it was in fact the God of Scripture. However, since others had already written whole books on it, I made my type A personality be okay with writing just the conclusion.

Next I wrote,

God is just.

In Christianity, there is no mitigating anything wrong we do. There is no way to do enough good things to cancel out the bad. There are no magic words, attitudes, or life changes that can erase all the things we do wrong. That's how life really works.

A smile played on my face as I remembered the little spats my siblings and I had growing up. One of us would do something that hurt the other—take a toy, lash out in anger, act selfishly, or say hurtful things—and when the injured one began to cry, the offending sibling, knowing the consequences that would soon result if a parent got wind of our action, would quickly begin piling on the sweetness in an effort to quell the tears and hide whatever childish wrong we'd just done. But it didn't matter how many My Little Ponies I offered to let my sister borrow, or how many books I promised to read my brother—I had still hurt them. I had still been wrong. I could try to do better in the future, but I couldn't go back and erase the past. Saying I was sorry and asking for forgiveness were important steps my parents taught us to take. They helped in moving forward, but they didn't erase the damage already done.

I curled up on the couch and let the memories come. It had been six years since I had last seen Larry. I didn't know what he'd done in that time, or what he would do in the future, but I did know that hearing him say "I'm sorry" wouldn't return me to the way I was before I was abused. Yet every other religion and deity, outside of Christianity, relied on some form of doing enough good things to outweigh the bad, as if life were just a balancing scale, and the damage from evil would go away if someone did enough charity work, said the right prayers, or took enough pilgrimages. But that's not justice. I knew Larry had helped create an autism foundation, which was great, but that good deed didn't stop my nightmares. The evil he did was there. The damage was done. Nothing could make that wrong disappear.

I picked up my pen again.

God is love.

Justice, all by itself, felt hopeless because there is nothing we can do to escape it. But I had to admit that God also loves, and He showed it when Christ chose to take on Himself the justice we deserved—not *erasing* what we've done, but *paying* for it. *That's a pretty crucial difference,* I thought.

I sighed and traced the lines on the plaid couch. I could still feel the war within me. There was so much I didn't understand about how God's love meshed with so much abuse in the world. I looked back at my simple diagram of circles. These truths I'd written—they applied to everything. If they were real, they were real. Period. That meant that whatever I didn't understand, whatever answers I hadn't yet found couldn't contradict what I *did* know. The answers to my questions fell within that first circle too, even if I didn't understand how.

There is good and evil.

There is a God who defines it.

He is just.

He is loving.

I leaned my head back on the couch and watched the wispy clouds moving across the brightly lit sky. I felt exhausted. But I also felt the tiniest bit of certainty. There was nowhere *else* to go, but there was *somewhere*. I didn't have *all* the answers, but I had *something*. I could say what happened to me was evil. I knew justice and love existed. It wasn't everything. But it was *something*. And I could hold on to that much.

10

FREE POMERANIA!!! The blog page I was reading at Xanga.com ended nearly every entry with this exclamation. I burst out laughing. *Who is this?*

I'd recently started maintaining my own blog at this social networking site and had stumbled upon these entries after following a comment trail left on one of my posts.

This blog page, however, appeared to be complete satire. There was no name associated with it, but it was run, purportedly, by a group of individuals professing their dedication to freeing the region of Pomerania. It was complete nonsense, but the writing was fast-paced and quick-witted, and I found it more than a little amusing.

Not long after I'd begun to read the musings of those committed to freeing Pomerania, another user left his first comment on an entry I'd written on the importance of examining our beliefs and the consequences that resulted from them. "Very good post," the commenter wrote. "What with all the books, histories, and commentaries, we should be the most informed generation the world has seen." The poster said his name was Jacob. He was posting through a mutual friend's Xanga, so the comment was all I had to go by.

Exactly one month later, the satire blog I'd been following left its first comment on my latest post. It ended with "Free Pomerania!!" and the notation "P.S. This is the Jacob who posted via your friend's site the last time."

A smile tugged at the corners of my mouth. I was amused to discover that the thoughtful person who'd commented on my blog post weeks ago was in fact the owner of the zany satire blog I'd been following.

Every few days when I opened my blog, I'd find more input from the unique "Free Pomerania" blogger, and I would respond. I discovered that Jacob came from a large family, one that included a two-year-old boy he had dubbed "The Right Honourable Minister Responsible for Destruction of Other People's Valuables." We shared a love for children, reading, learning, and faith. The more we communicated, the more we found to discuss. We exchanged book recommendations, debated current events, and talked about daily life—all in comments on each other's blogs.

Seven months after he had first appeared on my page, I learned yet another sibling had arrived in Jacob's family, and I asked to see baby photos. It was then that he pointed out that he didn't even know my name—in fact, we'd never even seen pictures of *each other*! I grinned as I read his message. I knew there was a remedy for that. Facebook had recently burst onto the scene, and just the day before, when I had gone to our mutual friend's Facebook wall to discuss his upcoming senior thesis for law school, I saw a post just above mine written by someone named Jacob. The writing style was too distinctive for it to be from anyone other than my new online friend.

"True, you don't know my name," I wrote back. "But if you look at Brian's Facebook, at the comment right under yours, you can find out at least that part."

I didn't mention the interesting addition of profile pictures—something we didn't have on our blogs. Mine was a senior photo taken on a wintry day in the snow by a river—as "elvish" a scene as I could find. Jacob's was a close-up shot of him twisting his face into an over-the-top skeptical expression that demonstrated, at minimum, amazingly flexible eyebrows. Like so much else, it made me laugh and seemed to fit the personality I was getting to know. Fortunately, most of his other photos were public, and I glanced over those too—a costume party at New Year's with him decked out as a mad scientist in a white lab coat and a fantastic wig that made him look like a cartoon character who'd stuck his finger in a light socket; wakeboarding (and wiping out rather painfully); a photo of a teddy bear passed on to him by a beloved younger sibling. One photo made me gasp with delight: Jacob, standing in front of a gorgeous display of books—old, thick, and beautifully gilded. I enlarged the photo as much as I could, straining unsuccessfully to make out any titles. My interest was piqued in the library, but I was also intrigued by the person in front of it.

We exchanged email addresses that day, and he sent me those baby pictures, which were every bit as precious as promised. And then much to his bewilderment (as I later discovered), I promptly forgot about him for more than a month in the rush of law school finals. When I finally resurfaced and remembered that such things as Facebook and Xanga existed, I discovered an old message from Jacob asking me what my motivation was for my writing, studying, and advocacy. *Now that's a discussion worth having!* I thought eagerly.

"Ideas have consequences"[5] was a phrase I often repeated to my own students each summer in the appellate advocacy course I was still teaching for SSI. Discussing ideas, examining the motivation behind them, and considering what resulted from them was my real passion. "The more you love, the harder you fight," I would tell my students. "Both your ideas and your motivation must be right." Ideas that weren't based on good facts or right beliefs had the potential to yield destructive consequences and damage real people. But the right ideas, divorced from love for people, would yield arrogance and a lack of compassion, and that wreaked destruction too.

"Love has to be your motivation," I explained. "Examine your beliefs and ideas; ensure they are right and good. Then do nothing out of an arrogant desire to win, but act out of love for those who pay the price when we believe the wrong things." More than anything for me, this flowed out of love for God—the One who defined goodness and love—and the lessons instilled in me by my parents.

Excitement flooded my mind as I sat at my little desk in the corner of our basement and typed my answer to Jacob's question: "This is my (short) life's story!" He wrote back, before launching into his own thoughts on the matter.

For the next eleven months, emails flew from Kalamazoo, Michigan, to the little town of Salmon Arm, British Columbia, and back again, nearly every day. I learned quite a bit about this Jacob who'd left the comment on my blog post. He was industrious. He'd learned finish carpentry and cabinet-making while young, and now worked for himself in the building industry while pursuing his bachelor's degree via a distance program.

We quickly found that our areas of interest complemented each other perfectly. I focused on advocacy, practical application, and the correct communication of ideas. Jacob, on the other hand, reminded me of the importance of theology, truth, and foundational ideas to avoid an "end justifies the means" approach to life.

●　●　●

Along with exchanging daily emails with Jacob, I invested time in the relationships I'd formed with my classmates, which were more impactful than I had ever anticipated. My class had dwindled to only nine students after the first year, me and eight guys around my age. A few graduates and a handful of students in the classes ahead of us rounded out my group of friends, and I'd grown to appreciate them in ways I never expected. A few times each year we met for review sessions or alumni events, and several of us met regularly via phone to study or just catch up.

Admittedly, I'd approached our first review conference with a mixture of eagerness and dread. By that time, I'd formed close friendships with several of the students who remained, but a general feeling of hypervigilance still pervaded most interactions no matter how good the friendship, especially because I knew we'd be reviewing material that threatened to bring everything to the surface. I was relieved to find that the student who had been such a problem a year earlier had dropped out, but many others remained—including the classmate who'd picked up enough of *something* to ask if I was afraid of him the last time we'd met. This time around, though, we had a different conversation. Chatting near the same elevators in the center's ornate lobby, we'd discovered a mutual love for athletics. Granted, gymnastics was nothing akin to the contact-heavy sport he'd pursued, and my athletic acuity outside of the gym amounted to exactly and precisely nothing, but it was enough to generate discussion at least.

"Why'd you quit?" I asked him. I presumed an injury, or perhaps simple practicalities like finances or the time commitment had ended his involvement, much as they had for me. "Just got to be too much?"

"No, not really," he said directly. "I still would really enjoy it. But honestly, the stuff that went on in the locker room wasn't good."

He didn't elaborate, but we both knew what he meant.

"I didn't want my mind filled with that," he continued. "Staying away from it was more important than continuing in the sport."

I felt almost numb. His answer seemed nearly incomprehensible. *That mattered to you? That doesn't matter to almost anyone.* My mind flashed back to the time I went out with a teen Bible study group and the guy sitting next to me, whom I didn't even know, put his arm around me and pretended to grope my breast. None of the other six guys I was with said a word. I recalled the lists I'd found at random teen events ranking each female student's body on a scale of 1 to 10, and the time my brother instructed my friends and me to stick with him at a summer camp. After four days of listening to the guys in his room talk, he was concerned about our safety. I thought about the blatant sexual discussions the guy sitting next to me in math class persisted in engaging in when we were supposed to be studying our college text. I remembered all the times I'd walked out of gymnastics practice or switched grocery store lines to avoid unwanted attention, and the hugs I'd permitted that were weaponized and by no means just "friendly." These were just top-of-mind memories. This list went on and on, and the acts were always written off by others as simply being "how guys are" or "just a joke."

That mattered to you? I almost said it out loud but bit back the question before it escaped. I was afraid that if I said anything at all, I might expose too much. But the brief conversation was enough to make tears—which I essentially *never* shed in front of others—an actual possibility. Our conversation had brought up so much grief over what usually was, and the tiniest bit of hope that sometimes it might be different.

The year Jacob and I were writing in earnest was the year I began to realize just how many walls I had put up and to face—at least in part—how much of myself had truly been damaged.

That year, my class and I gathered for a modular course on appellate advocacy. It was an intense week, and the rest of my class often engaged in a robust game of football when we had breaks. I only watched at first, but at some point my classmates determined that I *was* going to play with them at least once ("play" being very nicely put, rather like the way one references a toddler "helping"). When I finally agreed to join in a game, they did ensure that I caught the ball, treating me with the amused patience normally attributed to saints. After that, I was happily allowed to retire to the sidelines to observe for the remainder of the game. A rainstorm ended play prematurely, and we traipsed back to the conference center.

Soon afterward, we congregated in the common area to talk, lounging on a squared arrangement of couches. Between providing full-time childcare, doing my coursework, and working my second job as a teaching assistant, the weeks leading up to the forum had been exhausting. So much so that I inadvertently fell asleep and awoke just in time to hear a few comments being made about me while the rest of the group thought I was sleeping. Words like *gentle* were used, and I was appreciative. It also shook me. It was the first time since seeing Larry that I had not felt unsafe being perceived that way. Whenever I was coaching or caring for those who were smaller, weaker, or female, I felt it was incredibly important to demonstrate love, compassion, and gentleness. I wanted those around me to know they were safe. But I had not realized until that night how hard I fought to *not* be perceived that way by men. "Professional," "businesslike," "sharp," "intelligent"—descriptions that evoked some measure of strength and being untouchable—were the only adjectives I wanted to project. I desperately wanted to avoid any connotation of gentleness, femininity, innocence, or other "softer" adjectives. Those attributes would make me vulnerable. They could be manipulated, preyed upon. They were not safe. I'd been those things before. I hadn't learned my lesson when I was seven, and I stayed that way—I stayed soft. Larry saw it, and it had cost me everything. I'd failed—left myself exposed and vulnerable—and the consequence was violation. So I never ever wanted to be those things again.

But that night, for the first time, I'd been ascribed those adjectives and it didn't feel unsafe. Those attributes had been valued for what they could offer, *not* for how they could be exploited. If others could appreciate those things without seeking to manipulate them, maybe someday I could appreciate them again too.

• • •

Through it all, Jacob's emails kept coming. Hundreds of them. He eventually wrote and introduced himself to my parents, figuring that it wouldn't hurt for them to know who he was. That December, after I complained that we didn't have nearly enough snow in Michigan to suit my tastes, he informed me he was sending a box of Canadian snow via the US Postal Service, expressly to my front door. I laughed it off, but the next day, I came home to find a pink slip on my front door, informing me I'd missed a delivery. *What? He couldn't have really sent snow.* I was sure of that. I'd never even given him my address. Then two days later, amidst frozen mud and icy rain, the USPS delivered a package that did, in fact, bear Jacob's name and return address.

"Oh?" My mom said, a hint of teasing in her voice, eyebrows raised, as I put the wet cardboard box on the kitchen table and tried my level best to seem nonchalant. I peeled back the soggy tape, peered inside, and gasped in delight. I had been correct that it was not, in fact, snow inside the box. But much as I loved snow, what it did contain was even better, and seemed to perfectly capture both the sender and, somehow, me. I carefully lifted out a beautifully gilded and bound copy of Augustine's *Confessions* from Easton Press and a secondhand copy of P. G. Wodehouse's *Piccadilly Jim*.

"Oh!" I ran my fingers over the gold embossing on the front cover of *Confessions*, breathing in the delightful scent of a new book. I opened it to feel the thick pages, reveling in the slight cracking sound every new book makes when it first unfolds, and found an inscription. "To Rachael. From your friend Jacob." In my delight, I failed to notice that the inscription mirrored the words Professor Bhaer inscribed on the book he gave to Jo in Louisa May Alcott's *Little Women*. Jacob knew that book remained one of my favorite classics and those two characters in particular were some of my favorites from literature, so the mirroring wasn't an accident. If I'd realized the significance, I might have raised my eyebrows in teasing question the same way my mom did, but as it was, I viewed the gift as a gracious gesture from someone who had become a dear friend, and nothing more.

That night I curled up with a blanket, hot cocoa, and *Piccadilly Jim*. I was immediately lost in the hilarious, quirky world of P. G. Wodehouse—my introduction to the eccentric story lines he wove. This ridiculous tale was a romantic comedy filled with over-the-top personalities, including an easy-going but exceptionally quick-witted hero and a no-nonsense heroine with plenty of grit and spunk. Of course, they fall in love in the end (the way every story should conclude, as far as I'm concerned). I couldn't help but smile at the final picture Piccadilly Jim painted of (as he called it) "domestic happiness":

> Brisk give-and-take is the foundation of the happy marriage. . . .
> I seem to see us in our old age, you on one side of the radiator,
> I on the other, warming our old limbs and thinking up snappy
> stuff to hand to each other—sweethearts still![6]

I loved it. The idea of two lovers, grown old together, comfortable with who they are and who they've become, sitting side by side and still briskly exchanging ideas and snappy wit, was both sweet and merry. It was also very much what I hoped for someday.

As I worked my way through *Confessions*, I emailed Jacob about what I was learning, and we discussed our favorite parts—even where we'd disagree with the revered historical figure. The months flew by, and I remained content in the friendship we had. But late that spring, as Mom and I were driving around town running errands, she started poking a bit about my friendships with various guys. We had these conversations fairly often. I valued our relationship and my parents' insights, and I was grateful for open communication. Several guys in recent years had asked me to date them exclusively. Though they were good friends and great people, I'd never met anyone whose life, passions, and personality really meshed to the point of being a potential life partner, so I'd always said no.

Despite everything, I wasn't afraid to date. I actually loved the idea of being a wife and having a family. I knew there would be a lot to work through, and the reality of having to discuss something I could barely verbalize—even with someone I loved—*was* terrifying, but I also knew it could be worth it.

A saving grace through my abuse had been my parents' relationship with each other and with me. My mom was an abuse survivor, too, and she didn't hide that. I knew there were men out there who could walk through the grief and pain alongside survivors, who could help them heal instead of hurt them, because my dad had done that for my mom. From both my dad and my brother, I knew that healthy masculinity was a gift. But before dating someone, I wanted to have a deep enough friendship with him so that I knew marriage could be a possibility. I didn't see the point in getting involved romantically with someone I knew I couldn't stay with forever.

"What about so-and-so?" Mom asked, listing various friends I had. "Where are you with him?"

I watched the trees rushing by, bright green with new leaves, the promise of something awakening. Everyone Mom listed was a friend I deeply valued, but none of whom I had thought of being with permanently.

"What about Jacob?" Mom asked.

I smiled a little. "I mean, he lives on a mountain and has a library, along with multiple adorable younger siblings—doesn't that answer it?" I teased.

Mom laughed. "No, but really," she pressed.

"Honestly?" I responded. "I don't have any reason to think he's interested. But . . ." I paused. "I would have to know for sure he *wasn't* before I would date anyone else."

My answer came just a few weeks later.

"Hey." My dad poked his head into the living room. "Mom and I need to run something by you. Can you sit down for a second?"

"Yeah, sure." I took a seat on the couch.

"I got a letter," Dad said, smiling slightly, though clearly trying not to. "It was from Jacob."

I nodded. I knew that. He'd introduced himself to my parents months ago.

"Yeah, I knew he wrote to you," I said, plopping the navy blue throw pillow onto my lap.

"No . . . ," Dad said, still with a hint of merriment. "This was a new one. He wanted to talk about visiting." He explained that Jacob was considering a brief internship in Lansing—he had to do one somewhere anyway, before graduation—and needed to finalize his plans. "He knew you were in the middle of finals and wanted to respect that and not distract you, so he talked to us."

I appreciated that. I probably wouldn't have been able to focus very well had I known.

"So," Dad continued, "if you are okay with it, he has tentatively booked a plane ticket here for next week, while you're on break between semesters."

My jaw dropped. *Next week?*

"As in . . . five days away, next *week*?" I said in disbelief, completely incapable of hiding the excited smile that was spreading.

"Yeah," Dad said with a grin. "He'd like to stay about a week too—if you are comfortable with that. Then if you're both on board with the idea, he'll take the internship in June."

"Yes, I definitely would like that!"

That Sunday, for the first time since we'd "met" nearly two years before, we talked on the phone before he flew down to visit. We'd exchanged over nine hundred pages of emails by that point, but there remained no shortage of things to discuss, and when we hung up hours later, we were both eager to meet.

I smiled as I spun gently in my desk chair, glancing idly over the textbooks stacked on one end of the desktop, remnants of a completed semester. Jacob had made it clear that his desire for the next week was to prayerfully consider transitioning into a serious relationship. He didn't want to pressure me, but he also had no intent of leaving me wondering and unsure, and I was grateful for that.

Next week is going to be . . . interesting, I thought, with a sense of both contentment and anticipation.

I thought eagerly about all the questions I had, everything I wanted to know about who Jacob was and how we would navigate a serious relationship, if we decided to move in that direction. There was the distance between us and whether one or the other of us would be willing to move if things progressed, for starters. And . . . *that*. Fear and grief drowned out the joyful anticipation. *I'm going to have to tell him about that.* Even to myself, I used euphemisms still. Words that I rarely *thought*, I would now have to speak.

I could wait, I argued with myself, wanting a way out. *No, you can't. You really can't. This is going to affect a lot*, I reminded myself. *He's going to have to know.*

And it wasn't just for his sake; it was for mine, too. If Jacob didn't understand, he might add to the lies I heard in my head every day, and that would be crushing. I could barely fight the war within myself. I had no ability, nor any desire, to have to fight it with the person I let closest to me.

You have to know if he can handle it, I told myself firmly. *If he can't, there's no point in going any further.* There wasn't a choice. Not really. I was going to have to deal with it next week. I twisted back and forth in my chair, tense and on guard. *How do I even start that conversation?* I wondered with a sick feeling. The chair stopped spinning and I sat still, feeling half-frozen at the very thought of it.

I understood things now. In the two years prior, I'd journaled extensively, despite my inner protestations at my mom's suggestion. Mostly in pencil, which gave me the freedom to erase and hide whatever I put down. Memories flooded me as I wrestled with how and what to communicate. I flipped through my old entries.

> How do you explain to someone the confusion, sick feeling, and shame without knowing why, that swirls through your mind . . . when something is terribly wrong? How do you explain to someone who has never been that vulnerable that even though I wasn't "held down," I was still trapped? Even though I wasn't "physically overpowered," I was completely powerless? I can't forget any detail.

Two years earlier, I had stumbled across a news special on childhood sexual assault. It put words to what I had never understood—why I hadn't been able to move or speak during the abuse. There weren't just two responses to danger—fight or flight—as everyone casually said. There were three: fight, flight, or *freeze*.

> I know what freezing in fear is now. It's when you're so confused and ashamed and horrified and scared that you just . . . shut down, because reality is incomprehensible.

How could I even begin to let someone get close after that? I bit my lip just enough to feel a small pinch, enough to give me something in the present to focus on so I could think clearly. I'd journaled through the trust problem too.

> Because I trusted, I gave the benefit of the doubt. If I hadn't trusted these men enough to let them close, if I hadn't trusted enough to believe they wouldn't hurt me, it never would have happened. If they hadn't known I trusted, they never would have done it. It's my fault. I gave them the power to damage me when I gave them my trust.
>
> It was never the hand in the dark. It was always the hand I held. And it's my fault all over again, because it never would have happened if I hadn't trusted.

I rested my forehead in my hands. I had no idea how to deal with the conversation that I knew had to happen. I wanted it to go away. *No one will ever know* was the promise I'd made to myself over and over for years, ignoring the reality that someday, someone might have to. How much room could I leave for Jacob to not understand but to be willing to learn? I was steeling myself for the unintentional yet devastating response that was likely coming. I scanned the handwritten pages scattered on my pillow.

> I was too terrified and ashamed, too confused, to understand back then, but the price for not understanding then is that no one understands now. What I thought was my fault then, most think is my fault now.

I'd frozen. I'd trusted. I'd thought I had a dirty mind for thinking something was wrong. Almost no one understood those dynamics. All they could see was a girl who didn't fight back. So she must have wanted it. My fault.

As I stacked the loose collection of papers to put them back in the folder, another old entry slipped out. I'd titled it "Silent Battle," page after page of my attempt to put words to the internal war that rages within a victim when someone's actions don't match the person they are supposed to be. It was also my attempt to answer the resounding question I heard so often: *Why didn't you tell someone?* I felt exhausted. I knew this was the conversation that was coming, because it was the conversation I couldn't even get out of my own head.

Why didn't you cry out? He probably would have stopped if you had. In fact, if he thought you would, it probably wouldn't have happened at all. Why didn't you cry out?

Why? Because I trusted. I was a child. He was a doctor. He knows best. He had cared for me. He knew me. There had to be a reason. I must be reading too much into it. It isn't fair to assume he was being sexual. Think about who he is. Give the benefit of the doubt. I must be the one with the dirty mind if I can even think something like that.

Terror. Shame. Confusion. Shattered trust. Humiliation. Horror. Revulsion. Dirty. Used.

How could you not cry out?

I didn't know.

Foolish. How could you not know?

Because I trusted.

How could you let your guard down?

How could you trust so implicitly?

It's over. But it's not done. You didn't cry out.

I did inside.

Is that enough?

I inhaled sharply, closed the folder with a snap, and quickly shut the light off. There was no point in thinking about how Jacob would answer that unspoken question the following week. I couldn't change it. All I could do was live with the fallout.

11

THE NEXT WEEK I STOOD NEAR the baggage claim at the little airport in Kalamazoo, making every effort to appear completely casual, but completely failing. My parents had come with me, and my dad appeared to be using every ounce of self-control not to tease me.

Finally, the baggage carousel started up with a metallic grinding sound, and as if on cue, people began flooding the hallway. I stared intently in the direction of the passengers jostling through the door—totally calm, of course. Very, very calm. He told me he'd be wearing an "Opa hat"—the old-fashioned sort of cap that golfers wear—so dubbed because his grandfathers both wore them.

My stomach flipped as a gray cap emerged from the mass of travelers. I walked a few paces toward the young man who was striding swiftly in my direction.

Do we hug? I wondered. *I'm just meeting him. But I know him. Would that be weird?* I opted for the quick, safer handshake.

"It's so nice to finally meet you!" I offered, smiling up and meeting dark brown eyes that looked down warmly at me. (I would later find out he thought my greeting was hilariously formal, but I maintain that was his fault, because he didn't do something first.)

Impressively, he'd packed for the whole week in just a carry-on, so after my parents greeted him, we headed to the car.

During the ride home, I alternated between wondering, *How did we ever get here from Xanga?* and *What if we get to the end of the week and there's just . . . nothing?*

Late one afternoon a few days later, the house cleared out as family members went about their respective commitments, and Jacob and I were left alone. We sat in the living room. Outside the window, the bright sunlight had shifted to a soft gold, making everything seem calm and inviting. We discussed books and coursework, family and the little boy I cared for, and the goals and passions we each had. We even struck on a point of theology and philosophy where we disagreed. True to form, there was a good "give and take," exactly what I'd expected and hoped for. He became very animated, and his eyes lit up as he began discussing the truths he held dear. I was amused at the transformation.

"Here, let me show you!" He reached for the copy of the Bible resting on the coffee table and began excitedly flipping through it. I smiled as I watched him. He was so eager to learn and teach and grow, and so passionate about truth and its implications. *This is a man I could be with*, I thought with calm confidence. When we finally went our separate ways and headed to bed that night, I was certain where I wanted this relationship to go. But at some point, I still had to deal with *that*.

I woke up the next morning struggling to figure out how to talk about the one thing I felt we absolutely *had* to cover. I needed to find somewhere private to bring it up. Going somewhere for a date was no good. I definitely couldn't talk about *that* in a restaurant or coffee shop. Our home was wonderful, but small and busy. I had to be sure we wouldn't be interrupted.

That evening, as the sun was just beginning to set, Jacob and I went out for a walk. "Hey, is there any place nearby, like a park or something, that we could walk to and just sit and talk?" Jacob asked.

I thought for a moment. "Mmmm . . . yeah, there's a playground behind the school a few blocks away," I said.

Jacob nodded and we wandered off in that direction. The park was abandoned. We crossed the open field and each took a swing. I drifted lightly back and forth as we sat there together.

"While we're here . . . ," I started quietly, "there are some things I need to tell you because they might make a difference about whether you want to pursue this relationship." I pushed the toes of my shoes into the sand, shifting the swing gently back and forth. *Yeah, there's no delicate way to say this.* I kept my head down, took a deep breath, and just forced the words out. "I was sexually molested by a guy in my church when I was seven." I paused. *Annnd . . .* my thoughts prompted. "And by a doctor when I was fifteen. I never reported him because he's really famous and no one would believe me. If anything ever happens with it, though, it will be big—really big." I paused. *Connect the dots for him. He needs to know he has an out.* "If that changes things for you, I understand." I felt so vulnerable. I watched the sand move slowly under my shoe and didn't look up.

Jacob swung back and forth twice, keeping his feet tucked up behind him, the heaviness of what I'd said hanging in the air silently. "I am so sorry," he said. "I'm so, so sorry." I glanced up briefly. He was looking at me gently and with grief. I kept swinging slowly, watching the sand drift by. "This is not your fault," he said firmly but kindly.

"I don't expect you to say or believe that," I answered.

"But I know it's not," he said softly. "It was abuse. That's never your fault." He paused again. "I'm angry on your behalf, and I'm hurt for you. But no, that doesn't change anything for me."

We sat quietly for a moment. "You need to know," he started, "this does not diminish your value. This doesn't make me think less of you." He looked over at me and I glanced back briefly. "All this does is give me direction for how to best serve and care for you. Honestly . . ." He laughed just a bit. "I've been wondering this whole time what I could possibly bring to the relationship. You are intelligent, kind, accomplished; there's nothing I could add to that. But walking alongside you is something I *can* do. If God keeps leading us together, I can walk with you through this." He paused one more time. "And that would be a privilege."

We kept swinging slowly as the night grew dark. I felt sorrow, but I was thankful because I believed that Jacob meant what he said. Yet I also knew the depth of the damage done to me and how long it could take to overcome. The scars would always be there, and I knew that . . . well, sometimes things change when reality hits. I couldn't expect him to always be tender and patient or to understand. I took a deep breath and pushed a bit harder against the ground, the swing gently creaking in response. *But it's a start.*

The mosquitoes started to descend at twilight, and we reluctantly headed home. Once we arrived at the back door, I took a deep breath and pulled open the screen, light from the kitchen flooding the steps. When we stepped out of the dark and quiet and into the brightly lit house full of laughter and people, we quickly engaged in conversation with the rest of the family again. But for both of us, something changed that night.

Jacob returned to Canada a few days later after accepting the internship in Lansing. He promised he'd be back in eight weeks. He would be working with the Student Statesmanship Institute, the same organization that ran the camp I'd attended and where I now taught. By the time my week to teach rolled around, he'd be gone, but I'd go up as a chaperone one of the weeks he was there. Then we'd spend a few more days together and . . . well . . . we'd go from there.

The eight weeks in between felt like an eternity, but they were punctuated by daily emails and phone calls every weekend. I was busy with law school and both of my jobs, plus overseeing the school's mentoring programs. Jacob was working and in school too. We'd determined before he left that part of respecting and caring for each other would mean supporting each other's endeavors rather than selfishly distracting from them. So we studied and worked, learned more about each other, and interspersed it all with absolute mush.

Summer eventually came, despite our groanings that it never would, and we treasured every moment we had together. Between the two summer camps Jacob was working at, he had a weeklong break, which we spent at my house. One evening we returned to the playground swings in the nearby schoolyard as the sun was setting. "I've been thinking a lot about what happened the last time we were here," Jacob said softly. "I think I need to tell you something." He paused again, just for a moment. "I love you."

I froze. In our family, those words had serious power. *Love* wasn't thrown around at any given emotional moment. It wasn't used to describe the intense emotions or physical attractions that come along with dating. In our family, love meant commitment—a choice to care for, serve, and sacrifice for someone. *Can he really know that he loves me already?* My mind raced. *I can't say that yet.*

Jacob saw the look on my face and continued quickly. "I know that you aren't there yet and that you may never get there. I'm not presuming only one conclusion to this relationship. But—" he swung a few times—"because of what you've been through, it's important to me that you are not left wondering and trying to guess where I'm at. I want you to be able to do whatever you need to do in this relationship from a place of security. You need to know that I'm not going anywhere." He took a deep breath. "I'm committed to you, and to walking through everything that entails, without assuming where we'll end up. I want you to feel absolutely no pressure from me, but I also want you to know that I love you."

I pushed against the ground and drifted gently. "Thank you." I really didn't know what else to say yet. Jacob swung a few more times and then laughed softly.

"I'm thinking about what my friend Jesse told me about dating," he said. "He said, 'When you're cultivating a rose, you don't water it with a fire hose.' And I'm kinda wondering if I just did that."

I burst out laughing. It was such a funny, apt description. "No," I said with a soft smile, glancing over at him. "No. It was really good for me to hear, and I'm thankful you said it—more than I can explain." I thought for a moment. "You're right, I'm not there yet. And I'll probably be able to say that I love you long before I can say that I trust you. That last one is going to be a much bigger hurdle. But I'm really grateful that you aren't leaving me wondering and for everything you've communicated. It means a lot to me."

We swung in silence for a while and then headed home to escape the army of mosquitoes that were a quintessential part of the Michigan outdoors. Like the last time, we took a deep breath before pulling open the kitchen door and stepping out of the dark and quiet into the brightness and busyness of a full, cheerful house. And like the last time, we both knew something was different.

Our first real test came a week later when we were both working at the camp. After finishing our preparations for the next day, most of the staff split off for some late-night snacking and movie watching in the main classroom on campus. Jacob and I stayed in the student lounge, now quiet and deserted, to grab a few precious minutes together and to pray before bedtime. We hadn't so much as held hands yet. He was patiently waiting for me to take the lead when I felt ready and safe.

"Let's pray real quick," Jacob said as he closed the Bible we'd been reading together. "And then I'm heading for bed." We were both basically old people, or at least we acted like it, compared to the energetic group who had left to watch a movie. He sat forward on the couch. I paused for a moment, then reached out and took his hand. He stopped briefly, smiled at me, and closed his much larger hand around mine gently.

We prayed and then walked to the dormitories, fingers laced. We paused where the sidewalk split off in the separate directions of the men's and women's dorms, and I glanced down at our hands as we stood close. *It's never been the hand in the dark*, I remembered with a flash. *It's always the hand you hold.* I'd been keeping everything at bay, but before I even realized what I thought, my body began to automatically respond. I froze and started shaking. Jacob could immediately see in my face that something was very wrong.

"Are you okay?" he asked, backing up just a bit to give me space. I stood still for what seemed like an eternity. Finally, I nodded. He looked down at me with concern. "Okay. Let's get some rest for tonight." He paused. "I love you." Then he slipped his hand out and walked away.

The next day during an afternoon break, we went for a walk, finding a lone picnic table in a quiet spot. "Can we talk about what happened last night?" Jacob asked. I nodded but struggled to think of how to explain it.

"I could tell you were scared," he prompted, seeing that words were hard to come by. I listened to a bird chirping above us and pushed down the fear that was rising quickly again. Simply letting him know what I thought felt like too much. If he understood what I was thinking and feeling, that gave him *access* to me—*more* that could be manipulated. The one thing Larry had never had access to was my mind, so it felt like the one thing left I could protect. Still I knew that keeping those walls up forever would ruin me in the end.

"It's not just sexual stuff," I tried to explain. "The reason those guys could do what they did was because I trusted them. All the stuff they did that seemed totally innocent was all being used against me. So . . ." I searched for words again. "Innocent things don't feel innocent anymore. If I trust you and let you anywhere near me, I'm giving you access to me." I glanced up at him and bit my lip. "Do you realize what you could *do* with that?"

His eyes were full of grief. "Yeah. I do. You owe me nothing."

That night after everyone had left for the main classroom again, Jacob and I sat in the lounge and prayed, then walked back to the dorms together. I held his hand as we meandered down the sidewalk quietly. We reached the spot where the sidewalk split off and stood for a moment, feeling the cool night breeze that was a welcome respite from the sweltering heat earlier in the day. He glanced down at our hands and held them up ever so slightly. "I promise you," he said quietly and firmly, "this hand you hold will only ever be used to protect you." He whispered, "I love you," and slipped away.

The end of July came much faster than either of us wanted. Jacob returned home to Canada. The best news was that we wouldn't have *too* long to wait before my family and I would be heading his direction to meet his family and attend an annual camp with them that had been put together by area families. In the meantime, I had a senior thesis to finish and needed to sit for the MPRE (a nationwide ethics exam that aspiring attorneys are required to pass in addition to the bar exam).

Exactly twenty-four days after we said good-bye, my family and I were driving a rental car up a winding mountain driveway, and between the excitement of seeing Jacob again and the anxiety of meeting his family, my nerves were stretched to the max. My family was very close-knit, and I hoped to communicate my desire for that type of loving relationship with his family too. By the time the camp rolled around, I felt more at ease, and more certain that I was in love with this man. But it was the contrast between something that happened at camp, and the response from Jacob, that led me to communicate it.

Part of the camp's purpose was to offer families teaching on theology and family-related topics—often led by one of the men there. This year, the main focus was reaching the heart of your child—a topic worth discussion. At some point, one of the presenters decided that showing a video documentary titled *The Return of the Daughters* would be an excellent complement to that year's message, the camp's purpose, and the beliefs of these families. Neither Jacob nor I had seen it, but out of respect for those who wanted to show it, we went. We didn't last long. Within minutes of slipping in a bit late and taking our seats, one of the men teaching in the film turned his attention to the rape of Dinah—a story from the Old Testament about a woman who is raped while visiting women in town. Her brothers avenge her, while her father does nothing. As soon as I heard the name *Dinah* come out of the teacher's mouth, I went stiff. I knew exactly where this was heading. I'd heard it so many times before. *Don't go there. No no no no no.*

But he did. This rape, this abuse, he taught, is what happens when a daughter steps outside her father's protection.

I wanted to scream. It was a lie from the pit of hell, and I knew the damage it would do. No one else moved or registered any concern. I'd been here before. *Abuse is the woman's fault. It's a common assumption that if you are abused, it's because you did something wrong.* No blame on the rapist. No guilt for the father who shrugged it off. It's the daughter's fault. *This is what happens to girls who* _____. Society filled in that blank all the time: *to girls who drink; to girls who wear low-cut shirts; to girls who go to college, who go to bars, who freeze instead of fight back. One way or the other, the fault always falls on the girls, never on the person who actually committed the crime.* Christians dressed it up differently, but it was the same message. *Damaged. And it's your fault. This is what happens to girls who . . .*

Jacob squeezed my hand. We got up and left. We found an empty classroom, large and apparently used mainly for storage, and slipped inside to sit down and talk. We sat on the floor next to each other, backs against the wall. It wasn't exactly a romantic spot, but we were together, and that was enough. My mind was filled with the juxtaposition between Jacob and the teacher in the video. Between how Jacob valued me, and how the man in that video portrayed women. I smiled, squeezing Jacob's hand softly.

"I love you."

He sat up straighter. "What?"

I smiled. "I love you."

His face broke into a huge smile. "Well, then, I have a secret for you," he declared triumphantly. He leaned in and began to whisper in my ear. I smiled in anticipation. He opened his mouth to whisper what I was sure would be sweet nothings of affection. "I . . . ," he began. And then, much to his horror, he burped. I burst out laughing as he smacked himself in the forehead.

"Oh my gosh. That was going to be so nice! Oh man! I couldn't have planned that if I *tried*, but I never would have tried!"

I couldn't stop giggling.

"Let me try again," he said with determination, leaning in to whisper how much I was loved. This time it worked. We loved each other. We both knew I hadn't crossed the bigger hurdle yet, but we loved each other. And for now, that was enough.

Once the camp ended, we had just a few days before my family would head home. Jacob wanted to take me to the top of the mountain that overlooked Salmon Arm, so after lunch we grabbed two of his sweaters—because of course I'd forgotten to bring my own—and jumped into his rusty old pickup truck. The view from the mountaintop was breathtaking. As we sat down to enjoy the beauty together, I tucked my arm alongside his and held his hand. We weren't going to see each other again until January, and after that, we had no idea. Plane tickets were so expensive, we both had school to pay for, and I had to take the bar exam in February. He traced the back of my hand with his thumb and I smiled. I took a deep breath and said with resolve, "I trust you."

He looked down at me, cupped my hand in both of his, and exhaled. We still had a lot left to work through. We both knew that. And it still scared me to say that I trusted him. But I *could* say it, and that was a step. We sat together in silence a bit longer before returning home—once again reentering a busy, cheerful household. And again, we both knew something was different.

12

BY THE TIME OUR GRAY RENTAL car pulled away from Jacob's house and made its way down the long mountain driveway, my parents knew something had changed too. When we finally reached home after two long days of travel, my mom gave me a hug. "It's harder to be apart than it will be to move far away, isn't it?" she said, with tears in her eyes. "We can see it. We know it's time."

We also knew it was going to be a long wait. The bar exam was in February, and I had to get past that first. Jacob wouldn't even be back in Michigan until January, and I knew he wouldn't want to distract me with an engagement and wedding plans so close to the bar. So I threw myself into studying and coaching, determined to use the time well.

On the day I finished my law school finals, I closed my laptop with a sigh. Four years . . . It felt bittersweet to be done. I was excited, but I'd loved the coursework and had formed tight friendships with my classmates.

Jacob called that night to tell me how proud he was of me. "And hey," he added, "I sent you a package. It was just delivered. Go check your door and open it while you're on the phone with me."

I smiled and bit my lip excitedly. Butterflies in my stomach had become a familiar feeling over the past few months. I walked to the back door. It was already dark, and I couldn't see outside. I pulled the door open and shrieked in surprise and delight. He was *there*—holding a dozen roses. I felt as if my heart would burst!

The next few days were like a dream. That Saturday, when Jacob suggested we go out for coffee and a walk at one of our favorite places—a nearby park with winding trails and several bridges over the river—I jumped at the chance. I slipped my hand into his as we walked along the paved path, over the plank bridge, and through the trees. We paused for a moment at one of our favorite places—a massive stone bridge over the widest part of the river. I rested my elbows on the ledge and smiled as we watched the ducks glide by on the slow-moving river. We were deep in discussion but paused as a middle-aged guy in a sweatshirt approached, carrying a big black garbage bag in his arms.

Just as he passed us, the man turned. "Hey . . . ," he called out, "I left something in my car, and I need to go back and get it. This is really heavy," he said nodding at the bag, "and I don't really wanna carry it all the way back. Do you mind if I leave it here while I go grab the stuff I forgot?"

The skeptic in me was immediately on high alert, but Jacob shrugged. "Yeah, sure, you can set it here."

"Hey, thanks, I appreciate that." Then the guy set the bag on the stone ledge and hustled off back toward the parking lot. I watched the ducks for a few more seconds, but my tranquility had been shattered.

"That's really weird," I said.

Jacob just shrugged. "Ehhh. It won't hurt anything."

I was growing less sure. *What if there is something illegal in that bag? What if this is some bizarre form of a drop-off? What if that guy has something he isn't supposed to and didn't know how to get rid of it, so he gave it to us? What if someone finds us with it?*

I stretched up on my tiptoes and looked around. I could see the parking lot from the bridge, but there was no guy in a hoodie in sight.

"He's not coming back," I said nervously.

"Well, let me check and see what's in here then," Jacob said, as he started to rustle the bag open.

"*What? No!*" I hissed in a whisper. "You cannot go opening random strangers' garbage bags! What if it's something illegal and you aren't supposed to see it?" I stretched up again, straining for some glimpse of this very disturbing stranger.

"Hey, it's a wooden box!" Jacob said. I glanced at it quickly. Definitely handmade.

"Don't open the box!" I whispered fiercely as I kept scanning the area.

"Oh, there are old books in here!" Jacob said with delight. "Hey . . . your name is on one of them." I whipped around in absolute confusion.

"What?"

"Your name is on this one," he said, casually handing me a book.

"How . . . ? What . . . ?" I was so confused that I couldn't even finish the sentence. I had never seen that man before in my life, and Jacob definitely hadn't either. I was sure of that.

"Wow, it's a gorgeous copy of *Little Women*!" Jacob said.

I stared at the book he placed in my hands. I looked around again. *Where's that guy?*

"There's a bookmark," he prompted. I stared at the book. Something was tied to the end of the bookmark. It was round.

"Rachael."

I looked up quickly. Jacob took the book, set it down, and reached for both my hands. He knelt. Massive confusion melted away as I finally realized what was happening. I felt deeper joy than I imagined possible rushing over me as he spoke tender words that lifted me up, affirming everything he treasured about me and his desire to love me sacrificially. "Will you marry me?"

I found out later that Jacob had made the chest by hand and had shipped it to my dad weeks ago in preparation for this day. And that man in the hoodie? My dad later confessed that the stranger was a coworker of his who thought it would be great fun to help with the surprise.

Jacob and I would not see each other again until the wedding, which was scheduled for August 1. That spring, after weeks of intense studying, I passed the bar exam—a major milestone. I then focused on planning our wedding, and along with Jacob, saving money as we prepared to start our life together.

After what seemed like endless waiting, the night before our wedding finally arrived. We ran through the rehearsal, again marveling at how much love surrounded us. When I turned to Jacob to say one last good-bye the night before we were to be married and together *forever*, I found still more love awaiting me. He handed me an envelope and ran his fingertips over the side of my face. "I want you to know nothing but safety and love," he said.

When I was alone, I opened his letter, which promised that he was placing no expectations on me after marriage—that I owed him nothing. My safety and my ability to trust him were his first priorities, no matter what that looked like. I knew that would take work on both our parts— communicating fears and insecurities, listening and learning together. I would need to work to let him know what I was thinking and feeling, fighting the urge to shut down and shut him out. He would need patience and compassion, as healing slowly unfolded. We'd already laid the ground- work, communicating openly and candidly as we grew together, viewing physical intimacy as a way to serve and love each other, rather than him demanding that I meet his "needs." We had a foundation to build on. I was not without fear, but there was hope. Because we faced the damage from the abuse *together*. I went to bed and slept without nightmares.

● ● ●

The next day dawned bright and sunny. I scurried over to the church where my bridesmaids and I, plus a few friends who'd jumped in to help with hair and makeup, would congregate. Sunlight poured through the stained- glass windows, dancing on the rose-hued satin of the bridesmaids' gowns and catching the lace embroidery on my own dress. After we'd finished curling our hair and applying makeup, we surreptitiously hid tissues in our bouquets and prepared to line up at the back of the church.

As the soft piano chords of the prelude began to play, my heart raced. It was *finally time*! I watched as the precious little flower girls and ring bearers stepped out solemnly, followed by one of Jacob's younger sisters, bearing a lighted lamp. The bridesmaids moved toward the altar to the soft melody of the violin, and then the doors closed. I waited for the triumphant start of the organ, barely holding back tears of joy. When the doors opened again and my dad began walking me down the long aisle, Jacob's face, full of pure love, was all I could see. When we reached him, Dad placed my hand in Jacob's, and we faced each other, filled with more joy than I could have imagined possible. We had written our own vows in addition to the traditional promises, and as Jacob took my hands and began to repeat what he had written, I looked up to him with full trust, though months earlier I could not even meet his gaze.

By the grace and mercy of God, I do take you, Rachael, to be my wife.

I commit to lay down my life in sacrificial love for you. Not only in extraordinary circumstances, but in the ordinary circumstances of putting your needs ahead of my own.

In making sure you have the opportunities to use the gifts God has endowed you with . . .

In watching carefully over your health . . .

In choosing to listen . . .

In striving to make you feel secure, safe, and cherished . . .

In making your hopes and fears my hopes and fears . . .

I commit to be your safe place in times of trouble . . .

Your shoulder to cry on in times of grief . . .

I will be the one through whom every enemy and troublemaker must first come, be they the thoughtless gossip or the hand in the dark. I promise the type of relationship that elevates your stature, that tells the world of your preciousness to me . . .

Because Christ has promised to never leave, nor forsake, I pledge to you, by God's grace, the permanence of this covenant.

This is my solemn vow.

Every moment of that day was perfect—more beautiful and rich in what it was than it ever would have been if we had not first walked through so much. Family and friends from near and far had come, dear people from our childhood or from distances so great we never supposed they could actually be there to celebrate with us. The love we were surrounded with was overwhelming, and now Jacob and I were together, forever. New associations had been patiently formed with everything that had felt so unsafe and threatening. New memories began to help cover the old ones. A new life together was begun.

13

"Hang on, sweetie, I'll get you," I called softly. I dumped the last bit of laundry detergent in the washer and added a stray sock or two before closing the lid and starting the machine. *Soooo much laundry*, I thought. I turned around and smiled down at the barely-one-year-old clutching at my pant leg and whimpering.

"Are your teeth sore, sweet girl?" I asked, stooping down to pick up the distressed little waif and kissing her wispy hair. "Let's put you in the wrap," I suggested, "and we'll just cuddle for a bit."

As I walked through the small kitchen toward our bedroom, I paused to step around the two-year-old who was happily sorting her collection of pacifiers into various containers. It was almost seven years to the day that Jacob and I had begun our new life together, and as I glanced around our small home, I couldn't believe how much had changed.

Jacob finished his undergraduate degree not long after we were married, with a view to beginning seminary in Kentucky a few months later. The move to Louisville was delayed, however, when we were surprised by a little plus sign on a pregnancy test and a due date one month after his semester was supposed to start.

We were so excited to begin the journey of parenthood, but I quickly found that an unexpected darkness would come with the process. We'd enrolled in a birthing class where we were learning about the emotional signposts in labor, and we'd just gotten to one of the last ones, referred to as the "loses sense of modesty stage." *The what stage?* My mind raced as I politely smiled back at our teacher, who had no clue what she had unleashed. Basically, she explained, this was the stage in labor that is so intense that women simply don't care anymore and their inhibitions become essentially nonexistent. Our teacher presented this as a positive in that the revealing nature of birth wouldn't actually bother me when I got to that point. I, however, found it terrifying. Medical settings alone were still hard for me to navigate. To be in labor *and* unable to care anymore was almost unthinkable.

I'd selected a group of all female midwives, but not a single practice in the area was made up exclusively of female ob-gyns. If there were any complications, I'd likely be forced to see a male doctor. I wouldn't have a choice. And now we'd just been told I probably wouldn't be cognizant enough to care. The nightmares that had never completely left returned with a vengeance.

"I won't be able to defend myself if I need to," I said over and over to Jacob.

"But I will," he assured me. "I will." That brought some comfort, but it still cast a dark shadow over the joyful anticipation of our first child. *It isn't fair*, I thought in grief and frustration. *I shouldn't have to still deal with Larry every time I turn around. He shouldn't be there at every major milestone.* But the scars remained. All I could do was respond to the damage.

Jonathan Edward burst onto the scene in September 2011, nearly three weeks early and after just five pushes. The postpartum depression that followed, however, lasted quite a bit longer. I felt as if I were living in someone else's mind and peering out a little peephole at a world I could have recognized had I only been myself.

Just as the fog was lifting, a catastrophic stroke took the life of my grandma. She'd held Jonathan just once, two weeks before it happened, and that was a gift. But I ached from losing her. And the hits kept coming. Just weeks later, the company I'd been working for went belly-up, taking with it nearly one-quarter of our annual household income—a huge blow because it hadn't been a big income to begin with. The year that followed was difficult in every respect. We moved to Louisville, only to have the small company Jacob was working for close without warning. For the next year, Jacob worked a number of jobs and took a full course load, all as we adjusted to parenthood. But by the end of it we had a beautiful toddler and an even stronger marriage. And when the nightmares came, I had someone safe to wake up to.

Now that little plus sign was nearly five years old and running back and forth through our tiny home with seemingly endless energy.

"Mom! Mom! Do you know how I run so fast?" he called out. "I take in a *huuuge* breath and compress it tight in my lungs. The extra compression gives me a burst of power, like a turbo charger in an internal combustion engine!" Without a pause the little boy with brown eyes like his daddy's but a stubborn streak to match his mommy's took a massive gulp of air, squeezed the muscles in his wiry frame, and took off like a shot through the living room, blowing air back out his mouth as he went.

I nodded seriously. "Wow, that *is* quite fast! But your sister is in the kitchen, so I don't want you running in there, okay? If you crash into her, she could get really hurt."

He nodded again. "All right!"

I paused in the bedroom door. *Where is that baby wrap? How is it possible to lose something in a house this size?* It *was* a small home—barely one thousand square feet—but it served us well and already held beautiful memories, not the least of which was bringing home our second child, Annaliese Grace, a few months after we'd bought it.

I'd hoped that birth, my second one, wouldn't dig up so many memories, but once again, the specter of abuse reared its ugly head. Still, the blue-eyed baby who looked *just* like Jacob's mom was more than worth it, and watching Jonathan fall in love with his sister made for many beautiful moments. He was a protector, like his daddy, and delighted in her every little roll and dimple. And I was grateful because, just a few months later, I approached Jacob while cradling a barely four-month-old Annaliese with one hand and holding another positive pregnancy test in the other.

"Could it be a mistake?" my husband asked blankly.

"Well . . . I took four," I assured him, "so probably not."

Ellianna Hope was born in the summer of 2015, the chubbiest of them all, much to the delight of her big brother. The minute he walked into the hospital room, he unwrapped the blankets that swaddled her so he could count every tiny toe and finger. Annaliese immediately took to her little sister too, much to my delight. I'd been worried about how she'd adjust, being barely a year old, but Annaliese loved Ellie. Moreover, she was determined to take care of her—all by herself, shooting a glare at anyone caught supporting Ellie's little head while she rested in Annaliese's arms.

I popped my head back into the kitchen to check on my two-year-old. Annaliese was still happily sorting things into containers, but she was definitely the child who required the most "checking." In fact, just a few weeks earlier I'd found her sitting cross-legged on the counter next to a stove burner she'd lit. Her response to my horrified "What are you doing?" was a cool "I making tea," as she pointed to the teakettle on the burner that she'd filled and put on the stove herself.

"No, sweetheart. You could get burned so badly. It's too hot," I admonished her, only to have her declare, in the best "Duh, Mom" voice a barely-two-year-old can muster, "I *know* hot. It's *tea*!"

Now Jonathan passed me as he began another lap of his "race car race," Annaliese running not far behind him. "Be very careful not to crash, please!" I called. "Take turns!" Yes, our house was little, and yes, it was chaotic. Yes, I frequently misplaced things in the exhaustion of raising three children aged four and under while Jacob worked and studied. But we loved each other. We loved our children. And we loved the beautiful, busy life we'd been given.

● ● ●

I gave up looking for the wrap and resignedly buckled on the Ergobaby carrier instead, lifting Ellianna, in all her teething misery, onto my back. She giggled and laid her head down on my shoulder with a deep sigh. "I love you, baby girl. I am so glad God gave you to us," I whispered.

Not long after, I walked back to the washing machine, conveniently located in the small kitchen. Between laundry and cooking, I was pretty sure

I spent almost all my time in this one room. I began moving the wet laundry to the dryer and threw up my hands in mock exasperation when I pulled out the black Moby wrap.

Oh geez. How could I forget so fast that I'd put it in the wash? I craned my head to look at the baby on my back, happily playing with my ponytail. "You gotta start sleepin', little one! I'm going to lose my mind if you keep this up!" Jacob and I were both exhausted, but it was worth it. Each precious little soul was worth it.

Now, what should I make for care group this week? I mused, reviewing the contents of the freezer. Jacob had been a community group leader for our local church for about two years. We met in our home every Sunday to share dinner and friendship. The year we'd moved to Louisville had been so difficult. Between my postpartum depression, the death of my grandmother, and the loss of our income, we'd been exhausted and depleted for a long time, and our small group had been an incredible source of care and joy. Our kids had grown up with this group of families and loved them dearly. It was because of this group that we felt we were finally home in Louisville. Sunday afternoon, when the house was filled with love, laughter, and the noise of more than half a dozen children ages four and under, was our favorite time of the week.

I seemed to have all the major ingredients for Mexican. *Mmmm . . . not salsa, though*, I realized. I turned to my computer and popped it open. I kept a running grocery list in my email so that I could quickly send it to myself when running out to the store. I'd left my Internet browser open the night before, and my Facebook page filled the screen. I went to minimize it, and that's when I saw the story trending in my news feed. I briefly wondered why, because I hadn't done or searched for anything that should have made it a relevant story for me, but nonetheless, there it was: "A Blind Eye to Sex Abuse: How USA Gymnastics Failed to Report Cases." My heart sank.

Again. It is happening again. Why can't we get this right? I wondered, with a deep, desperate ache. *It's everywhere.* By and large, I was doing well. With Jacob's patient care, I'd formed new associations with physical touch and intimacy, and new memories were layered over the bad ones. Yes, every once in a while a flashback or nightmare would come without warning and shake me, but Jacob was always there to work through it with me. I'd gotten to the point where I had told a few select, close friends that I'd been sexually abused and was now focused on helping others who'd been through something similar. It still hurt, but I had answers—and I had peace—about my situation.

Over the last year, however, the issue had begun to feel very raw again, ironically, because of our current church. They'd formed a working relationship with a new church plant in Louisville, the flagship of a network of churches that had recently been renamed Sovereign Grace Churches (SGC). The Louisville church and the ministry as a whole were led by a big-name pastor whom I'd greatly respected—from a distance, anyway—growing up. The problem was that just a few years earlier, that network of churches had numerous allegations come out that pastors and leaders were routinely mishandling sexual assault allegations—counseling victims to forgive and forget, not listening when alarm bells were sounded about someone's behavior, and even, many victims alleged, interfering with or being negative toward police investigations. In more than one instance, women alleged being counseled to stay with husbands who were sexually abusing their daughters or to have sex more frequently with their husbands as an attempted cure for severe addictions to pornography or pedophilia. Former members brought abuse allegations against a few of the pastors, some of whom remained in leadership.[7] For those of us trained in evidentiary law or familiar with abusive dynamics, it was the type of evidence that carried a lot of weight. At a minimum, an investigation was warranted.

Yet a number of prominent Christian leaders immediately surrounded this high-profile pastor and his ministry—defending him publicly and bringing him back on the national speaking circuit. It was the mistake made by all too many communities. "Not him." Community protectionism. Everyone hates abuse and doesn't want it covered up—until it happens in their own community, and then it's "different."

In the meantime, the church's leaders missed something critical: All the survivors attributed the mishandling of their cases to the church's theology. They alleged dynamics like an excessive view of pastoral authority; a refusal to engage with secular authorities or abuse educators outside the church; teachings on concepts like unity, forgiveness, and grace that resulted in abusers being "forgiven" while victims were silenced by being characterized as "bitter." It wasn't a new story—not to me nor to anyone who understood the reasons churches typically mishandle abuse. The information was there for anyone who really wanted to see it. In fact, I'd written numerous Facebook posts on conservative and evangelical scandals in recent years—whether at big-name universities like Baylor or within fundamentalist groups. Experts had warned for decades that predators sought out churches because of the exact dynamics the victims at the SGC churches had identified. But no one was listening—including our own church.

Jacob and I didn't realize that until we sat in church one morning and listened as one of our pastors prayed that the SGC leaders would be able to endure these false assertions. I felt sick. I'd already received calls from more than one sexual assault survivor in the church who had been deeply hurt and felt very unsafe because of how our church was handling the scandal within SGC, and I knew there were likely more who wouldn't feel safe enough to speak up. Jacob and I were also concerned about the message the leaders were sending about abuse by allying with the SGC churches and even praying *against* the survivors.

Jacob talked to a few of our elders and discovered that no one he spoke with had even a basic knowledge of the allegations. As far as we could tell, they'd relied on the investigation a small committee of elders had done before deciding to work with this church. That didn't surprise us; it had been said both from the pulpit and in writing that the elders had carefully interviewed the head pastor about these allegations and determined there was no reason *not* to align with him and his ministry. Some leaders in the church had even used their personal social media platforms to urge Christians to stand with the pastor and his ministry, including statements that were factually incorrect— errors we'd already brought to the elders' attention.

We figured our church must have information that would clear the matter up, so we asked to meet with one of the men most involved in the interview of SGC's head pastor. He'd agreed right away, and we were grateful.

When we first sat down to discuss our concerns, I said, "I want to be very careful how I express our concerns—" only to be cut off by the leader.

"I definitely suggest that you should be," he said with a firm nod of his head.

I was shocked. *What is that supposed to mean? I've never even talked to this pastor before. He doesn't even know me.*

Our church, the man confirmed, was relying on the personal word of a prominent pastor who had supposedly looked into and then overseen the SGC pastor's return to authority. We couldn't get any information, however, on what *that* pastor had done to consider the concerns. We weren't asking our elders to resolve the dispute, we told him, but we were deeply troubled about what their support was communicating to survivors and what it revealed about their own understanding of the dynamics of abuse.

We reached an impasse pretty quickly. Our conversation was painful and exhausting. I left the meeting feeling empty and full of grief. I knew it wasn't malicious, and that almost made it worse. It was well-intentioned and very, very wrong. There simply was a complete inability to understand the evidence or the impact of abuse.

We contacted another pastor for a follow-up meeting, but it hadn't happened yet, and I felt it hanging over us like a weight. And now similar concerns were back in the gymnastics world too. The church and the gym—the two places I knew best.

Why can't we get this right? The combined grief from the two settings felt overwhelming. Now, in my kitchen, I looked around to make sure Jonathan was occupied and clicked on the link. Several sentences from the article jumped out at me:

> Top executives . . . failed to alert authorities to many allegations of sexual abuse by coaches—relying on a policy that enabled predators to abuse gymnasts long after USA Gymnastics had received warnings. . . .
>
> Two former USA Gymnastics officials admitted under oath that the organization routinely dismissed sexual abuse allegations. . . .
>
> [Steve] Penny, the USA Gymnastics president since 2005, testified . . . that the possibility of a witch hunt is "very real" and officials have to move carefully on complaints.[8]

I gripped the washing machine as I read, hearing the anguish in the statements from the gymnasts' parents, my mind seeing the little girls I knew were behind every notation of "victim." But this report—these reporters—got it. They understood the dynamics. They knew best practices. They weren't fooled by USAG's conflation, deflection, and excuses. They'd hit the truth hard, even though USAG was headquartered in their own city. The report was explosive. It hit every note, and the damage to the families and these little girls wasn't hidden under layers of nice verbiage.

They understand the devastation. They know why this matters.

I scanned the story three times, looking for any hint they knew about more than just the coaches. Looking for Larry. There was nothing. But they understood. And they were pursuing those files.

If they exposed the coaches, maybe they can expose Larry. I glanced back at my Facebook page. The story was still trending. People were paying attention. They were listening.

This is it. Now. This is it. Ellianna began fussing. I'd been still too long. I took a deep breath and resumed my bouncing as she laid her head back on my shoulder. Then I opened my email.

There will be a price to pay if this gets out. If the church finds out, they'll think you've just imposed your situation on them.

I shook my head. It didn't matter. I felt physically ill at what I knew would unfold if the *IndyStar* picked this up.

It doesn't matter.

Now. This was it. Now.

I started typing.

I am emailing to report an incident. . . . I was not molested by my coach, but I was molested by Dr. Larry Nassar, the team doctor for USAG. I was fifteen years old. . . . I have the medical records showing my treatment. . . . They are in a file cabinet at my parents' house, which is several hours away. I did not ever report Nassar to anyone, except my own coach, some years later. . . . I was told not to tell the owner of the gym . . . it would come back on me. I decided against going to the police . . . it was my word against his. . . . I was confident I would not be believed. . . .

I have seen little hope that any light would be shed by coming forward, so I have remained quiet. If there is a possibility that is changing, I will come forward as publicly as necessary.

And I hit Send.

14

I TOOK A DEEP BREATH after sending the email and turned around to face my half-cleaned kitchen, unfolded laundry, and two small faces smiling up at me. *Focus on the now. Be faithful with the now.* I'd done what I could. I couldn't do anything else yet.

When Jacob made it home that night, we talked about what I'd done. He took a deep breath and pulled me close.

"Okay," he said calmly. "This was the right thing to do. If anything comes of it, we'll do it together."

I'd gotten a quick automated response back from the *IndyStar*, thanking me for my tip. That was it. All I could do was wait. I thought it would be hard to think about anything else, but as it happened, two days later something else took our full attention.

Adam, the leader from our church whom we'd asked to talk with, finally got back to us; not only that, in his email he asked to meet with us that very night. Something didn't feel right. Adam confirmed my suspicions when we sat down to talk with him in our living room after we'd settled the kids in bed. He told me that the church leaders felt that I had disparaged the elders by expressing my concerns about their support of SGC when two close friends of ours, also church members, had asked about it.

I was taken aback as Adam, not unkindly but firmly, explained the church's position: I had been divisive by expressing my concerns to other members of the congregation. I could have talked with an elder's wife, perhaps, but I should have gone no further than that. "People have raised concerns about your Facebook posts—that they are divisive."

"I haven't said anything about our church on Facebook," I replied in confusion. "I've only ever posted about abuse issues in the church as a whole." I offered to show every Facebook post, which listed numerous organizations embroiled in scandal and clearly referenced the cultural issues only. I'd been advocating on this issue long before our church took a position on SGC. It didn't matter.

"But you've posted about this issue," he reiterated. "It doesn't matter that it wasn't about *our* church or that it was in the context of the broader issue. You've posted on this issue of SGC, and your position is different from the position the elders have taken."

I opened my mouth and then closed it again, unable to find the right thing to say. Adam's words left no doubt. "You cannot discuss SGC in any context where another member might hear that your position differs from the leadership's." He paused.

"You need to know that your posts are significant enough that we had a discussion about them in our elders meetings," Adam continued. "We discussed whether Jacob should even be a care group leader because of them."

What? *You had a discussion about my concerns and my husband's role in the church without ever talking to me—to us—about them?* My mind was reeling.

"If we believed there was a deliberate cover-up," I said, "we wouldn't be here. We wouldn't be trying to discuss it with the elders. I have email communications with those church members explicitly saying that we don't believe the elders are doing something *wrong*. We simply believe there is a blind spot." I paused. "You are welcome to see the emails."

Adam leaned back in his chair and looked at me and Jacob. "Why does this matter to you? Why is this such a big deal to you two?"

I felt my heart sink. He'd asked the right question. No one else had even bothered to ask why it mattered. I took a deep breath and explained the damage handling this improperly could do.

"I care about the survivors. I care about the church. I care about the integrity of the gospel. When we get this wrong, it does terrible damage." I felt frustrated. We'd explained all this before.

Adam nodded. "Is that all?"

I felt Jacob looking at me. We'd talked many times about whether I should explain my personal experience. Jacob thought it might help. I was certain it wouldn't. "They will immediately presume I've projected my experience. All communication will shut down," I'd warned Jacob. Then again, Adam was the one elder we trusted to potentially be able to see things clearly.

"No. That's not all." I kept my voice as even as I could. "I have personal experience with this, in the church when I was around seven and again with a doctor when I was fifteen. I've spent a long time studying this."

He nodded. "Thank you for sharing that with me. I will keep it in confidence unless you direct otherwise."

Our discussion waned after that. We told Adam we would write an apology to the entire elder board and asked him to deliver it at their next meeting. After he left, I sat on the couch with my head in my hands. I knew it wasn't going to be that simple.

I drafted the apology: We understood the elders' concerns; we wanted to make sure they knew we had never alleged sin, malice, or ill intent by anyone at our church; we were grieved at the harm we'd caused; we reaffirmed our love for the church.

Our letter was distributed to the elders the next day. The following Monday, we met with three of them for hours. They had brought a list of four things I was believed to have said that troubled them. In the end, they agreed it was a misunderstanding caused by my use of the word *inaccurate* to describe the posts our elders had put up that were, in fact, inaccurate. They'd even *acknowledged* they were inaccurate. I felt helpless.

"You're a very intelligent woman, Rachael," one of the elders said. "It would be easy for you to plant ideas without directly saying something. Are you sure you haven't used your communication skills to do that?"

My intelligence hadn't counted for much when I'd raised the concerns. It was a liability. Not an asset. "No. I could do that, but I have not. I have no need to be indirect." I thought about my email to the *IndyStar* and what I would need to do if the paper moved forward.

I was told not to post about SGC anymore in any context and not to discuss it with anyone in the church, or anywhere a churchgoer might see or hear. I scrubbed my Facebook of all my posts on the church and sexual assault, since most listed numerous scandals that included that one. We didn't want to lose the church we loved so dearly.

Jacob was asked to meet again two days later about the future of our care group. When he got home from his meeting, I could read the shock and disappointment in his eyes.

"They're shutting down our care group," he said.

"What?" I gasped in disbelief. "I don't understand." Jacob had been immediately removed from leadership after that first meeting with Adam, but we'd been assured the group would stay together.

I felt empty. I remembered what it felt like to have my first church torn from me. I didn't want that to happen to my children. But the decision was final. The appeals we made went nowhere. We were told there was no one else who could lead the group, but we were not to tell anyone about the leaders' decision. An elder would come to our group to make the announcement. Apparently I'd created "too much baggage" to let the group continue.

• • •

Forty-eight hours later, still reeling from the loss of our care group, I opened my email.

> I'm Mark Alesia, one of the reporters who worked on the investigation of USA Gymnastics. I'm hoping to speak with you about Dr. Nassar.

I froze in disbelief and fear. I had given up hope after two weeks of silence, but suddenly, there it was—there was still a chance.

> We can start off the record, and you can decide later what—if anything—you're okay with us publishing.

I appreciated his caution, but the decision had been made a long time ago. I glanced quickly around the kitchen. I was just getting dinner ready for the kids and was running behind. *A quick email is better than none*, I decided.

> I am willing to do anything you need. I want this to end, and if it ever will, it will now, when people are watching and maybe more willing to believe.
>   I live in Louisville, KY. Do you want to talk via phone or in person?

I closed the computer. I didn't expect to hear anything more until the next workday, but around 11 p.m., I heard from Mark again—he'd like to come down to Louisville if a phone interview went well. Could I talk by phone sometime tomorrow? And then he said it.

> We have heard from someone else who mentioned the same guy.

I wasn't alone. I was *not alone*.

Not only that, but it might now be possible to get police to investigate Larry Nassar. I pulled up the Michigan Penal Code and began searching the statute of limitations. I'd checked them when I first realized I'd been abused. At the time, I didn't realize the penetration was abuse, but I knew the groping was. So after determining which class of crime I *knew* Larry had committed, I'd researched how long the law gave me to file a police report. I discovered I had ten years from the event.

As my twenty-fifth birthday had approached several years before, the cutoff date weighed on me like a dark cloud. I had sat up the night before, wondering if there was any hope I'd be believed if I filed a report. And I just didn't see it. When I woke up the next morning, all I could think was *That's it. I've lost my chance.* I could no longer file a police report.

But now Mark was saying there was another survivor. I was too old to file the report, but maybe she wasn't. Maybe she could press charges. I could offer to be a witness in the case. I could offer to be the public face. I stopped my research to begin typing my response to Mark:

Tell her I will take the risk and the heat.

I would take the pressure and the public risk if this second survivor would just file the police report. I went back to the penal code to continue my search for information on how long a victim had to initiate legal action against an abuser.

Then I froze. I realized I'd made an error years ago. Larry's abuse was so much more than "just" groping. The penetration was assault too. And that made the assault first degree. I'd realized that over the years but hadn't reviewed the statute of limitations since then. And the statute of limitations on first-degree sexual assault was gone. There was no longer any time limit for reporting first-degree sexual assault. That change had been made after my last recorded visit with Larry but long before the ten years I would have had to file a police report expired. I scanned the text of the penal code. Although the statute was not written to apply to crimes that were committed before the law changed, I knew courts typically extended new provisions to include any claims that could have been filed at the time of the change. I needed to know if the crimes against me fell under the new law or the old.

Can I still file? Hope shot through me. I didn't want to do it—I hated the idea—but if I *could*, no one else would be forced to make that decision. I could do it myself.

I needed to know for sure how the court had interpreted that statute, but I no longer had access to the research systems needed to pull court cases. I was going to have to ask for help from someone who did.

That night at nearly 2 a.m., after trying every avenue I could think of to find answers, I finished my email to Mark. After confirming the time for our phone call the following afternoon, I wrote:

Yes, I will meet in person. I will do whatever it takes.

At 4:30 p.m. the next day, I was sitting in an overstuffed rocking chair in the kids' bedroom—the most secluded room in our little house—with Jacob perched on the toddler-sized bed across from me. My parents were in town and had offered to watch the kids so he could be with me for this first interview.

When the phone finally rang, my heart practically leaped out of my chest.

"Hi, Rachael. Thank you so much for talking with me." Mark's voice was kind. "What can you tell me?"

I leaned forward, clenched my fists firmly, and launched in. *Clear. Explicit. Every detail. Clinical. Precise.* I had to be as accurate as possible. I glanced up at Jacob as I recounted what had taken place and realized this was the first time I had ever described the abuse to anyone. Jacob had never heard these details. My mom hadn't even heard some of them. I'd never put it in words.

I went through the evidence with Mark: the prior disclosures; what my medical records did and didn't show; the two therapists my mom and I had spoken with years ago; the possibility that I could file a criminal complaint; what the legal status was; the questions I still needed answers to; and what Larry would likely say in response. I told him about the status Larry held, how Michigan State and USAG would have many reasons to make sure this never saw the light of day, how many victims there likely were—hundreds, probably more. *Every detail.* Finally, I paused. I heard Mark take a deep breath.

"I am so sorry." He paused again. "Your story is very similar to the other woman who came forward. We may be able to do something with this. Your voice matters, and this is important, Rachael."

I believed him. More important—*he believed me.*

"Check out the story we did on Becca Seaborn,"[9] he encouraged me. "She was one of the first survivors I talked to. She was abused by her coach. She helped make this whole investigation with USAG happen. See what you think of how her story was handled and what you might be okay with. We will always respect your choices."

I nodded again, but there wasn't a question in my mind about how to do this.

"I will do whatever it takes, Mark. When do you want to come down?"

We set up a tentative time one week later when we would review my records, record an interview, and take photos. After we hung up, Jacob came over and sat down next to me. I kept my eyes on the floor as he folded me in close to him—every muscle in my body rigid in reactive tension.

"I am so sorry, honey," he whispered. He reached down into Annaliese's crib near the chair, pulled out a blanket, and wrapped me in it. We sat there until the shaking stopped. But the sick, burning feeling in the pit of my stomach remained.

Still, I had three children to take care of, dinner to make, books to read, and bedtime cuddles to give. My continued research and collection of evidence would have to wait. We exited the room to the noise, chaos, and smiles of three energetic children, and for the next few hours, focused on "right now."

When the children were tucked into bed, I stepped outside, sat down on our cement porch, and called an old family friend—Keith, my third-grade Sunday school teacher, someone I'd grown up around and trusted. He also happened to be the assistant prosecuting attorney in a county near my hometown. If there was one person I trusted to seek legal counsel from, it was him. I dialed his number and waited, silently pleading for him to be home. I wasn't sure I could handle any more tension. He picked up, but as I began to speak, I realized I could not take one more disclosure tonight. I asked for help "for someone I know" and explained the situation briefly.

After a brief pause, Keith said, "I want to be very sure I get the correct answer. Let me pull the case law for you tomorrow, and I'll get back to you ASAP."

I thanked him and we hung up. A few moments later, Jacob came out and sat next to me.

"Let's pray," he offered, taking my hand in his. But all I could manage was a whispered "Please help."

We turned to go inside. "What are we going to do about church?" I asked.

Jacob bowed his head and sighed. "One thing at a time, honey. Let's just take one thing at a time."

I tried, but it wasn't *happening* one thing at a time. I wasn't sure how much more I could take.

• • •

I spent the next day alternating between compiling evidence and managing daily tasks. A lengthy trip down into the cellar yielded the medical file my mom had wisely procured more than a decade earlier in the event we ever had the chance to speak out and be believed. I pored over the records, cross-checked them with current and past medical journals on pelvic floor therapy, updated Mark via email, and then took another shot in the dark. I called the physical therapist I'd seen during my last pregnancy a year earlier. She specialized in lower back and pelvic pain, and her whole practice specialized in pelvic floor therapy.

How do I explain this to the receptionist and make sure I get a call back? I wondered as I heard the phone ringing. I closed my eyes in exhaustion. *Just get it out. You've got to get answers. Just get it out.*

"So . . . I have an unorthodox question," I said in response to the receptionist's cheery "How can I help you?"

It worked. My physical therapist called me back not long after, and I explained it again to her. "I need to be very accurate in what I report," I said. "Can I please describe to you what happened and just hear your perspective on it?"

She readily agreed, and I launched in. Every detail, every movement.

"I'm so sorry," she said when I finished. "Nothing you described resembles any legitimate medical techniques." She identified every discrepancy I'd already found. Wrong fingers. Wrong movements. What Larry did wasn't . . . wasn't anything. Anything medical, at least. "You aren't missing something. That wasn't treatment in any way."

It was the answer I never wanted but desperately needed. I thanked her and walked out of the bedroom, just as Jacob needed to leave for a class. As he left, I tried to clear the memories and focus on the little people who needed so much attention, but I felt as if I were carrying a weight that just kept getting heavier. The next morning, I received an email from Keith. It was full of case citations and headnotes, and the conclusion I'd been waiting for.

The action is not time-barred. A prosecution can proceed.

In other words, even though the new law hadn't been passed when I was fifteen and seeing Larry, the crimes he committed against me could be prosecuted because the old time period hadn't expired when the new law was passed. I could *still* file against him! I quickly settled the kids with quiet toys and an audiobook and slipped into our bedroom, dialing Keith's number as I went.

"It's me," I said when he answered. "That case is mine, and I need to know if there's a chance a prosecutor would pick this up. Can I go through the law and the evidence with you and hear your opinion?"

And for the second time that day, I went through it all again—every detail that pointed to first-degree assault.

"We're only going to get one shot at this," I cautioned him. "If it gets buried, he'll know he can't be caught. I don't want to pull that thread until I know it's a case that has a chance of succeeding. Keith, what would you do?"

He paused, then told me what we both knew. "It's going to be a long shot. These cases are hard enough to prosecute as it is, and the process is going to be very difficult on you. But if it were me . . . I would give it a shot. I would try." Without pausing, he added, "And I'll do whatever I can to help you."

I wanted to cry. I'd been too afraid to ask anyone to step into this mess with me—knowing what was likely to unfold—and especially unwilling to ask anyone to use their reputation or credentials on a case with so much risk. And yet it was what I had so desperately wanted someone to say.

"If this goes to trial," Keith continued, "I am more than willing to testify as a character witness for you, and I'll write a letter vouching for your character and asking the investigators to take this seriously. You can bring it straight to the police when you report." He paused again. "Justice is God's work, Rachael. And I'm going to pray with you that you see it—as completely as we can reach it here on earth."

15

THE NEXT DAYS WERE FILLED with compiling the evidence for my case. In between changing diapers, washing dishes, and reading bedtime stories to my kids, I buried myself in case law, medical records, lists of people I needed to contact, and medical research I had to catalog. I was determined that I would put together the most complete case file I could.

Whenever the baby finally napped and Annaliese and Jonathan did their quiet time with an audiobook, I transitioned from mommy mode to attorney mode and began making phone calls. There was a chance I'd be able to make the initial report in Kentucky and have the local police collaborate with the police in Michigan to get the ball rolling. This would be the fastest way to move, *if* the departments were willing to coordinate. But I was bounced around from department to department, first in Kentucky and then Michigan, as we struggled to figure out who had jurisdiction to investigate the claim.

"I'm calling to make a delayed disclosure of sexual assault," I said over and over as yet another officer picked up my calls. Each time, a rush of nausea and fear would follow, since I knew that if I'd finally found the right department, a painful conversation would quickly become necessary. Each time, they'd take a message and I'd wait for a callback. The last message I left before Mark Alesia showed up at our front door with videographer Robert Scheer was with yet another police department in Michigan, and I still had no answers for where to bring the case file I was amassing.

In addition to making all the phone calls, researching, compiling evidence, and doing my best to maintain normalcy as a mom, I agonized over and meticulously planned which details to share in the *IndyStar* report. I had seen enough accusations buried or ignored to know what going public meant. Not only would I be verbalizing my trauma and relinquishing every shred of my privacy by having those details out there forever, but it also opened me up to the immediate attack of having done this for fame or money.

As much as I tried to keep my feelings at bay while I collected evidence for my case file and tried to anticipate any move Larry could make to derail my efforts, the stress of reliving my abuse every day and of knowing what my family was about to undergo took its toll. In the week between my phone and videotaped interviews with Mark, my five-foot-six-inch frame shrank to barely one hundred pounds. I lost more than ten pounds in six days from the constant stomach pain and stress.

But I knew how it needed to be done. I knew that if I did not give explicit detail very publicly, Larry wouldn't be forced to answer publicly, and that *had* to happen. I was absolutely certain the only way this could be done was to meet him where he was most confident—in the public eye—and to do it without flinching. And I had to offer enough detail that other survivors could hear the story and realize that what they'd been through wasn't medical treatment. I needed them to be able to hear what I said and then realize, *Wait . . . that happened to me.* Just as important, I needed the institutions that surrounded Larry, which had undoubtedly protected him for years, to be subject to swift public pressure and scrutiny, making it impossible to dismiss and bury the allegations again.

By the time Mark and Robert arrived, I'd had to decide exactly which details to release and how to release them. Each detail was chosen and framed to reach a specific goal. My parents had taken the kids out for a fun day so we'd have plenty of space, and my sister had come to lend and apply makeup (my collection was woefully inadequate), leaving shortly afterward. Now only Jacob and I were home.

I'd critiqued every aspect of my appearance, right down to what I wore. I assumed Larry would hire defense attorneys who would attempt to weaponize everything I did. I anticipated the attack that I, as an attorney, had used my legal training to fabricate a story or lie about details in order to meet the legal requirements. And I needed other survivors to know that I could be approached and that I understood the confusion and pain that were likely to follow.

Not too sharp or professional . . . relatable. I passed over the business suits. But I also needed to project mastery of the subject matter and story, and a high level of competence and tenacity. I needed to make it clear to Larry and the institutions surrounding him that these allegations were credible, handled professionally, and weren't going to be easily dismissed. *No jeans or casual clothes.* I ditched the gray blazer that matched my pencil skirt and paired it with a soft, lacy top instead. It was absurd to have to calculate how my clothing choices would be analyzed when I spoke up, yet this was the forced reality of a sexual assault survivor.

"Are you afraid you'll cry?" Jacob asked before Mark and Robert arrived.

I shook my head. "No. I can't cry, so I won't." I knew crying would lead to my being judged as an overly emotional person trying to manipulate the situation, or as someone who was too unstable to be credible. I had to avoid that to the best of my ability. I'd been abused before Larry, and a swift line of attack would be to argue that I had projected my first abuse onto an innocent party. *No. No tears allowed, period.* And yet I also knew that if I showed *no* emotion, I would be attacked for not "looking" like a survivor should look—not showing "real" hurt. And a lack of tears could be used to argue that my story was a made-up claim. I knew very well that in many ways, the dynamics survivors have to navigate just to be heard are no-win situations. Tears are attacked; no tears are attacked. Too much education and you're smart enough to manipulate (hadn't one of my own church elders asked that question about my advocacy for other victims?), yet victims from marginalized communities are often written off as "those kinds of people" who are just looking for attention or a quick buck. Every look, every word, every mannerism, every alleged fact could and likely would be scrutinized and attacked, weaponized and used to try to discredit me. I was walking a tightrope. The community surrounding Larry would attack immediately, and he would surely hire attorneys skilled in this type of manipulation and mind game. I had to think both short- and long-term.

• • •

"They're here," Jacob said softly, glancing out the window. I took a deep breath and opened the door, smiling as Mark and Robert came up the sidewalk. *Do your job. Do it well. No regrets. Pick up the pieces later.* I shook their hands and invited them into the living room, with their camera equipment in tow.

Robert eyed the lighting in the living room. "Set up anywhere you need," Jacob reminded him. "We know it's not the best backdrop."

Mark got right down to business, but did so kindly.

"We've heard again from the second survivor," he said. "She's going to be filing a civil suit."

Oh! I thought in shock. "That's good. That's really good. That will give this additional legal weight. When is it being filed? Does Larry know?" My questions came pouring out.

Mark shook his head and informed me that the suit hadn't been filed yet but was in the works. "She is definitely going to remain anonymous for now," he confirmed, "but that suit will get us one step closer."

I nodded. Mark had told me by now that she was an elite gymnast—an Olympian. That much would be in the civil suit, and I ached for her, knowing what she was going to face.

"I'm really glad she feels the freedom to remain anonymous," I said. I knew the community backlash would be fierce, and having more name recognition, she'd have more to lose if this went south. "I am so grateful she is willing to speak at all."

Mark nodded. "It's going to be tough. A lot has to happen before we make it to print, so I can't promise anything, but this will help." He paused. The entire reason we were having this discussion felt like the proverbial elephant in the room, and I wasn't sure if it was worse to try to make small talk around it or to deal with it head-on.

"Have you decided what you are comfortable with?" he asked, nodding toward where Robert was setting up video equipment.

I laughed. *Comfortable with? Umm . . . nothing? I don't want any of this out there.* But I knew what he meant.

"All of it," I answered out loud. "Everything needs to be public. Survivors won't feel safe to come forward unless they have a name and a face—unless they know someone out there is going to believe them and understand what they've been through."

Mark paused again. "Okay. You know this is *your* call. If you change your mind, we will always respect that decision."

I smiled a bit. I did know that. I'd researched how they had handled the USAG story and others, and I trusted them to do this right.

"I appreciate that, but it's not a real choice. It has to be done this way. I have always known it would have to be done this way. I'm simply grateful someone is listening."

I pulled out the medical file that contained my complete records from my time with Larry, grateful once again that my mom had had the foresight to request every piece of my file years earlier, just in case I ever had the chance to speak and be heard.

"The records are here," I said, setting the file on the table. "Like I said before, you are welcome to photograph them, or we can take them and get copies made." Robert came over and started snapping photos of each page while Mark and I discussed my situation.

"I have confirmed that I can file a police report," I explained, "so I have to keep the originals with me, but we'll do whatever we need to get you what helps the story too."

Mark raised his eyebrows. "Are you filing a report?"

"Absolutely," I responded with emphasis. "A police report is the only way to have a shot at really preventing him from continuing to abuse. I've got calls in to a police department in Michigan. We're just waiting for confirmation of where to report, and then we'll head up there immediately."

Mark nodded. "That would be huge. Long process, though."

"I anticipate around five years with appeals—*if* we are relatively lucky," I confirmed. "And quite possibly parole hearings every few years from that point on. It's a long-term commitment, but it's a chance, and a chance is worth it." As Robert finished photographing the medical files, I explained the research I'd done so far and where the law stood in Michigan. Then we sat down to do the interview.

"Let's just start with a basic sound check," Robert suggested after fiddling a bit with the camera focus. "Say something, anything."

I hesitated a bit and laughed softly, suddenly unsure of what to say.

"Just say the ABCs for me," he said, smiling, and I began reciting in an amused tone.

"A, B, C . . ."

After a few more he held up his hand. "All right, got it."

Then Mark started explaining the basics to me—where to look, how to let them know if I needed to change an answer or wanted to rephrase something. "No pressure," he reminded me. Then he nodded at Robert and started recording. I took a deep breath. *No regrets. Give it everything you've got. Pick up the pieces later.* And I began to tell my story.

Mark's questions started out almost as small talk—where had I grown up, when did I start gymnastics, when and why did I first see Larry—open-ended questions that were designed to give me room to draw out the dynamics and narratives people would need in order to understand my story.

"Tell me about Larry. Can you describe him to me?"

I thought about the tight-knit gymnastics community. The stories we'd all told about Larry. The videos and pictures of him helping Kerri Strug off the mat at the 1996 Olympics. His outstretched hand, seemingly eager to help and care for us. To understand the abuse, people needed to recognize Larry's prominence in our sport. They needed to see how Larry gained our admiration and confidence. They needed to realize how impossible it was for survivors to speak up.

The first question I would get from the community and the first attack from Larry's defense attorneys would be why I hadn't spoken up earlier. I knew this interview wasn't just about facts; it was about helping the community understand grooming and trust. It was about proactively combating the assumption that survivors automatically speak up if they've really been abused. And it was about communicating to the survivors who would see this that I understood. I knew what it felt like to trust him. I knew what it felt like when the world was turned upside down. If they spoke up, I would hear them and I would understand. Jacob was right. I could do this. I'd been trained to do this. I had *taught* this.

How many times in the last ten years had I told my appellate advocacy students, "It's a conversation. You are having a professional conversation with a justice." I kept my hands relaxed and open on my lap, remembering my own instruction. "Stand up straight and professionally, but be relaxed and calm. Engage respectfully and relationally. Make them want to hear you. Make it easy for them to change their minds."

I'd taught my students what I learned in law school—how to synthesize massive amounts of information and distill it down to concise, memorable themes. How to use key words to signpost and provide a road map; how to reflect the law and the conclusion their audience needed to reach; and how to imprint their message on the mind of a justice so that when the oral argument was over, the theme remained clear in the justice's memory. I'd explained how to use words as hooks so that information was easily recalled and accessed by a jury or judge when certain terms came up and reflected the law they needed to evaluate. I'd taught my students how to recognize their cases' weaknesses, the arguments they were likely to encounter from the other attorneys, and how to use that information to diffuse and preemptively handle potential problems. And I'd taught them how to answer questions: "You've got to hear the real issue behind the question being asked—to be able to see where the mental hang-up is—and respond clearly and concisely in a way that addresses the concern behind the question."

I told my students over and over, "Be able to use your themes and key words, memory hooks, and road maps as you answer. Guide your listener through the information so they don't just *hear* the answer to their question, they *understand* the answer to their question. Give your listeners the tools and words they need to answer their own objections."

And I told them always to balance the immediate and end goals. "You've got to answer the question you're asked—you've got to see the real concern the justice is expressing that is keeping them from reaching the right conclusion. There is always an immediate goal, but you also have to know how that question and your answer relate to the conclusion you need the judge to reach." I wanted to help them understand that they needed to respond to the issue at hand and then transition seamlessly back into the overall narrative, moving their listeners closer to the end goal.

Now it was my turn. I relaxed into the interview and relied on what I knew how to do. I'd already laid the groundwork—distilling the facts of my own case down to themes, key words, and ideas designed to reflect the legal elements of the crime, combat cultural misunderstandings, and communicate the dynamics of abuse to anyone who read the story. Now I needed to communicate it. Much of what I said would go into print; only a bit would make it into the video piece. But every word mattered. Every movement, every facial expression, my tone, my body language—everything communicated something, and I needed it all to communicate the right things.

"Can you tell me about Larry?"

I answered with a smile. "Everybody who's a gymnast knows who Nassar is." *Let survivors know you are one of them. You understand the dynamics. We speak the same language.* "He's not just a normal sports med doc," I continued. *The community outside the gymnastics world needs to understand why a survivor would never dare to speak up. He has power and is surrounded by people with power.* "He's extremely personable. Extremely gregarious. Very warm. Very caring."[10]

Reference grooming. Advocates and investigators will recognize it. Victims will know you understand. Don't attack. Attacking shuts people down. Speak to the dynamics. "He's the type of person that knows how to make you want to trust him. There's a reason he's risen to his place of prominence." I carefully emphasized that last phrase. *He knows how to make you want to trust him. He knows. It is intentional. It is calculated. It is manipulative.* A direct and harsh attack on a beloved abuser never works. The community and even victims flock to defend against harshness. But other survivors needed that seed of doubt planted too. The community needed that seed of doubt planted. Larry is a very nice guy. *And he knows it.* He makes you want to trust him. He calculates it. He doesn't just engender trust; he makes you *desire* to trust him by creating careful physical and emotional connections. Nothing Larry did was an accident, so nothing I was going to do could be either. I wanted to send *that* message to survivors too. *I understand.* Survivors want to trust the abuser. They are groomed to want to. *It is not your fault,* I silently breathed into that sentence. *I understand why you trusted. I did too. Larry did it on purpose. It is not your fault.*

Mark nodded, letting me continue. The cultural dynamics and interpersonal relationships between victim and abuser played in my mind. *Let your honest grief show.* Grief communicates and invites people in. Harshness and anger create instinctive protective reflexes. Grief, more than anything, was what I hated to show, because it felt so vulnerable. But I felt it, and I needed to communicate it, no matter how much it hurt.

"Honestly, part of what grieves me so much is that he has everything he needs to be an incredible leader," I continued. "He has the personality, he has the skill, he has the knowledge. And he's using that to prey on people." I paused and for a brief moment allowed my grief to come through, despite how vulnerable that made me feel. "What a waste."

I knew his victims were, by and large, going to love Larry. Truly love him. Because he had calculated that. His friends, coworkers, and the community loved him. Because he had calculated that, too. I needed to identify with that emotion. What Larry had done with the skills he had was grief-worthy. It was heartbreaking. I needed survivors to know it grieved me, too. I didn't *want* this to be Larry. With every word I spoke, I saw other survivors in my mind—the little girls and women I couldn't protect; the ones who had been silenced; the ones whose lives were about to be turned upside down as they fought the idea that someone they cared for and trusted had wielded their innocence against them. And many would fight that reality. Their parents would fight that reality. Because it was devastating. I wanted them to know, in every way I could communicate it, that they were not alone in that grief.

"Why did you see Larry?" Mark asked.

"I had a lot of pain in my wrists and in my back. I have a couple of vertebrae that don't bend, and so that put a lot of extra pressure on my wrists and on my back. . . . It got to a point where it was just very chronically painful. Very difficult to do anything." I knew gymnasts would understand this. Anyone who saw Larry would understand the desire to be out of pain. They would have been in that place too.

"There were several gymnasts at my gym who had gone up to see Nassar, and their parents recommended that we head up there, so we did." *It was reasonable to trust his reputation. He helped so many. All of us knew about Larry.*

I knew the questions would come. How could I not have known? Why did I not suspect? How could I be so easily fooled? The same questions that had haunted me for years would be the barriers to everyone else believing me too. I had to tell my story in a way that explained those dynamics and helped walk the listener through the mind of a survivor and the methods of an abuser. "He suggested that he could do myofascial release and sports massage to help with those dynamics," I said.

Then Mark asked the question I dreaded the most: "What happened?"

"I'd had myofascial release done before by a physical therapist, so I consented. But as he was doing that, he also began to massage internally as well." I pressed each clinical detail out, forcing the recital to be technical. Precise. Accurate. Graphic. No room for misinterpreting. No ability to second-guess what I was describing. I needed Larry to have to confront each of these dynamics specifically. I needed survivors to hear his answers. I needed Larry to see this interview and know I was not mincing words. Not flinching. Not shying away from the reality. I needed him to know that *I knew* exactly what he did and that I was going to tell it publicly, without hesitation, every chance I got. He was confident, and rightly so. He had gotten away with this for decades, and I wanted him to know I was equally confident. He could not talk his way out so easily this time.

I used the technical terms Larry had used—the terms other survivors were likely to have heard. And I used the legal terms that would need to be proven if we got that far. I used that language for survivors. I used it to set myself up for testifying in a criminal trial—likely years down the road—and I used it to send a message to Larry and his attorneys. *I know the law and the medical aspects of what happened, and I will handle them both well.*

"He would continue to progress in what he touched, and where he touched, and how he touched, and nothing was off limits for him. He never wore gloves. Never." I picked details that would indicate to anyone willing to hear that this did not follow normal medical procedure. It escalated. It lacked standard best practices like wearing gloves. Something was wrong. The facts didn't add up. There was a reason to ask questions.

"My mom was actually in the room at the time," I began explaining to Mark, shifting the focus again to answer the cultural questions I would be asked—How was this possible? How could I not know? "He would just position me and position himself so that she couldn't see what he was doing. I didn't realize that she couldn't see and so that was also part of the dynamic that kept me quiet. I thought if there was something wrong, surely my mom would speak up. But Mom couldn't see what he was doing." I spoke softly, knowing how many other parents would soon find themselves in my mom's situation, realizing they had been witnesses to their own daughters' sexual abuse and had not seen it. I ached for them. And I needed these parents, these survivors to know—it happened right there in the open. To not assume their situation was different because a parent was in the room, or for parents to downplay a daughter's concerns with the mistaken belief that they would have seen the abuse happening. I needed the public to see how Larry had wielded the beautiful bond between parent and child to manipulate and cover evil.

Mark nodded. The truth that parents had been in the room was difficult for everyone to swallow. So brazen. So calculated. So much damage to everyone.

"What was going through your mind?" he asked quietly.

I took a deep breath and concentrated on responding calmly, with the right amount of emotion. This was the other question I dreaded the most. Larry had tried to gain access to my mind, and I had shut him down. He would frequently ask me, during the abuse, how I felt. Describing what was happening in my mind at the moment felt like yielding the last bit of protection I had left. The last bit of privacy and security, and I hated it. Yet it was the question I most needed to answer. This was one of the most important things we had to reckon with as a culture—the mind-set of victims during and after abuse, the damage that is caused—why they cannot speak up. It was what we'd gotten wrong as a society almost every time. It was the question that would, more than anything, help other survivors be able to examine their own confusion and what they felt in that moment and realize they weren't alone—and they weren't crazy. There was a reason something didn't feel right.

"I was terrified," I answered honestly. "I was ashamed. I was very embarrassed. And I was very confused, trying to reconcile what was happening with the person he was supposed to be.

"He's this famous doctor. He's trusted by my friends. He's trusted by these other gymnasts. How could he reach this position in the medical profession, how could he reach this kind of prominence and stature if this is who he is?"

I wanted to help the readers of the *IndyStar* article understand how survivors could be unaware of what was happening to them, unable to trust their own instincts. The questions that made it so difficult for a community to identify an abuser were the same questions that kept victims silent. The dynamics that made it seem impossible for an abuser to really be an abuser were the very same dynamics that allowed the abuse to continue.

"It's much easier in some ways to hide from what's happening and just go somewhere else mentally. It was easier to not have to verbalize and recognize what was happening."

I wanted the readers and viewers to understand what had taken me so long to realize, that victims' responses—especially in the moment—aren't just fight or flight. There's also freeze. Few people really understand that third response, even though it is arguably the most prevalent. I knew what it felt like to be so overwhelmed with shock, confusion, and fear that I literally shut down to try to survive the reality. And I knew that many survivors would, as I had, blame themselves—*and be blamed* for that response. They needed to know this reaction was common, and it didn't mean they'd consented to the abuse. For years I hadn't understood that my response was normal—even biological and outside my control—and I'd felt so much guilt for not being able to fight back. I wanted to spare these women and little girls the years of self-blame I went through. I understood why they couldn't put words to it and why they would have pushed through the feeling of uneasiness and defended Larry even in their own minds. I knew, because I did it too. *You are not crazy. This. Is. Not. Your. Fault.*

Finally, Mark referenced the original *IndyStar* article. Did I think USAG was responsible for my abuse? I answered honestly and without hesitation. "If they truly didn't know, hands clean, then no, I don't hold them responsible." I was immediately going to be attacked for wanting money, even though I hadn't filed a civil suit and had no intention of doing so, and I needed to make it clear that there was only liability if the wrong things were done. *You are not on a warpath. Be reasonable. Be precise. Be accurate.* The attacks would come anyway, but accuracy and a calm, reasonable position would make my allegations easier to consider.

And yet I needed to leave room to deal with the strong likelihood that USAG needed serious cultural reform. "If they did with him what they did with those other coaches, I absolutely do." I paused. "I think time will tell."

By the end, I felt the interview was what it needed to be, and now I had to trust Mark and his team to tell it right—and hope and pray we even made it to print. The police report would be happening. Whether the story would follow wasn't certain at all. A high bar of proof had to be met before a press outlet could publish allegations like this without fear of being sued. And news by its nature is dependent on circumstances. Anything considered more newsworthy than this story could easily bump it from publication.

When we'd finished, Mark said, "You communicate really well, Rachael. If this makes it out, a lot more people are going to want to hear from you." I laughed. I rather doubted that.

"You know I can't promise anything, but I'm going to do my best," he added. I nodded. I did know the uphill battle we faced. I'd been mulling it over for more than a decade.

"I know," I said, taking a deep breath. "Nothing is guaranteed. I get that. But you are listening, and that's a first. And the police report is happening regardless. Hopefully that will get us one step closer."

After Mark and Robert packed up and drove away, I stepped back inside, looked at Jacob, and smiled tentatively. He pulled me close. I felt numb, exhausted, unsure what to do next.

That night, the nightmares that had started with the first phone interview a week earlier came back with a vengeance.

16

THE DAY FOLLOWING THE INTERVIEW was exhausting, and it became more so when I picked up a phone call from a Lansing, Michigan, area code. It was the Ingham County Police Department.

"Hi . . . Yes, I left a message about a delayed disclosure of sexual assault." I steeled myself for answering even the most basic questions as we prepared to set up an interview. What I heard in response was not what I expected.

"Can you read me the address again of the medical building you were in?" the male officer asked. I scrambled to pull out the evidence file, flipped to the first page of my medical records, and gave him the address.

"Yeah, that's in Ingham County," he confirmed. *I know; that's why I called. I checked already.* "But was that an MSU building?" he asked.

I glanced down at the sheet again. "Mmmm . . . I think it was." I paused and glanced through the sheets. "Yeah, it definitely was." I read him the name of the complex where I'd been treated.

"Okay, that makes a difference," he said. I froze at his next words. "Because the incident technically happened on campus, the Michigan State University Police Department has jurisdiction over this. The school will have to handle the investigation."

"What?" I asked blankly. *How does a school investigate itself?*

"Universities typically have their own police departments," he repeated. "They have jurisdiction over anything that happens on campus. Your report will need to go to them. We take calls for them, so I've forwarded everything on to MSU PD, and they'll call you back."

I felt as if the room were spinning. How had I missed this? Why hadn't that occurred to me? I knew universities had their own police departments, but I'd never even considered that MSU might have jurisdiction over *itself*. I swallowed the anger rising up inside at this unexpected and *very* unwelcome development.

"Okay, thank you. I will wait to hear from them," I replied, trying to keep my voice calm. As soon as I hung up, I called Jacob.

"It's MSU PD," I said, trying to control the shaking in my voice.

"What do you mean?" His response was tinged with a combination of confusion and concern.

"I got a call back from the police department in Ingham County. Larry abused me on MSU property, and that means I have to report it to the university's own police department. He's going to be investigated by one of his own." I pushed down the feeling of panic and hopelessness that was threatening to settle in. I'd been concerned enough about a local PD simply because of Larry's reputation and community pull, not to mention his association with the university as a whole. But I'd never considered that the university itself might be tasked with the investigation.

"We don't know that they won't do a good job," Jacob said soothingly, trying to help calm my fear.

"You don't understand. I was never afraid of reporting because of Larry. It was the investigators and the prosecutor. That's where it breaks down, and now I have to report to the very university that hasn't paid attention before." For the first time in a very long time, I was more than fearful. I was angry.

"You don't know that they haven't listened," Jacob tried again.

"Yes, yes, I do. Because he's been abusing for at least sixteen years. There is no way that someone hasn't spoken up before and been ignored by *someone* in that school—quite possibly even the police department. And now I have to report in his backyard." I paused, trying to explain how much of a problem this could be. "There's a very good chance at least some of the investigators will know him or will have been to that office for medical care."

Jacob took a deep breath. "I'm really sorry, honey. You have every right to be concerned. But we don't know it will be a problem yet. If it is, we'll deal with it together, and we'll watch carefully, but right now, this is the next step. Let's do the next step and not worry until we *know* it is a problem. Cautious and on guard, yes. Worried—not yet."

In frustration, I leaned into the counter, pressing my palm into its smooth surface as hard as I could. He was right. I knew he was right. I could not change it. I could only deal with it. One more instance in which I didn't have a choice.

"I love you," he said firmly. We hung up, and I took a deep breath, pushing the anger and fear back down. All I could do now was wait.

I glanced at the clock. I had about twenty minutes before the kids were done with quiet time. Enough time for one more "next step." I emailed Jackie, the head coach at the gym I'd worked at. As my first official disclosure, she would be a key witness. I needed to know if she even remembered my talking to her about this, and I also needed to tell her what I was doing so she would know to call the investigators back. My conversation with her years ago was a critical piece of evidence that proved I wasn't just now making this up and that my story had been consistent.

"I have a question for you that goes back to our gymnastics days," I typed. "Is there a time I could call you really quickly?" Then I closed the computer. Time to shift gears. I watched my phone like a hawk as I made lunch and then kept it within earshot while we sat at the table and I read *Alice in Wonderland* aloud to my small troop of diminutive and highly energetic humans.

I had a case to put together, but I also had three little souls and minds that needed to be nurtured and grown. They needed my every effort too. So for now, it was lunch, *Alice in Wonderland,* and little people to love and care for.

• • •

I was exhausted as I anticipated not just the police interview, but also the final week of our care group, when an elder was scheduled to come and explain to the group that they had decided to break us up. Our support system was gone, and it was over the issue of sexual assault. It never ended. It just never ended.

That Sunday meeting never came, though, because the next day I answered another phone call with a Lansing area code. The woman on the other end identified herself as Detective Munford. She was returning my call about a report of sexual assault. I gave a very brief overview, careful not to mention Larry's name or any details.

"We live in Louisville, Kentucky, now," I explained, "but we can come up to Michigan. I'd like to schedule a time to come in and file an official report."

The detective responded calmly. "We can definitely do that. I can also take a report over the phone. What would you like to do?"

My mind raced. I was adamant that I did not want to report over the phone. I had no idea who this woman was, her level of training, her understanding of the dynamics of abuse, or her approach to cases. First impressions mattered, and I wanted to do what I could to establish good personal rapport. Face-to-face communication would be much more effective in demonstrating the reliability of my story, as well as my own stability, education, and background. I didn't know the types of questions she would ask. If I needed to push back on doubting or skeptical questions, I'd rather do it in person so I could keep it less combative. I needed her not to feel that I was being threatening, caustic, or dismissive. I wanted to walk her through the case law and evidence myself to make sure she understood the medical and legal complexities. I wanted her to be able to read my medical files. And I knew publicity was generally discouraged, so I wanted to be able to have a face-to-face conversation about my decision to go public.

And the truth was, I wanted to size her up too. I'd already talked to Keith about options for removing the case to another department or agency if the MSU PD didn't handle it properly. I needed to see how she conducted herself and responded to what I brought. Her body language, facial expressions, tone of voice, the interest she showed in the evidence—I wanted to be able to assess all of it. I needed to report in person. I'd seen too many interactions with authority figures—doctors, legislators, attorneys, law enforcement officers—quickly go south if they felt their expertise was not respected the way it should be.

I grasped for how to make my desire to make a report in person clear, while not striking any sour notes. The realities of reporting sexual abuse played in my mind constantly—out of every 230 rapes reported, only nine are even referred to a prosecutor. Only five result in conviction. The numbers are worse for nonrape sexual assaults. There are hundreds of thousands of untested rape kits sitting in police departments across the country[11]—each representing a woman who went through the trauma of having her violated genitals examined, swabbed, and photographed, only to have investigators never even *consider* the evidence. I knew that most people have no idea what survivors are up against when reporting. Trying to explain those dynamics was frustrating. Survivors are often judged as overdramatic or "too damaged to trust." The vast majority of survivors are dismissed, with their abusers allowed to walk free. I needed to see how Detective Munford handled what I brought.

"Mmmm . . . I have all my medical files and some other documentation here in Kentucky. I would need to get those to you anyway, wouldn't I?" She responded affirmatively. "Okay, since I'll need to bring those in at some point, I think I'd prefer an in-person meeting where you can go over anything you want to see as we're discussing it. If you can find a time that works in your schedule, we'll be as flexible as necessary."

The detective quickly assented and pulled up her calendar. The earliest appointment was the following Monday, five days away.

"Perfect. We will be there," I agreed immediately. She offered to send her contact information and address to my email, and I spelled out the address.

Then she asked one more thing. "Would you be comfortable telling me the name of the person you are reporting? I can start reviewing files to see if anyone has reported him before and digging around a little bit if you're okay giving me a name."

I actually hadn't wanted to. I'd wanted to perceive the physical response, if any, when I gave the name. But I also needed to be seen as cooperative and calm, not overly suspicious or unstable, so I responded as easily as I could.

"Sure. His name is Larry Nassar. He's a doctor of osteopathy in the sports medicine clinic."

"Okay, thanks." And then she continued calmly, "I think I've heard of him before. We have some officers who go to that clinic."

I exhaled softly. Of course she had. Of course there were. Isn't that what I was concerned about right from the beginning? *Do the next thing. Be on guard. Don't borrow trouble until you have it.*

"I'm not surprised," I said in an effort to be lighthearted. "He's a pretty famous doctor." I thanked her for her time and we hung up.

I glanced at the clock. The entire conversation had taken less than fifteen minutes, so I had plenty of time before the kids' quiet time ended to get yet another painful conversation out of the way. Jackie had messaged me back with her phone number and a note that she was free all afternoon. I had been dreading this conversation as much as anything else because I knew it was going to hurt—and not just me this time.

I heard the phone ringing, and then she answered in a cheerful voice. We made small talk for a few minutes, and then I launched in.

"Do you remember the conversation we had years ago about Larry, when you wanted one of the little girls I coached to go see him?"

She responded that she did, a note of confusion in her voice.

"Can I ask what you remember?" I questioned, leaning against the washing machine. I squeezed my free hand tightly to vent nervous energy and try to still the shaking. When she answered, I breathed a sigh of relief. She remembered it well—well enough, in fact, to verify my story.

"Thanks." I paused. "Well, I'm calling because I need to let you know, I was telling the truth, and something has happened that's made it possible to report Larry." I briefly explained the *IndyStar* article. "I'm reporting him on Monday. I wanted to call you to let you know because you were my first disclosure and that conversation with you is a huge part of the evidence verifying my story. I know the detectives will need to talk to you, and I didn't want you to be blindsided by this." I paused. "I'm going to keep your name out of everything as much as I can, but it's really, really important that you call the detectives back." I stopped, unsure of what else to say.

Jackie's voice came hesitatingly over the phone. "I . . . I mean, I always believed you, Rach . . . I just figured that if this was a big deal, you'd . . . do something about it." I dropped my head into my hands and closed my eyes. She didn't understand. *I did. I did do something. I told you and, through you, a police officer. I told two friends. And you sent another gymnast to Larry anyway and cautioned me against saying anything else. That* was *me doing something about it.* This was exactly the part I'd been dreading. I knew Jackie cared. I knew she'd have wanted to do the right thing. What I was about to do was going to be terrible for me, but it was going to be painful for a lot of people, and I hated that.

"I'm really sorry, Rach . . . I hope this hasn't been too big of a deal for you." I could hear the hesitation in her voice as she searched for words. I bit my lip before saying, as steadily as I could manage with tears—for both of us—pressing in, "It was first-degree assault, Jackie. It's been a *really* big deal." She was quiet for a moment.

"I'm really sorry . . . ," she began.

I stopped the conversation there, for both our sakes.

"Thanks. I know you are. I just wanted to let you know because you'll get a call, and it's important that you return it." I paused one more time. "And if this gets to trial, your name will have to come out. I won't be able to help it." I wanted to give her time to come to grips with everything. If we got that far, I'd need to find a way to tell her she was in my journal, of the impact that conversation had, and everything I was going to have to testify to. But she didn't need to hear it right now. That much, maybe, she could be spared.

We hung up and I made one last phone call before switching back into mommy mode.

"Hey, honey," Jacob answered. I could hear a saw in the background. He was in the middle of a kitchen installation.

"I've got an appointment to file the police report on Monday," I said quickly.

"In Michigan?"

"Yeah . . . it was the first appointment they had," I said apologetically. It wasn't much notice given his work and class schedule. The PhD program had just started.

"No, no, that's really good, I'm glad. We can leave on Saturday."

That night we sat out on the front porch again, baby monitor in hand. I knew the storm that was coming, and everything felt so, so dark.

"Everyone is going to know," I whispered. Jacob pulled me close.

"I know. And I am so sorry. It's not fair." He paused. "But it is right. It is the right thing to do, honey. And I'm so proud of you." He paused again. "If there is one person who can do this and actually make it stop, it's you. You have the background, intellect, skill set, and conviction to see this through and do it well." He tilted back and looked down at me. "You can do this," he said firmly.

• • •

During the next few days, I drafted a basic legal memorandum that walked through each legal element of the case and the available evidence. I drafted it as a letter, not knowing the background of anyone who might read it. Keith had sent me the case law, and I'd thoroughly studied the statutes, interpretive guidelines, and relevant cases. Armed with that framework, I developed a basic outline of the case. I explained the dynamics that led me to stay silent and the reason I'd chosen to speak up now:

> This decision cannot center around what is easiest for me, or protecting myself. I do believe Dr. Nassar is still a risk to every girl who unknowingly walks into his office, and I also believe there are likely many other women and teens still living in silence. I now have three children of my own, and I understand more completely how much protecting our children depends on the actions of the adults in their lives.

I headnoted each element of the statutory definition. Penetration. By an authority figure. Personal injury through the subcategory of mental anguish. Age requirements. I noted the court's interpretation of the statutes and cataloged the evidence to prove each prong. I also explained how to counter the responsive arguments Larry was likely to make. Then I outlined the available evidence I had, including the emails from the *IndyStar* showing the existence of two more survivors and the consistency of my story.

The following Saturday, we headed to Michigan, case file in hand, our three children beyond excited to "take a family trip to see Grandma and Grandpa." My parents still lived in my childhood home in Kalamazoo, so we explained to the kids that we were going for a visit, and Mommy had a few errands to run while we were there.

In between playing I Spy with the kids and tossing them snack bags as we drove, I made a list of the many tasks that remained in front of me. When we got to Kalamazoo, the kids tumbled out of the car and made a beeline, first to my parents and then to the backyard, where swings and a yellow plastic slide—staples of my childhood—still stood. We played for a bit, and then I retreated to a corner of the small yard to make a phone call to Tim Evans.

Like all the *IndyStar* reporters, Tim was professional and kind, and I appreciated his clear desire to capture the story the way it needed to be told. I watched my children sliding and swinging, running and shouting in their delight to be out of the minivan, and I walked Tim through more evidence and a quick fact-check. We still didn't know if the story would be published at all, much less when, but they were putting every effort into getting there, and quickly, knowing that my report would go in by Monday, and at that point, I'd be out there alone. Mark had promised that he'd ask the other two survivors for permission to release their identities just to me, after the story published, so that I could encourage them to file police reports. But if the story wasn't published, he couldn't even make the ask, and I would be speaking out on my own. The unknown made me tense at every turn.

The next morning we walked a few short blocks to the small church Jacob and I had settled into shortly after we were married. I took a deep breath as we entered. Here I felt safe. These people had loved us so well, poured into us so much, and there were many families in the congregation who were raising adopted children from traumatic backgrounds, which I knew gave them a level of knowledge that yielded compassion and understanding. I wanted to cry with relief simply to be in a church that felt safe.

After the service, Jacob pulled one of the pastors aside. "Can we talk to you for a brief moment privately? We'd like to update you all on a few things."

Andrew nodded congenially. "Yeah, yeah. Let me grab one of the other guys. Come on in," he said, gesturing to his office. Jacob turned to me once the two pastors had sat down across from us. We'd agreed earlier that I would explain the situation. I hated having to tell my story again, but it made me feel more in control to be the one to speak.

"When I was fifteen, I was repeatedly sexually assaulted by a very high-profile doctor," I said directly, forcing eye contact. There simply was no nice way to broach a topic like this. "I never reported him because he is very prominent and surrounded by two very powerful institutions." I explained a bit about Larry's position within MSU and USAG, and how that related even to the power and money involved in the United States Olympic Committee.

"But a few weeks ago, the door opened for me to finally speak out." I referenced the *IndyStar* article and explained how that had provided the press coverage and public pressure I needed to move forward. "I am filing a police report tomorrow, and there will likely be a big news story coming out shortly thereafter. I don't know how far it will go for sure, but at least around here, you will see it, and we felt it was wise to let you know what is coming. I can't keep it quiet any longer anyway."

Andrew bowed his head briefly and looked back up. "I am so sorry, Rachael," he said, grief evident in his voice.

Zach, the second pastor, spoke up. "How are you two doing handling this? This has got to be incredibly difficult."

I answered honestly. It was very difficult.

"Are you going to have good church support in Kentucky through this process?" Andrew asked, resting his index finger on his chin thoughtfully.

I looked at Jacob. *No. We weren't.*

Jacob was more hopeful. "I think so," he said cautiously. "We've had some bumps, but we're doing everything we can to make sure those are smoothed . . ." He paused again. "I think so." I hoped he would be proven correct.

Andrew looked squarely at Jacob. "How are *you* doing with this? How is your marriage holding up?" I was so grateful for knowledgeable, direct, caring questions—ones with thought behind them and a realization of the weight we were carrying.

They asked our preferences for communicating to the church. How could they pray for us? How could they support us? Finally, Andrew paused and looked at me again.

"Is there anything you feel you need to get out of this process, besides stopping an abuser?" I paused. It was a powerful and insightful question.

I thought back over the journey I had been on for so many years. The tears. The anger. The impassioned pleading for answers and dreams of finally confronting Larry. The frustrated prayers. The circle diagram I drew that sunny day so many years ago. Despite the pain, I felt peace dawning as I answered.

"I really appreciate that question," I said slowly. "Years ago, I would have said yes, that there was a lot I needed." I paused again, searching for the right words. "But now . . . no. I had to wrestle through all those questions and desires for years. I had to reach a place where my identity and healing weren't bound up in anything I get here. I can't be dependent on how this ends; I can only be faithful." I paused again, filled with deep gratitude for how far I'd come and the ability to answer his question honestly.

"I don't need anything from this," I continued. "This is not about me, my healing, or what I want. But I do need to do everything in my power to stop him."

Andrew nodded. "Okay," he said. "We will be holding you up."

17

THE NEXT DAY, Jacob and I drove to the MSU Police Department in Lansing to meet Detective Munford. The hour-and-a-half trip seemed as if it would never end. I'd felt too sick to eat or drink anything that morning, and we drove in silence. There just wasn't anything left to say.

In my hand, I held the cream-colored file folder with copies of my medical records. (I was loath to release my only original copy until I was confident the MSU PD would handle the investigation properly.) The folder also contained my correspondence with the *IndyStar* and the cover letter explaining the steps I was taking and why. In it, I had laid out the evidence to prove first-degree criminal sexual assault and provided a brief treatment of the statute of limitations and the related case law to prove that my claim was not time-barred. I also included a list of evidence and witnesses. On top of it all was the letter of reference from Keith, the one outside person so far who'd offered to enter the mess with me and stand on my behalf.

I hadn't yet been able to get a copy of the medical report from the day I disclosed to a nurse practitioner in 2004, and I silently prayed she had transcribed what I'd told her. I had calls in to the physical therapist and therapy assistant my mom had spoken with years ago, but I hadn't heard back from them yet either. But I'd brought what I could, and on my computer was a list of articles and links on legitimate pelvic floor therapy, which I planned to send to the investigator after the interview.

Today was a business suit day. Unlike the day I recorded the *IndyStar* interview, my goal was to relate to Detective Munford as professionally and articulately as possible. If this investigator wasn't motivated to handle the case well, I wanted it made subtly clear that I was capable of pushing the issue and had no intention of letting it go. External pressure and fear of negative publicity might motivate where ethics did not.

•   •   •

We arrived at the MSU PD and parked in the lot Detective Munford had directed us to.

"Wow. What's going on here?" Jacob mused quietly. The sidewalks and office were filled with a steady line of college students flocking in and out of the doors, looping around the walkway. I shrugged. I had no emotional, physical, or mental energy for anything other than my case. We wound our way past the line of students who, we learned, were attempting to procure parking passes for the semester. When we informed the officer at the desk that we had an appointment with Detective Munford, she picked up the phone to notify her and directed us to sit in the chairs lined up near a window.

Jacob and I sat silently, side by side, in the small lobby. I mentally ran through the checklist of evidence and the layout of the case, feeling as if the words I was about to speak were written across my forehead and visible to every student who walked by with a curious glance. Finally, the door opened and a petite woman with dark-brown hair walked toward us.

"Rachael?" she said, smiling. "I'm Detective Munford. Come on back." She wound us through a hallway and around a few corners.

"How are you doing? How was the drive?"

I answered as pleasantly as I could, appreciative of her attempt to normalize our interactions. She opened a door to a small room with a stuffed couch and a few chairs arranged in a cozy fashion. Detective Munford took a seat in a chair opposite the couch where Jacob and I sat down, and she made a few casual remarks. How did the kids do on the drive? Did we have any trouble finding the building? I answered the chitchat and took note of the room. Throw pillows softened the room's appearance, and a Kleenex box sat on the table. The department at least seemed to make an effort to conduct interviews in a victim-centered fashion. I hoped that meant the training and standards were up to best practices and that the department was committed to investigating cases thoroughly.

"Do you mind if I record this?" the detective asked as we settled in.

"No, not at all," I answered cheerfully. *In fact, I'd prefer it, so if the right things aren't in the report, I can prove what I said and point out any problems with the investigation.*

"Great. So can you explain to me what happened and the background?" Detective Munford asked.

"Yeah, absolutely." *Calm. Even pace. Relaxed demeanor.* And I began to explain. I'd been a gymnast. Doctors in my hometown hadn't been able to resolve my chronic wrist and back pain, so a mom from my gym recommended we see Larry.

I explained who Larry was and the position he occupied in the community. I talked about his patent. His book on conditioning. The story that went around the local gyms that Larry had told a gymnast who'd broken her neck that if she'd done his conditioning her injury could have been avoided.

"At the point we considered seeing Larry, my mom and I also talked about another recommendation we'd received for a physical therapist who did internal pelvic floor work. We decided to go ahead and start with Larry because he specialized in gymnastics, but we actually had a conversation about how we might need to consider something like that other form of therapy." I took a deep breath. "So we made an appointment. I was asked to dress in loose-fitting athletic shorts and a comfortable top, and I changed when we got there."

Detective Munford sat calmly, letting the story simply come out.

"When Larry entered the room, he was warm and gregarious. He asked a lot of general information, small-talk questions." *Describe the personal interactions, the beginning of the grooming process.* "And then he began the exam.

He did a very thorough assessment and immediately found some issues that I knew were legitimate but that other sports medicine doctors didn't find."

I explained how Larry had diagnosed my spinal problems and rotated pelvis, issues that other physical therapists would confirm. "My shoulders were also abnormally tight, and Larry explained that it was causing me to arch in the wrong place in my lower back, putting extra pressure on both my wrists and my lower back because of the angle those joints had to be at when I tumbled." *It was reasonable to believe him* . . . "And when he was finished with the evaluation, he recommended a few types of treatment." I paused, considering how best to explain the "soft tissue work" Larry recommended to relieve the pain in my lower back.

I described with clinical sterility exactly what Larry had done. I would need to differentiate Larry's behavior from normal pelvic floor therapy. I chose my key words, terminology, and descriptions precisely.

Detective Munford began to ask more detailed questions. "Could you tell which fingers he was using?"

"How far in?"

"Can you describe the movements?"

I made eye contact and forced every word out. Every sensation. Every movement.

"How many times did he penetrate per minute?"

"Can you describe exact finger positions?"

I used my own hands to demonstrate.

"How long did it last?"

"Did he say anything?"

It felt as if the questions went on forever, but they were expertly framed, seeking precise clarity, and I was thankful to see that level of attention paid to what I'd described. When I paused, I realized we'd covered only the first appointment. And there were so many more.

"As things were happening," I explained, "my thought process was that it was clear Larry did this regularly, and if he did, someone would have stopped him if there was any question about it. I was sure it wasn't possible that no one had ever described what Larry did, and if they *had*, surely the proper steps would have been taken to ensure the procedure was legitimate." *I thought the problem was me*. And then I said that out loud too.

"Were there other visits?" Detective Munford asked.

Yes . . . so many more. . . . I began describing the escalation in abuse using accurate medical terms and precise descriptions. I gestured and described and answered question after question after question.

"And then on the second to last visit . . . ," I began. Again, I forced eye contact. I described the initial abuse. Larry turning me on my side. "He was breathing heavily. His face was flushed. He was clearly sexually aroused." I described the clear bulge in the front of his pants. "He had an obvious erection." And I described the abuse. Graphic. Clear. Precise. No room for misinterpretation or confusion. "And I froze . . ."

Detective Munford nodded. "Exactly where were his hands?"

"Can you describe the motion?"

"How long did it last?"

"What happened when he was done?"

"Who rehooked your bra?"

The questions came calmly but regularly—defining, clarifying, and open-ended, drawing on my senses and full memory experience. I recognized forensic interview techniques and breathed a quiet prayer of thanks. Those techniques were best practices, designed to fully draw out memory and experience without leading or suggesting information. I glanced at Jacob as I spoke, his presence helping me stay grounded and calm.

Detective Munford paused. "Was there ever anything he said or did regularly?"

I nodded. "Yes, there were clear grooming techniques. I didn't recognize them at the time."

I described Larry's fascination with my button-up boots, the way he used innocent touch. His compliments and small talk.

Referring back to my description of the way Larry abused me, she asked, "Did anyone ever witness this?" She kept her pen poised over the notepad.

I told her how Larry would send students or trainees out of the room before the abuse. How he blocked my mom's view, hid his hand. How he engaged with her, talking about anything and everything, often in a steady stream, as he was molesting me. How he diverted her attention. Ensured her trust. Made it appear to me that she knew what was going on and thought it was fine.

"He weaponized my own mom against me," I said with an ache, knowing full well how many parents were going to find the ground falling out from under them very soon. My heart broke for every mom and dad who would come to discover the truth about what was happening to their precious daughters as they were watching.

"It wasn't until much later that I began to fully realize what happened, but I am confident now that nothing he did internally was medical."

She leaned back in her chair a bit. "Okay, let's talk a bit about that. How did you begin to realize that?"

I nodded and clasped my hands over my knee. "Well, I knew that last time was abuse, but it took a while before I let myself consider that there might be more." I began to take her through the process my mom and I had been through, highlighting the parts that would be important evidence and carry probative value. "One of my earliest disclosures came through my mom to a physical therapist and therapy assistant. Around the time we started having questions about what Larry was doing, I was in physical therapy at a practice that had expertise in pelvic floor treatment." I was careful to accurately describe what we had communicated to these therapists.

"Mom didn't give much detail. I hadn't given her much, and I don't know that these therapists even remember the conversation, but we told them that I'd been receiving pelvic floor treatment and began to work around the issue of standard practices and procedures for pelvic floor therapy."

Detective Munford nodded. "Did they provide any input?"

"Yes, they did. They did not specifically state it was abuse, but they were very concerned about what we reported—the lack of gloves and lack of consent specifically." I described to her what we now knew about standard practice for internal pelvic floor work. I focused on the lack of consent and lack of gloves, knowing that understanding these practices would be key. I wanted to be absolutely clear about the differences between Larry's techniques and acceptable and expected practice.

"It's normal for therapists not to wear gloves for certain procedures—

myofascial release is very touch sensitive. Meaning, therapists are often really concentrating on the response of the muscles as they work on them. It's not even unusual for them to close their eyes at times as they try to focus."

I wanted the detective to have a sense of the range of normal for these types of therapies and be able to clearly see where that line had been crossed. I wanted her to know that *I* knew there was a range of normal. I wasn't hypersensitive. I wasn't overreacting. I wasn't "reading into it."

"So the lack of gloves while doing massage, even massage lower down, like on the external surfaces of the glute muscles, isn't abnormal. But the failure to wear gloves during internal and genital contact absolutely is. Wearing gloves is standard practice for any kind of genital contact or penetration. Larry never used gloves."

I detailed the types of standard consent procedures I now knew would be followed for legitimate internal pelvic floor work and contrasted that with Larry's absolute lack of either consent or explanation.

"Both therapists we spoke to advised us not to go back." I paused. "I didn't realize that the type of touching Larry was doing was so far outside the realm of what is normal therapy, so I never explained the details. I wish I had at that time, but I just didn't know enough to do so."

I gave her the name of the nurse practitioner I'd also disclosed to and explained the paperwork she'd given me, along with the suggestion that I file a complaint with the medical board so someone could investigate whether Larry's practices were normal or abusive.

"Did you do that?" Detective Munford asked calmly.

I shook my head. "I didn't. I researched it and discovered the investigation would be done by a group of doctors—Larry's peers, essentially. There was no real appeals process, no protections in place, nothing to resort to. I was—and am—sure they would have cleared him, making it harder to come forward at a time when I had a real chance of being heard. Out of all my options for reporting, this one was the least likely to succeed—it was the worst option." I paused. "I did save the paperwork, though, and I did disclose more detail to her."

I described what I'd told the nurse practitioner, and why. It was because of her that we'd retrieved my medical file from MSU. She was the first person to offer to help—she volunteered to go over my medical records with me to examine if anything had been charted that would indicate what I was describing. She had, and there wasn't. Larry hadn't charted anything about internal pelvic floor work. "I don't know what she transcribed after that appointment, but I've been working on tracking that file down to see if what I told her was recorded."

I kept working my way through the evidence and my file. The conversation with Jackie, the emails from the *IndyStar* showing that two other women had contacted them about Larry.

"What about your friend from the gym—the one who went with you to some appointments—would she be a witness?"

I shook my head. "No. She's in denial right now. I understand why, and I didn't expect any different. I don't even want to provide her name. I feel very strongly that her choice and ability to face this in her own time has to be respected."

Detective Munford nodded, and I was grateful that she did not press the issue. We kept moving through the evidence.

"How has this affected you?" she asked.

I hated that question. Almost more than any of the others.

"It's . . . it's changed everything." I began detailing the impact of abuse, focusing most on details where I had external corroboration or on elements I knew would be an issue at trial. I explained how it affected me in the workplace. In interpersonal relationships, dating and marriage. Having children. All of it.

"I journaled a fair bit," I told her.

"Do you still have those journals?" she asked, eyebrows raised just a bit.

"Yes," I said with a sick feeling. I'd known she would ask. I'd have to produce them. I'd listed them in the legal memorandum under the appropriate elements that could be used to prove my allegations. But still it felt unbelievably violating to be forced to turn them over.

"I haven't located them yet. I thought they were in a file cabinet at my parents' house, but I couldn't find them. I think I must have been mistaken and already transferred them to Louisville." *Just keep going.* "You should know I'd actually been abused before, by a pedophile in my church. I know that can and probably will be used against me if we were to make it to trial, so I'm giving you a heads-up. You'll see references to that abuse in my journal too. Larry really . . . it really made it all come back."

I took a deep breath and stepped back into the chain of my research. "When I started realizing something didn't seem right and Mom and I started asking questions, I slowly began researching what pelvic floor therapy looks like." Memories flooded my mind—memories of sitting in our basement, poring over medical journals, blogs, websites, anything reputable, and desperately looking, over and over, for something, anything, that resembled what Larry had done; memories of the sick feeling in the pit of my stomach every time I found nothing.

"What I did discover is what real pelvic floor therapy is." I began detailing the differences for her. Differences in movement. Length. Type of touch. Which fingers are used. Where fingers are placed. Everything. "And I have now spoken with a therapist who confirmed those differences." I explained the conversation I'd had with my physical therapist in Louisville. The one who began by saying, "I'm so sorry . . ."

"I know this is going to be an uphill battle," I said, after I'd finished going over almost every shred of the file I'd brought. "But I do think this is a case that can be won. I've already consulted with a very respected prosecutor to go over the evidence. He's told me that, in his professional judgment, he would try this case. He sent a letter of character reference." I pulled out Keith's letter, filled with gratitude again that someone from the outside who hadn't had to enter the mess with me had done so willingly. Keith had a reputation and credentials built on his education, experience, professionalism, and integrity, and he used that to speak for me. Detective Munford took the paper and glanced over it.

"Thank you," she said. "Okay, let's talk about where we go from here."

I nodded, sitting straight up, trying with all my effort to stay relaxed.

"I will open an investigation. As part of that, I'll be interviewing Larry pretty quickly. You also have a second investigative route open to you. Because this happened on campus, you can file a Title IX claim, if you so choose."

This was the first surprise in the process, and something I didn't know very much about.

"Can you explain more about that?" I asked. "How is it conducted, and what's the difference between that investigation and yours?"

Detective Munford nodded. "Yeah. So Title IX prevents schools from discriminating on the basis of sex. Part of that is ensuring that the campus environment isn't abusive or harassing. It's another layer of protection, basically. The police work pretty closely with the Title IX office because many times there is overlap—it's both a crime and a Title IX violation—so we interface to make sure there's good coordination and that the investigations are done well, but they proceed independently."

She began describing the Title IX process. I became particularly interested when she stated that it would result in Larry immediately being put on desk duty for the duration of the Title IX investigation, while a police report didn't necessarily mandate that. It also had a lower burden of proof, and the probe would likely be finished before the police investigation.

I took a deep breath. A lower burden of proof and quicker resolution meant that there was a higher chance a violation would be found whether or not we made it to trial. In the public eye, the finding of a violation would bolster my credibility and claims. It would add pressure to a police investigation and potential prosecution. And it would ensure that Larry was away from patients immediately—for a few months at least. That was worth a lot. On the flip side, if the investigation wasn't done well and we failed to meet the lower burden of proof, it would crush my credibility and the hopes of any survivors who might otherwise come forward. It would also incentivize a prosecutor to never take the risk of bringing charges.

I ran through the possibilities as I considered my answer. I needed to know more to weigh it properly, so I began asking follow-up questions. Who are the investigators? What types of evidence are considered? Is there an appeals process? Is it public? By the end, I decided to take a calculated risk and begin a parallel investigation. Detective Munford seemed, as best I could tell at this point, to be current on best practices for investigations and interviews, and well versed in the dynamics of abuse and trauma. If she was working closely with the Title IX office, hopefully that would be a check and balance to any problems with their investigation. And there was another significant benefit. During the process, Larry and I would both be interviewed, and we'd get to see each other's responses. I would be able to see, very early on, how he was defending himself and plan accordingly. This, I felt, was worth the risk.

"Yes, let's begin. What do I need to do?"

She nodded. "We'll need to set up another full interview. I think the investigator can come down to Kalamazoo this time. If I can, I'll come as well to do a follow-up."

She added that a meeting with the Title IX team, part of the normal course of business, was scheduled for later that afternoon. She'd go over the case with them and get the process started within a matter of hours.

"We'll give you a call and get everything set up."

Detective Munford walked me and Jacob back down the winding hallways with the promise that she'd begin acting on my complaint right away. As we walked out to the car silently, I was simultaneously exhausted and hyper-vigilant, unable to relax or rest despite the weariness.

"What did you think?" Jacob finally asked as we pulled out of the parking space nearly three hours after we'd arrived.

"I think it went as well as it could have gone for the stage that we are in," I replied cautiously. "She may be taking this seriously. Or she may be very good at simply playing that part. Or very passionate but lacking the practical skills necessary for a solid investigation. It is going to be a complex case from a legal perspective because the medical dynamics are very technical."

Jacob nodded. "She seemed to be taking it seriously," he offered. I did agree with that much at least.

"She did seem to be," I relented. "Her questions and techniques for the interview were very well informed, and she seemed to have a really good grasp of abusive dynamics and trauma, which is encouraging." Focusing on the positive, while being aware of the long road ahead and on guard for problems, would make things better for all of us.

"Do you want to grab some lunch?" he asked, quickly following with, "You really need to eat, honey," after seeing me start to shake my head. I sighed and acquiesced. I did need to eat. I just felt far too exhausted and sick to care.

Jacob quickly googled a few options, and we soon ended up at a pizza place on campus. I felt glaringly out of place in a business suit and heels, so we left in relatively short order but at least we'd had really good pizza.

"So . . . what are you thinking about traveling back home?" Jacob broached as we drove. I sighed in frustration. For the same reasons that I felt it was vital to meet with the police in person, I was convinced it was equally necessary to meet face-to-face with the Title IX investigator.

"I think I have to stay until all the right parts are moving," I said hesitatingly. I knew he couldn't. It just wasn't an option.

"Yeah, I know you do," he agreed. "I think . . . if it's okay with you, I may actually just head back to Louisville as soon as we get to your parents' house." He paused and glanced at me. "Are you going to be okay?"

Okay? No. Nothing is okay. I desperately wanted him to stay. I didn't want to go to bed alone that night. I didn't want to wake up from the nightmares I knew were coming without him next to me. I knew he'd stay if I asked. But I also knew it would mean a very early morning the next day, and another day off work. And we had a very long road ahead of us. We needed to save those emergency days for the times we really needed them. My parents were incredibly supportive, so I wouldn't be alone, much as I wanted Jacob there.

• • •

Two hours later, Jacob was on the road, and I was outside in the backyard, pushing my babies on the swings, trying to pull myself out of the exhaustion and fog. I felt physically light-headed from the weariness and stress. But my little people needed me, and there were tiny bodies to cuddle, little cheeks to kiss, stories to read, and walks to go on.

My parents did everything they could to lighten the load. And I started making phone calls and leaving messages. I needed answers, and I needed them fast. I didn't have the luxury of leaving vague messages with random receptionists and hoping doctors, medical records offices, and physical therapists would be motivated to call back quickly. So I left plenty of details every time, on every phone call.

The day I reported felt as if it would never end. By that night, I'd left messages with everyone possible, and Detective Munford and I had scheduled a meeting for Thursday morning at 10 a.m. in Kalamazoo. I'd written to ask our pastors if we could use a church classroom. I couldn't think of anywhere else to go. A coffee shop or public place was inappropriate for this type of discussion, and I didn't consider my parents' house an option either—not with the kids around. They would interview my mom that day too, Detective Munford explained, probably after talking to me.

The two days in between felt like a blur, and juggling normal life while keeping all the investigative parts spinning was exhausting. My medical records from the nurse practitioner still existed, I discovered much to my relief. But because they were more than ten years old, they were locked away in a vault and wouldn't be available until at least Friday. The *IndyStar* was still working on the story, and I kept them up to date on the progress.

On Tuesday afternoon, I received an email informing me that Larry was coming in for a police interview at 4:30. I glanced at the clock. In less than two hours, he would know about my report. I tightened all the security settings on my social media accounts, as much as they could be. I'd opted not to disable Facebook, so I could direct any survivors who might contact me to the MSU PD, but I knew Larry and his attorneys would search for me immediately, so I made my profile as private as possible.

Later that day, Sue, the physical therapist my mom had talked to years earlier, returned my call. She confirmed that she remembered our conversation from more than a decade ago—and remembered it well.

"Can I tell you what happened and just hear your professional opinion on whether any or all parts were legitimate treatment?" I asked, being cautious not to leave room for accusations that I planted ideas in how I phrased the question.

"Absolutely," she said without hesitation. I launched into my descriptions again. After not allowing myself to put the details into words for sixteen years, I was telling them over and over and over again.

"He used his *thumb*? Oh, no no no . . ."

I kept describing his actions. "What? No. No," she repeated over and over. Sue had always been a get-down-to-business, call-it-like-it-is physical therapist. I smiled just a bit. Her personality hadn't changed at all since she was whipping me back into shape nearly fifteen years ago.

"Oh, no," she said when I finished. "Absolutely not. I not only practice this therapy and have continued with my education as it's grown, I actually teach and certify therapists in pelvic floor work now, and uh-uh, this is *not* pelvic floor therapy. *Nothing* you are describing is pelvic floor therapy."

Relief flooded me. I knew that, but every time a definitive answer was given, I felt awash both in grief and gratefulness. *I wasn't crazy. I hadn't ever been crazy. There was no debate.*

"Can I ask what you'd identify as the differences?" I asked. I was looking for patterns, key similarities between Sue's explanations, the explanations of my own therapist in Kentucky, and what I'd found in my own medical research.

She launched in descriptively. Wrong movements. Wrong fingers. No gloves. Lack of consent. There was no relation to real pelvic floor work, she said over and over. I breathed yet another sigh of relief. Those patterns were obviously emerging, and the more clearly I could explain them and highlight them to investigators, the better.

Later, I heard from Detective Munford again. Larry was firm in his medical technique defense, and that was all she could say for now.

Since it looked like I'd be there at least until Saturday, Mom and I put together a shopping list and headed to the grocery store the next day. But Larry was *there*, too. Shortly after I popped my two-year-old into the shopping cart, with the baby wrapped in a carrier, happily riding on my waist, my phone rang. I picked it up and paused in the middle of the aisle when I heard, "Hey, this is Kathy. I got your message about having some questions for me. How are you?"

It was the physical therapy assistant I'd spoken with, the one whom Sue had pointed me to years ago when we first sought her input.

"Yeah, did anyone explain to you why I was calling?" I asked, beginning to push the cart again, looking for a relatively empty aisle before launching into graphic descriptions of my sexual assault once more.

"I just heard your message," she said. I nodded, ignoring the fact that gestures were useless while on a cell phone. And I said it all again for what felt like the millionth time.

"Do you happen to remember a conversation my mom had with you years ago about a doctor I was getting pelvic floor treatment from?"

She did. I continued to be amazed at how many people actually remembered what I needed them to.

"Can I just ask what you remember from that?" I said, pausing in my aimless strolling, tense with anticipation. I needed her to remember. I needed everyone to remember. She did. She remembered the lack of gloves. No explanation. No consent. Everything we'd told her. Everything that had made her so concerned years before.

"Thanks, I really appreciate you taking the time to go through all that again," I said with a bit of a pause. "Circumstances have opened the door for me to file a police report about this, but I want to be very accurate in what I report. Can I simply describe to you what happened, and hear your professional opinion about it?" Kathy readily agreed. Wandering the aisles of the grocery store, I described it all in detail, inserting strategic pauses and uttering "ummm" when I needed to walk past other shoppers and didn't want them to overhear what I was reciting. Kathy's response, too, was just what I'd anticipated, and as much in line with the personality I remembered as Sue's was.

"Well, first I need to say I am so sorry, Rachael. And I am so proud of you for taking this step. I do believe this is going to save other girls and women. No, none of this is medical. Absolutely nothing you are describing bears any resemblance to real pelvic floor treatment."

I nodded with thankfulness. Like Sue, she was ready to step into the mess with me. Both offered to speak to and meet with investigators. Both offered to go to court as witnesses. Both provided more insight regarding training and certification, as well as leads on experts in the field, and served as a check on the medical research I'd done. They gave me their personal contact information and said they'd do whatever they could to help.

Our shopping trip took much longer than normal that day, and I constantly felt like I had whiplash, trying to move fluidly from investigations and graphic descriptions of my abuse back to parenting and grocery shopping. But the pieces were coming together, and I was deeply grateful.

And I had the information in time to meet with Lin-Chi Wang, the Title IX investigator, and Detective Munford at 10 a.m. the next day, when I would need to go through this all . . . over . . . again.

18

I TOOK A DEEP BREATH and peeked into the silent, dark rooms of our church in Kalamazoo, looking for one that seemed appropriate for the interview.

"Feel free to use any of the rooms," Andrew had said. I opened one door and smiled at the kid-sized chairs dotted throughout the classroom. Detective Munford was petite, but not *that* petite. The metal folding chairs or stackable plastic chairs in the other rooms, while at least full-size, didn't look particularly comfortable to sit on for what was sure to be at least a few hours. Plus, they were very near the pastors' offices. I'd rather not risk being overheard.

The nursery has rocking chairs, I thought. Unconventional for an interview, perhaps, but at least more inviting? I headed down to the lower level and opened a door near the play area for the older toddlers. A table with about a dozen padded office chairs filled the small space. The room seemed relatively soundproof, too, and was close to the entrance. I'd completely forgotten about this meeting room, but it seemed the best option by far.

Just a few minutes later, a car pulled into the parking lot. Detective

Munford stepped out of the driver's side, and Lin-Chi Wang, the Title IX investigator, exited through the passenger's door.

"Is this all right?" I asked, after greeting them and ushering them into the meeting room.

"Oh yeah, this is perfect," Detective Munford said, taking a seat opposite me while Lin-Chi sat at the head of the table.

Lin-Chi pulled out a packet of paperwork and slid it over to me. "This is the Title IX information. Before we start, I'd like to go over the process with you, and then we can sign the forms."

I nodded as we went through them page by page. The college wasn't my advocate. I could not be anonymous. A panel would review the witness statements. Larry would see my statement, and I would see his. We would each get the chance to respond or make corrections.

I signed the paperwork, the words "We are not your advocate" ringing in my ears. I knew that, but it was still a stark reminder that seemed to scream, "You are on your own!"

"Okay," Lin-Chi began. "Why don't you tell me what happened." And I launched in—again. Detail after detail. The clarifying questions the last time had been difficult; this time the depth required was even more significant because this time Larry had already been interviewed.

"Wait," Detective Munford said, pausing me after I attempted to explain exact finger movements. "Can you explain to me how far in his fingers were and how you knew that again?"

And I did. Again.

"Okay." She glanced at Lin-Chi. "When I interviewed Larry, he denied penetration. He said he's outside and pressing into the muscles, but always from outside."

Lin-Chi nodded. "Yeah, he was very specific about denying penetration with me, too."

I furrowed my eyebrows in confusion. "He's denying it? Like, he just . . . says he doesn't do it?"

Detective Munford nodded. "Yes, he says he's external."

Lin-Chi agreed with her again. "When I interviewed him, he was specific that he doesn't penetrate."

I blinked in confusion. "He's not arguing that he does internal pelvic floor work?" It felt repetitive to ask again, but this was so unexpected, I couldn't wrap my mind around it.

Detective Munford shook her head. "No, he doesn't seem to be making that claim. You?" she asked, turning back to Lin-Chi.

"No, no, he's clearly not, based on my interview."

I shook my head. "Huh . . ." *He must not really understand what I'm saying . . . That doesn't make sense.* I'd expected Larry to immediately produce his training and certification for internal pelvic floor work, and then to get into a heated debate about the extremely technical aspects of what that could and couldn't look like. I couldn't fathom why he hadn't done that. *He'll figure it out pretty soon. Then it's really going to get rough . . .*

I took Lin-Chi through everything Detective Munford and I had discussed, through the medical evidence, my case file, what other witnesses could testify to, and statements I was still trying to track down. By the time we were done more than two and a half hours later, I felt completely drained just like before—but this time, Jacob wasn't here.

Detective Munford looked down. "What's the time?" she mused briefly. "Okay, let's grab some lunch, and then we can catch up with your mom." She paused again. "Would it work to just meet at her house since it's right down the road?"

I thought fast. Having them at the house would be the opportunity to show more stability in our family and personal life, hopefully gaining additional credibility. Plus, a more interpersonal relationship could help form a feeling of loyalty. *On the flip side . . .* The house was very small, and my three children had no doubt been keeping my mom hopping at a time when she was already emotionally exhausted from all of this. It was entirely possible that their home, right then, might look like a tornado had swept through its one-thousand-square-foot frame. Or to be more accurate . . . three tornadoes.

"Let me give her a call and see where they're at today," I answered after a brief pause. The benefits probably outweighed the risks. "I think that should work fine."

"Great," said Detective Munford. "And then do you just want to come along to lunch with us?"

"That would be great." I stepped back and dialed the number, keeping my voice soft as she answered and I explained what we were considering. I heard laughter on the other end.

"Here? We've barely finished breakfast and the toys have basically become a full-blown obstacle course." *And the two-year-old is probably wearing half the breakfast in her curls*, I mentally added to Mom's description.

"But yeah, that can work," my mom said. "Maybe give me an hour and call me before you guys head over!" She paused. "And be on guard during lunch."

When we arrived at my parents' house that afternoon, I was relieved to find my two-year-old not wearing her breakfast and my mom more put together than I felt just then.

After briefly introducing her to Detective Munford and Lin-Chi, I turned my attention back to my kids. I was exhausted and immersed in my memories. Not only that, but after being questioned so intensely about my abuse, I bristled at the thought of anyone touching me. Now I had to stifle that aversion so I could hold and hug the three little people who were so excited to have me back (after three whole hours). I then whisked them downstairs to play.

"Let's read some books!" I said eagerly, leaving Detective Munford and Lin-Chi alone to speak with my mom. Reading was a favorite pastime for all of us, and I theorized it would be quiet and they wouldn't fight. Annaliese Grace was the little girl I'd dubbed my "fire and ice princess" because to her everything was either very wonderful or very, very *not*, and I was hoping to avoid a scene. Jonathan was very mild mannered, but he was finally learning to match Annaliese in volume, and there was always the real possibility that a situation could devolve rapidly.

I wasn't mistaken. Halfway through the second Berenstain Bears book, Jonathan managed to do something to tick his sister off. I didn't even see it coming, but I *heard* it as soon as the unperceived issue arose. I attempted to gently scoop Annaliese back into my lap so I could calm her down, which immediately backfired as she started screaming for me not to touch her. *Oooh my gosh. Please do not scream like I am harming you while there is a detective in my kitchen! I'm going to wind up under investigation myself.*

In less than an hour, Mom called down that they were done, and I ascended the stairs to say good-bye to Detective Munford and Lin-Chi, baby in one arm, guiding the two older kids in front of me. *See? Not hurt. Just really, really stubborn and loud.* Detective Munford introduced herself to all of the kids with a smile.

"Sounds like you had fun down there," she said with just a hint of tease in her voice.

"Oh . . . always an adventure!" I replied.

She laughed. "I have kids. I remember!"

I sincerely hoped she did. I thanked them for making the drive, and they left. Mom smiled, the exhaustion and stress obvious on her face.

"Did everything go okay?" I asked.

"Yeah, it did. They were really nice." Mom teared up just a little bit. "Detective Munford suggested I consider getting counseling. 'You're going to need to be the mom,' she said, because she knows this process will be especially hard on you." She paused. "I appreciated her insight and care."

I smiled back. "She does seem to understand." I remembered the detective making a similar recommendation to me at the end of my interview. "Consider it, okay?" Detective Munford had said to me with compassion in her voice. "I know you've healed a lot. You are clearly very strong and prepared. But going through this process has a way of making things come back up. It kind of feels like losing control again, you know? Because the story is out there. You gotta take care of yourself."

I nodded, and my mom and I stared at one another. *What now?* We were both so exhausted and also both jittery from the stress. And . . . there were three small children wanting our attention.

"Let's take the kids for a walk," Mom suggested. And so we did. We filled the rest of the week with visits to the nature center, my dad providing much-needed stability for all of us.

* * *

A few days later, we all headed back to Louisville. My mom stayed a few days to spend time with us and my other siblings. Keith continued to check in regularly to offer suggestions and encourage me. And my family surrounded us with practical and emotional support. My sister-in-law, Christa, and my brother came over with a supply of precooked food and numerous hand-lettered notecards filled with comforting Scripture verses. I finally procured my medical records from the nurse practitioner and wanted to cry with relief when I saw that she had, in fact, charted every detail I told her. The thankfulness I felt for statutory requirements regarding medical records couldn't be overstated. Though I'd never told her Larry's name and she'd gotten a few identifying details incorrect, she'd charted enough specifics about him that he was easily identifiable.

I kept in touch with the reporters at the *IndyStar* and was told in early September that a story was tentatively planned for some time around the ninth, though that could change at any moment. So on September 2, I finally did what I'd been avoiding for weeks—years, actually. I sat down to write an email to close friends and family telling them what had happened and preparing them before it hit the news.

How do I even start an email like this? I wondered, typing as fast as I could because I knew if I stopped, I might never finish it. Then I read, reread, and reread my email again before hitting Send with a sick feeling. The nightmares kept coming. But so did replies of support from those who received the email, as well as from Mark, the *IndyStar* reporter, who checked in with me regularly, often just to give me an update or see how I was doing.

"You are not alone, Rachael," he wrote that day. "*IndyStar* will scrutinize every aspect of the Title IX proceeding and the criminal case. They will know we're watching."

Every time I received an email, I was overwhelmed with grief, but also gratitude. Someone finally cared. Someone saw that it mattered. Someone else was fighting for the truth too.

Jacob and I continued to be isolated from our church. That week, we discovered others in our care group had been told I'd "done too much damage" to allow for the group to continue. The pain from that experience ran deep and greatly compounded the exclusion and grief Jacob and I felt. But I wasn't alone, and after sixteen years of waiting, being in this position felt surreal.

A few days after coming home, I stood in my kitchen on the phone with

Detective Munford when she told me, "I couldn't tell you this earlier, but I wanted to let you know, this isn't the first time we've received a report about Dr. Nassar. Someone filed a police report in 2014, too."

I froze. I had been right. Someone had already tried to do this and hadn't been believed. The police had already cleared Larry, just two short years ago. What I did not know at the time was that he'd actually been officially cleared only a few months before—despite the report coming in 2014—because the investigator at the time had essentially sat on the investigation for around a year and a half. *They already cleared him once.*

"Your case may be different," Detective Munford hastened to say. "What you are alleging goes further than what the other woman alleged because she'd only seen him once. But I wanted you to know."

This was exactly what I'd been afraid of. This exact department had already not listened. I tried to keep my voice steady.

"Were you involved the first time?" I had to know if she'd been the one to clear Larry before.

"No, I wasn't," she replied. "But I have talked to the woman who filed the report. She says she's willing to speak with us again and will help however she can."

I exhaled slowly and with relief. I felt profound, unspeakable appreciation for this unnamed woman who had already been through the trauma of an investigation, only to be told she was wrong. And she was willing to come back and talk to police *again*. She had to be incredibly strong and committed to fighting back if she would even consider it. *Thank you*, I whispered to her, wondering if I'd ever be able to meet her and tell her that in person. I thanked the detective for letting me know and then called Jacob.

"I was right," I said, the anger at being in this position seeping through my words. "I was right. He's been reported and cleared before. He could have been stopped sooner."

The days that followed felt unbearably long, yet too short to accomplish everything I needed to do. I was in contact every day with investigators and journalists, and it felt like a nightmare from which I could not wake. The mental whiplash of navigating the details of my abuse and parenting small children was exhausting. Even the brightly lit, sunny days felt physically dark. In addition, Detective Munford needed my journal, and I was struggling to find the will to turn it over. It was so deeply personal—and Larry would get to pore over every word of it. I had tried so hard to protect my thoughts from him, and now in an attempt to stop him from abusing others, I was forced to turn over a record of my pain that was so deep I'd never shown it to another person. *I* couldn't even read it, and now I had to give it to my abuser.

• • •

September 9—the day the article was set to come out—dawned clear and bright, but I could not see the sun. I refused to check my phone for updates, knowing I wouldn't be able to handle the emotional turmoil of the story and still parent well. But by the time Jacob got home from work, there was still no news, and I felt the stress in every fiber of my being.

That night was supposed to be one of our favorite nights of the year—the Fall Festival. Once a year our seminary put on a huge fair that was a highlight for its families. Jonathan had been looking forward to it for months. We packed up and went, but I was so light-headed from the stress that I felt as if I were barely present.

Mark called soon after we'd arrived. They were still waiting for the court to confirm that the civil lawsuit from the other survivor had been filed, he said. They couldn't print the article if that didn't happen. A sick feeling grew in my stomach. I knew how this often worked. USAG was named in that lawsuit, and they'd have every reason to try to bury it.

A nagging fear kept my mind spinning—*What if everyone settled the suit quietly with a nondisclosure agreement, binding the other victim to silence?* It was a common tool, and one I'd been worried about from the beginning. Survivors are frequently too exhausted and traumatized to push through a public lawsuit, and enablers and abusers know this. Some attorneys will suggest a quiet settlement with a nondisclosure agreement (NDA), promising the victim fast relief and a smoother process. Getting abusers and enablers to agree is rarely a problem because an NDA ensures the victim's silence. Everyone can carry on with no public pressure or substantial repercussions. Attorneys who don't want to put much time and effort into the process can bind survivors to silence at a time when they are too vulnerable to fight back or even know better, and then those lawyers walk away with a windfall payment. If that happened in this instance, the article wouldn't go to print. The second survivor's identity wouldn't be released, even to me. She would be bound to silence, and it would be my voice against Larry's.

"Mark," I asked, incapable of not pushing a little, "is it possible they are trying to reach an out-of-court settlement?" I heard him sigh on the other end.

"I don't know, Rachael. I'm not in touch with the attorney. He says they filed, but nothing is showing up. I think that question needs to be asked, for your sake as much as anything else." He paused. "But I don't know. I've been afraid of the same thing."

The night wore on, and I struggled to enjoy the evening we'd looked forward to for months—the one that came only once per year. *Be present now. Be present now*, I whispered over and over to myself, forcing my eyes to rest on the delighted faces of my children and to absorb their laughter. But I felt robbed of the special moments we'd been waiting to enjoy together. It was yet another stark reminder that abuse follows you everywhere, and that everyone pays the price.

Finally, well after 9 p.m., Mark called again. "I'm so sorry, Rachael. It's not going to be tonight. We're still waiting on confirmation." He said the court's spokesperson did say they were backlogged. In any event, the paper wouldn't run the article over the weekend. The earliest it would appear would be Monday.

I nodded. "Thanks, Mark. I really appreciate it. I know you're doing everything you can."

Icy fear followed me all that weekend. *What if it doesn't print? What if there's a settlement and the other survivor promises her silence?*

Shortly thereafter, I heard from Lin-Chi—Larry had sent dozens of files, videos, photos, and articles showing his techniques. Could I watch them and give my perspective on whether it was what I experienced?

I jumped at the chance. It would give me clear insight into his line of defense. So the following day, Jacob took time off work and school to stay with the kids, and I sat down in our little bedroom with my computer and the Google Drive link that Lin-Chi had sent. I downloaded every file and every video onto my computer first. I wanted to be able to refer back to them if the link was ever taken down. Then I clicked the first video and nearly threw up. It was Larry, doing treatment. I hadn't understood that I would have to watch *him* treating patients when Lin-Chi asked me to watch the videos. I thought he had sent her footage from the school or some outside source, but he hadn't. It was him. Hands all over young gymnasts. I jerked backward as he swiftly slid his hands up the rib cage of a young girl, nearly to her breasts, while her arms were positioned over her head, and then I quickly turned the video off. I hadn't heard his voice in more than a decade. But I had to hear the explanations. I had to watch his hand movements closely. Every aspect needed to be analyzed, contrasted with my experience, compared to current medical practice, and explained to investigators. I shook my head. It had to be done, and the sooner the better. I could discuss this with the *IndyStar*, too, if I could get it done before the article was posted. I pulled the quilt off our bed, wrapped myself up tightly, and pushed Play.

Listen. Watch. Pause. Rewind. Focus on his hands. Transcribe his explanations. Watch it again. I watched more than half a dozen videos over and over, confusion growing as I did. *This was all external treatment. All of it.* I recognized every bit of what he presented in the medical research I'd already done, and this wasn't internal treatment. Not even close. *Why isn't he just saying he did internal pelvic floor work?*

I knew from talking to both Detective Munford and Lin-Chi that they had questions. But to me, after years of studying internal and external pelvic floor work, this was clear-cut. I could swiftly point them to articles that would show these methods and this hand placement, all of which was external. And I could clearly differentiate it from what he did to me, and from real internal pelvic floor work.

Along with the videos, Larry had sent PDFs and two PowerPoint presentations. I clicked open the PDF on rib treatment and analyzed every word—cross-checking with my own research as I did so, just as I had with the videos. Again, it was clearly defined, normal treatment. And it was obviously nothing like what I had described. I was relieved but also very confused. *When is he just going to say he does internal pelvic floor work?* I wondered.

I clicked open the last PDF and scanned through the pages. On the very last page was what looked like a video. I clicked the gray arrow and watched with trepidation. The theme music from *Star Trek* came floating over my computer with the narrator's voice reading the intro script to the show. But across the screen ran Larry's version: "Pelvic Floor—The Final Frontier." More text followed: "These are the voyages of the sports pelvic floor special-ist, whose lifetime mission is to explore strange fascial relationships. To seek out new treatments and tape applications."

I almost begrudgingly granted the humor of it, having been a *Star Trek* fan years ago, until the final line ran across the screen: "To boldly go where no man has gone before (in most of our young gymnasts—hopefully)."

I froze. *He just made a pedophile rape joke in his lecture.* I wanted to throw up. *Where no man has gone before . . .* He'd written those words into his slide, about himself, knowing he was doing exactly that. Going where no man had gone before. Without permission. Without consent. He was doing this to *children*. It was bold. It was brazen. He had done exactly what he'd joked about—right in front of my own mom.

And he'd ended it with "hopefully." *Why "hopefully," Larry?* I wondered. *So you could be the first? So you could take what we'd never given? Take it before we had a chance to make the choice with anyone?*

I burned with anger. Even if Larry had not been advertising, right then and there, what he was doing, this lecture was being given to med students and doctors. The slides were filled with graphic depictions of his hands on the pelvises of little girls—externally, yes, but still very close to their most private areas. In each photo, their shorts were tightly pulled aside and barely covering their genitals—sometimes bunched up so tightly on either side that their full buttocks were exposed. And as these slides of little girls—barely clothed, his hands near their groins—were flashing across the screen, he was joking about going where no man had gone before. The disrespect shown to these young women, the level of perversion necessary to find this funny, filled me with revulsion and anger. Had these children consented properly to these photos? Had their parents? Did any of them know the images of their daughters, barely clothed, with Larry's hands all over them, would be played over and over for other men while jokes about touching their daughters "where no man has gone before" played?

And how had MSU missed this? What kind of ethical standards allowed a professor to lecture and train students using sexual jokes at all, much less sexual jokes about *children*? I wondered, did anyone at MSU ask Larry for the consent forms for all these minor children? Had anyone told him this wasn't appropriate?

In all my years of research, I'd never found another doctor with expertise in these techniques who exposed his patients the way Larry exposed these little girls. When others demonstrated these same methods, they did so on fully clothed patients. And while the treatment he performed in these materials was external, Larry worked dangerously close to the vaginal area, and he was clearly not wearing gloves. The techniques themselves were legitimate, yes— but this presentation should have raised many red flags, not been a staple of conferences and lectures. Yet Larry was passing on these materials as if they cleared him. I was furious. Tears burned in my eyes for all of us. Because Larry had done exactly what he advertised. And none of us had had a choice.

* * *

Two days later, on the following Monday, the *IndyStar* article came out. I screened myself from it until Jacob could come home and watch the kids. The emotional load of trying to switch back and forth was too much, so I just waited. I was grateful that a break from class meant I didn't have to wait more than a few hours. Yet the frustration of almost always being the last to find out or see anything—even about my own case—as I sought to balance parenting with my efforts to push the case forward became an ever-present reality from that moment on.

I slipped off to our bedroom to watch the video and read the article. The *IndyStar* had gotten it right. They'd nailed it. The cultural dynamics. The abusive mind-set at USAG. The important facts. The pattern. It was everything I'd dared to hope for. I was horrified to see the words in print and hear my voice coming over my speakers, but it was exactly, precisely what we needed.

But I was stunned by two disclosures: First, USAG had learned of complaints against Larry and reported him to law enforcement, allegedly more than a year before. *He's been under investigation for a year? But he's been seeing patients . . . Nobody stopped him . . . Nothing has been done . . . How is this possible?* And this line: "Nassar's attorney said his client never used a procedure that involved penetration."[12]

I'd been told that he'd been denying it, but until I saw it in print, I could not comprehend it. I immediately dialed Mark's number.

"He's publicly denying doing internal vaginal procedures?" I asked in disbelief.

"Yeah," Mark said, his voice also tinged with disbelief, "he is, Rachael. He just flat-out denies it. Says he's never done them. He's adamant."

I felt out of breath. "I . . . I don't understand. Why would he do that?"

"I don't know," Mark replied. "But he's insistent that he doesn't do internal pelvic floor work. He's never used penetration."

It had never—not once—occurred to me that Larry might not even be *trained* in internal work. That he might not even be *pretending* to do internal work. I had researched internal pelvic floor procedures because I thought he had to be operating at least under the pretense of being trained and certified. And he wasn't. He couldn't be, or he would have produced evidence of that training immediately. There was only one reason why he would deny doing internal pelvic floor work: because *he had never been qualified to do it at all.*

I felt as if the floor had fallen out from under me. I had spent sixteen years wondering at what point I'd transitioned from patient to victim, never expecting a clear-cut answer. But I had one now. I had been a victim right away. From the very first moment. From the very beginning. I'd never been a patient. I had always and only been his victim.

Part of me was relieved to realize that Larry wasn't claiming to have done internal pelvic floor therapy. This would make my allegations much easier to prove. It turned the case from a technical medical case to a simple he-said, she-said—*if* the investigators and prosecutors realized that. But I was also horrified. I thanked Mark and hung up, and then tried to resume daily life. But a short time later he called again. His next words flooded me with grief—and hope.

"We're getting calls, Rachael. I can't say any more than that, but I wanted you to know. We're getting calls." He paused. "It's working."

19

THE STORY BEGAN SPREADING LIKE WILDFIRE. By that evening, it was a headline story on the website of the Canadian Broadcasting Corporation (CBC), and other international outlets were beginning to pick it up as well.

When they read that Larry had denied doing internal treatments, some of his former patients clearly realized that they may have been abused too. Within thirty-six hours, more than twenty women had come forward either to the *IndyStar*, the police, or the civil attorney named in the lawsuit, asking where to go to report. Two of them came to me.

Late in the morning on September 15, I picked up the phone for a Michigan number. The *IndyStar* team had let me know a survivor was going to be calling. Sitting on my son's toddler bed while holding the baby, I talked to another Nassar survivor for the first time.

"I can't believe this," she said. She said she'd seen Larry for years, both at his office and his home. "He has a massage table in his basement," she told me.

I dropped my head into my hands, coming face-to-face with my own baby girl cradled in my lap—innocent and trusting. The way all of us used to be.

"When I saw your article, I was like, 'Oh that's normal; he does it all the time.' But then he said he didn't do internal work, and that's when I knew. I was like, no way . . . no. You are lying. You did it to me."

I exhaled in relief. I'd been right to release those details. *It worked. I'd wanted him to respond publicly to that specific detail. I needed him to do that so other survivors could see inconsistencies. And he did.*

She laughed a little, as if not knowing what else to do. I knew how she felt.

"The only reason he would lie is because you are telling the truth," she added with conviction. "I don't even know what to think anymore." She paused. "But I want to help. Tell me what I can do." I suggested she speak to Detective Munford, and she agreed to call her right away.

After we hung up, I sat on the bed and reflected on the conversation. This woman had seen Larry from age thirteen on, but she recognized the truth of what Larry had done that quickly and was ready to speak out. I was amazed at her strength.

Later that night, I picked up the phone again for a call from Seattle. Another survivor.

"I knew it," she told me. "I *knew it*. I reported him, but he said it was medical—that I just wasn't comfortable with my body because I wasn't a gymnast. The police talked to him but never really opened an investigation."

I felt a wave of grief wash over me. This must be the woman Detective Munford had told me about.

"I went to the hospital and got a rape kit done and everything," she said, her voice tinged with heartache and disbelief. "And after everything I went through, the police just called him in and believed him."

I nodded in empathy. "I am so sorry. I can't imagine how incredibly traumatizing that had to have been." It made me feel sick just thinking about it. "Thank you so much for coming forward. I honestly can't express how thankful I am." And I was. To be willing to go through everything all over again, after not being believed . . . I was *so thankful.*

"Absolutely!" she exclaimed energetically. "I just can't even believe this is happening. I struggled so much after I reported him in 2004, and I was right the whole time . . ." Her voice trailed off.

I froze. "Wait . . . 2004?" I asked in disbelief.

"Yeah," she answered confidently. "I was a high school student and saw him for a sports injury in 2004."

My mind was racing in disbelief. "You're . . . you're *not* the one who reported Larry in 2014? To the MSU PD?" *There were two police reports?*

"No!" the woman exclaimed. "I didn't report to MSU PD. I reported to my own local police department. Do you mean there was someone else who reported him?" She sounded as shocked as I felt.

"Yeah . . . ," I answered in disgust. "He was reported to the MSU police in 2014. He got cleared then, too." I stood still in the middle of my kitchen floor, and we were both silent for a moment. *He could have been stopped. He could have been stopped.* It was in 2004 that I reported to Jackie, and Mike checked for other police reports. Right near the end of that year, actually. *If this police department had even properly filed an investigation, Mike would have seen it when I reported to Jackie.* But they hadn't, and so I was told I was all alone. But not anymore. Her voice came over the phone again.

"What can I do? I will do anything." I gave her Detective Munford's number, and she called right away.

* * *

As the days unfolded, I felt like time was moving in slow motion, yet without giving me a break to breathe. At one point, Detective Munford emailed me to ask how I was doing and received in response the outpouring of emotional exhaustion I'd been living in. I'd grown increasingly frustrated by the clear perception, even of many people close to me, that I'd done this for my own benefit—that it was my step toward healing. Nothing could have been further from the truth.

"There is nothing in the world I could want from this process for *me* that would make any of this worth it," I wrote her. "All this accomplishes for me is being forced to relive it, but with an audience, which is far worse than living it in private. I don't even need a jury verdict for myself. I find this process to be entirely counterproductive to healing."

The idea that I'd had a bee in my bonnet about assault and finally gotten the platform I'd wanted was repulsive to me. *People have no idea what it costs survivors to stop an abuser.* And I knew I wasn't alone. In fact, I had far more support than many survivors do simply because I had a loving, stable family, and yet somehow everything was *still* so dark. *Imagine what survivors who have no one go through.* As much as my sorrow weighed on me, knowing what so many others lived with weighed far heavier.

Over the next several days, the *IndyStar* began working on a follow-up piece, and I began fielding press calls like it was a second job. I turned down offers from a few teams that leaned more toward sensational reporting, I helped others behind the scenes, and I allowed NBC to record an interview in our home.

In the middle of it all, daily life continued. Jacob and I tried to work through things with our church, but we made no progress. Jacob tried to keep up with a full load of PhD coursework as well. At night, after the kids were in bed, I was supposed to be working on marketing and outreach for my law school, but more often I wound up answering emails that had accumulated during the kids' waking hours from police, the Title IX office, or journalists. I had nightmares every night, but keeping a protective wall up wasn't an option when each morning started with three kids who needed me.

When corresponding with authorities, I tried to carefully ask questions about where the investigation was at. There were specific things that had to happen, and I simply didn't know yet if the MSU PD would handle them correctly. Larry's computers needed to be searched. Child porn would almost certainly be there, but if they didn't hurry, he might destroy it, and we needed it to be found. Search warrants had to be obtained properly and executed correctly or legal technicalities could result in the evidence being inadmissible in court. I checked and double-checked everything I had access to. Under a federal statute known as the Clery Act, all universities are required to track and make public reports of crimes reported on campus. I pulled the MSU log one day and cross-checked it to identify my case report. It was logged as third-degree assault. I took a deep breath and tried to remain calm. It wasn't third degree; it was first. If it were third degree, I'd be time-barred and unable to proceed with the case.

I wrote a legal memo to explain why Larry's abuse qualified as first-degree assault. I quickly emailed Detective Munford, trying to sound casual. "Just wondering—why third and not first? It meets all the elements of first, and if it's third, it's time-barred. I wouldn't have brought it if it was only third because I know that falls under the statute of limitations. I'm presuming a DA can change that?"

I hoped I wasn't driving her crazy. She replied that it had already been updated, and I was thankful, but the constant reality that we could find ourselves years down the road and losing a trial because of mistakes made within even the first few days weighed heavily on me.

"Are you able to get hold of his computers?" I tentatively asked her when she called to update me one day.

"Oh yeah, we'll be looking at all of that," she responded reassuringly.

I had to step back and let everyone do their jobs. The feeling of being at the mercy of everyone else was one of the worst parts of the process. I had no choice but to divulge my most painful experiences, yet I could only hope it was handled correctly. I wasn't owed an explanation for every little decision or daily occurrence, but it was draining and frustrating nonetheless to have decisions made without any dialogue or input. For sixteen years I'd researched and put the case together, but I had no part in the decisions being made or even the conversations surrounding them. All I could do was wait. More often than not, I had to wait and read about what was happening in the newspaper, and it was beyond frustrating.

Slowly but surely, however, progress was made. Eight days after the *IndyStar* report ran, Michigan State fired Larry. Evidence had arisen showing he'd failed to comply with basic office protocol he'd agreed to implement after being reported in 2014. He was still free. He still had access to kids—his own and those gymnasts who came to his house for treatment. But he was out of the official exam room, and that was a small victory.

●　●　●

And then Larry did what I'd been waiting for. He realized the massive mistake he had made in flat-out denying penetration. He fired his attorney and hired two new attorneys—Shannon Smith and Matt Newburg—who immediately issued a statement that created confusion and obfuscated the real issues. They said that the former attorney had been incorrect—Nassar *did* use techniques that resulted in technical penetration. The first attorney, they argued, hadn't understood the legal term correctly.

Confusion was already growing in the public eye. Was Larry certified in internal pelvic floor therapy? Journalists released stories on the statement, consulting medical experts who used internal techniques and pointing out that they are real medical procedures—missing that Larry did not claim to be doing them.

I would find out later that when I came forward with my medical evidence, Larry began googling "internal pelvic floor therapy," trying to educate himself on what the appropriate boundaries and techniques were. While I was educating investigators and journalists, Larry was desperately trying to educate himself. Of all the things I expected, I had not even considered that I would know more about the therapy I had presumed he was doing than he would.

I called Mark. "Is it your perspective that Larry is backtracking and changing his story?" I didn't think he was. "Technical penetration is *any* entrance into the *outside* genitalia," I said. "That's not at all the same thing as internal pelvic floor work, which uses actual penetration the way we normally think of it. If he's only using *technical* penetration, that's still actually a denial of internal work."

Mark adamantly agreed. "No, he's not changing his position, Rachael. He's trying to bank on a technicality. We pushed him on the medical procedures, and he denied doing internal pelvic floor work again."

I shook my head. It was a shrewd move on the part of his attorneys. They were hoping to confuse the issues, confident no one would understand either the law or the medical procedures well enough to differentiate between the two. *But I know. I can tell the difference. And I can explain it too.*

I fed the kids lunch, read them a story, got them settled in for quiet time, and then emailed Detective Munford and Lin-Chi.

Nassar is NOT claiming he does intervaginal/interpelvic release. He specifically disclaimed that. . . . He's just claiming that some slight penetration occurs in the treatment he shows you in the videos, and that the videos are still consistent with what he did with all of us. That's still radically different than the argument that he does what is classified as internal release.

Later that afternoon, we got on the phone and discussed the law and the medical procedures. I pulled up every news article I could find and contacted each journalist directly.

"Larry is not claiming to do internal procedures. It's really important that you report this correctly." I walked them through his responses to the police and the Title IX investigator, as well as the facts in the first *IndyStar* report. I explained the law and emailed the relevant statutes to any journalists who wanted them. I described internal pelvic floor work and external work, and how those procedures meshed with the legal definitions of penetration.

"Why don't I send you medical information on both types of procedures so you can see for yourself?" I offered repeatedly, emailing them the best articles and overviews I could find so they could understand the medical technicalities. I stopped being selective about interviews and talked to every single person who called or put up a story that wasn't absolutely accurate, especially if they were connected to widespread media outlets.

"He can 'vigorously defend' as his attorney says," I wrote to Detective Munford one night, "but his desire to protect himself is not as strong as mine to see it end."

I thought about what I told my students: *The more you love, the harder you fight.*

*   *   *

Almost two weeks to the day when the first article appeared, the *IndyStar* published the first of many follow-up pieces: "16 More Women Accuse Former USA Gymnastics Doctor of Sexual Abuse."[13] It reminded me again why I'd trusted these journalists. The reporting was precise and accurate. It highlighted the most important dynamics of abuse, demonstrated the pattern, and included statements from Larry that made clear he was still denying penetration and using internal techniques. They got it right. Again. They *nailed it.* I was overwhelmed with gratitude for the reporting team and for each woman willing to speak in that article. They'd all remained anonymous so far—with the exception of one woman who'd used her first name—but that didn't change the impact they'd had, and I hoped they knew it.

On October 6, I received the welcome news that Michigan's attorney general had decided to take over the case. What I didn't know then but would later hear from numerous independent sources was how close we had come to losing everything we'd worked for that week. Just a few days earlier, child pornography had been found on Larry's hard drives. The MSU police had executed search warrants on Larry's house days after the *IndyStar* piece ran, made possible because of two women who came forward soon after reading the news report. They spoke to Detective Munford within hours of each other, linking Larry's abuse to his house. The first woman was the daughter of a family friend and the only known survivor abused outside of a medical context. The second was a longtime patient—the woman who had called me—and she was the first to tell investigators that Larry "treated" girls in his home. The MSU PD wanted to turn the evidence over to the federal government in an effort to obtain much stiffer charges and sentencing. (Michigan law was, at the time, extremely lax on justice for child pornography victims.) The county prosecutors had other ideas.

So on October 4, while I was helping another mom select books for her homeschool program, juggling the needs of my own children, and talking to reporters, a crucial meeting was happening between Detective Munford, MSU police chief Jim Dunlap, and members of the county prosecutor's office. And it wasn't pleasant. The county prosecutor didn't want the chief and Detective Munford to turn the child porn evidence over to federal law enforcement. They wanted to charge the child porn under state statutes instead and offer Larry a plea deal: plead guilty to the porn, and they wouldn't bring the sexual assault charges. *Any of them.* It would be neat. Clean. Done quickly. The survivors might not be strong enough to withstand a trial anyway, they argued, though it was national news by now. International, in fact.

During the discussion, the county prosecutor pushed a file across the desk. "I can't prosecute this. It's full of holes." The file bore the name of the young woman whose case eventually led to the first charges filed against Larry, the family friend whose abuse did not fall under the guise of treatment. If Chief Dunlap and Detective Munford had acquiesced, right then and there everything I'd worked for would have ended. Larry would have served minimal jail time; most likely, he would even have kept his medical license and continued to practice. He would have been unstoppable, and he would have known it.

Fortunately, I had a team that was committed to fighting for us, including a police chief who picked up the phone and called the attorney general, asking him to take the case. We had an attorney general who answered and sent his very best. And his very best was an assistant attorney general named Angela Povilaitis. She looked at those case files and said, "I will take them all. And I will fight for all of them."

And she did. Later that day, though I didn't know it, MSU's president contacted the police chief after the local prosecutor called to ask her to require that the chief leave the cases with their office. After talking with the police chief, the university president told him to do whatever needed to be done and said she supported the investigation and prosecution. More than a year later, the MSU president, along with several others, would confirm that phone call during a private meeting I had with her the night she resigned. Publicly, the case was transferred to the attorney general because it crossed jurisdictional lines. Privately, it was the chess move that ensured Larry would face the full force of the law, and it saved our cases.

But in early October, I didn't know any of that was happening. I didn't know how close we'd come to being silenced again. But I did know that when the attorney general took over the case on October 6, an election was coming up. I was hopeful the attorney general's office would do the right thing for the right reasons, but I knew better than to count on it.

So I kept taking every phone call. I followed every article and mapped each survivor's story and place in the time line by cross-referencing other articles, so that when I spoke, I could present a robust and complete picture of how all the pieces connected.

● ● ●

We celebrated Jonathan's birthday weeks late, and the Roald Dahl *Charlie and the Chocolate Factory* party I'd planned for him lacked some of the planning and decorations we'd dreamed of. I was exhausted, straining to grab hold of and be able to see the joy still around me as I relived graphic memories over and over. Much as I had spent the long-anticipated Fall Festival waiting for a story that wasn't actually published that night, I felt robbed and cheated of the memories and time with my precious children. Larry had already stolen so much that I ached at the thought of losing anything more—especially moments with my young children that would never come again.

I traveled back to Michigan for a friend's wedding and instantly regretted having done the second police interview and Title IX process in our church building. I hadn't counted on the memories that would flood back when I entered the building again. By this point, my sexual abuse had achieved "casual dinner conversation" status, and I felt at a loss for how to interact with lifelong friends who now possessed every graphic detail. I appreciated those who didn't ignore the elephant in the room and asked informed questions, but I still felt unsure how to handle them.

The next afternoon, Jacob, who'd stayed in Kentucky, called. His van had been broken into overnight, and more than three thousand dollars' worth of tools had been stolen—everything he needed to work. We were now involved in *two* police investigations.

"I posted about it on Facebook," he said, bemused. "Four leaders in the church called to see if we needed anything."

I exhaled slowly. "Four leaders called to check up on us because of the van?"

"Yeah," he said, irony in his voice. "Within two hours."

I dropped my head into my hands. "Are we even on the prayer chain for this national investigation?"

He let out a soft laugh. "Nope. We've never heard a word."

I shook my head. "Do they realize that the damage done to me, to us, through this investigation is so much worse than the damage done to your van?"

I heard him sigh. "I don't think they understand. Or know what to do."

He was right. We knew their silence wasn't malicious. But no one had any idea what to do, and they weren't asking. It was okay not to know what to do. It wasn't okay not to ask what they could do.

By and large, the events of the last few months had been a sharp reminder of the uphill battle survivors face. To find justice. To be heard. To be understood. To have anyone even care. And I constantly wondered, as I reflected on how hard the process was for me, despite healthy relationships on both sides of the family, *Who is going to find the survivors who have no one? Who is even going to see the survivor who isn't on the news? Who will find these hurting people and tell them how much they are worth?*

20

I RETURNED HOME after the trip to Michigan still struggling to find "normal" and feeling very lost.

Someone on the *IndyStar* team texted to ask if it would be all right if they passed on my cell number to the civil attorney who had filed a lawsuit in California on behalf of another victim. He had some information he thought might help my case. *Finally*, I thought. I appreciated the importance of the civil process, but did anyone realize we had a criminal conviction to get first?

Like I did with everything else, I ran this request through a cost-benefit analysis. I had contributed little to the civil process up to this point, other than to add the available facts into the narrative to help journalists identify patterns and time lines. There simply hadn't been enough information in the press about this attorney, John Manly, to get a good sense of who he was or how he did business. He was right, of course, that Larry was a predator. Whether he had the skill to handle this case and grasp both the medical and legal complexities, I had no idea. His TV interviews were fine, and the court briefs were good—journalists frequently sent me the briefs or motions they legally obtained—but that wasn't enough to be sure. And his professional ethics were a significant consideration from my perspective. *How* he did things mattered as much to me as *what* he did. I suspected that he just wanted another client or hoped to ferret information out of me that would bolster his case. He wouldn't be getting that—not unless I knew it would help with the end goal: stopping a predator.

I had no intention of filing a civil suit when I began this process. The additional weight and strain on me and our family wasn't worth it. I'd reviewed the law in Michigan, and even if I had wanted to go that route, my claim was time-barred. On the other hand, I might be able to get some help from John, whether he gave it intentionally or not. And a criminal conviction would help his case, so if he knew what he was doing, he would be motivated to help me, too.

"Sure, that's fine. I'd love to catch up with him," I texted back. A few nights later, John and I finally talked.

He started out by thanking me. "I want you to know how many women and little girls you've helped," he said. "And I know this is an incredible load on you."

I thanked him a little awkwardly.

"No." He paused. "I'm a survivor, Rachael. And I know what this is like. I am so proud of you." I thanked him again but didn't yet realize that one of the most incredible parts of the next two years would be watching how John worked: taking frightened victims and showing them their own strength, teaching them how to advocate and speak, giving them the tools to move themselves from victim to survivor.[14] "The way to healing," he told me then, "is to take what you've been through and make it mean something. And you've done that." And I remembered one more time: *The more you love, the harder you fight.*

He passed on information he had about the time lines regarding Larry's abuse and some witnesses who would be speaking to the police, but he carefully guarded their confidentiality. I was grateful for his attention to ethical attorney-client relationships. It wasn't until after we hung up that I realized he hadn't asked me for anything. And it had been a welcome relief to be able to talk over the case on a technical level.

John was true to his word. He passed on useful information whenever he had it, and he offered his help freely, without mentioning the civil suit. "I've dealt with the press a lot on these issues. If you ever have questions or concerns about a reporter or outlet who contacts you, feel free to shoot me a message."

That I needed. Detective Munford couldn't give input, and I hadn't even talked to the prosecutor yet. No one else I knew had much experience with the press—especially on this issue—and as much as I researched reporters, shows, and outlets before agreeing to go on, having someone to bounce these requests off meant a lot.

When Election Day rolled around on November 8, 2016, Larry walked away with 21 percent of the vote in his race to be elected to the school board—despite the many sexual assault allegations against him.[15] I intentionally didn't look up the results, knowing what they were likely to show, but a friend passed them on anyway. Local journalists were doing a great job of reporting on the allegations, but popular opinion wasn't yielding much ground. Community protectionism is a strong force, and I wasn't surprised to frequently see Larry portrayed on social media and in news reports by his friends as the real victim, while my parents and I received no mercy in the court of public opinion.

I'd enjoyed a calm, simple, full, and beautiful life before coming forward. I'd reached a good place of healing. But facts rarely got in the way of the traditional narrative: "She's bitter and angry—just wants money and attention." As if I were somehow benefiting from upending our lives and turning the sexual assault on my body into casual conversation.

Less than two weeks later, I was changing the very messy diaper of my seventeen-month-old when my phone rang. It was one of the many journalists I'd been working with for the past few months. When the reporter called, I picked up immediately—deadlines were tight, and stories had to be accurate.

"Hey," he greeted me. "Have you heard anything? The attorney general just announced a press conference, and we're hearing rumors that it has to do with Larry."

I sighed. "No, I haven't. I think I would have if it's about charges related to my case, so I can pretty much guarantee it's not related to me directly. It's totally possible he is being charged for actions against someone else." I felt exhausted. Detectives and investigators always kept things close, and I knew this was the way it had to be. Even though I'd brought the evidence and put myself out there to ensure others would come forward, I was entirely uninvolved in what was being done with that information. Conversations *about* me and *around* me—though rarely *with* me—happened all the time. It was terribly draining to have no part in the process or conversations around the case. At times, I struggled not to simply feel used.

I swallowed my exhaustion and frustration as I lifted my toddler down from the changing table. The journalist had promised to call if he heard anything more, so all I could do was wait. Just like every other day. A few moments later, my phone rang again. This time is was Detective Munford—whom I'd begun calling Andrea by this time.

"I wanted to let you know we have a development in the case," she said. "I won't be able to call everyone, but I felt like it was important to call you at least, and I wanted to reach you before you heard it anywhere else." I covered my mouth with my hand and stifled a laugh. *Oh, you'll have to call* way *earlier if you want to update me before anyone else*, I thought in amusement.

"The attorney general has called a press conference," Andrea said. "Larry is going to be charged with sexual assault today. We picked him up just a little bit ago, and he's in custody now." She paused. "We were able to proceed faster with this victim because she wasn't a patient of his. She was a family friend."

My heart sank, and tears flooded my eyes. One of the biggest questions I'd had for sixteen years was whether he'd brought his abuse home. He had an endless supply of victims through his medical work, so I'd held out the tiniest hope that somehow the evil had stayed in his office—that he'd had some boundaries.

She explained, almost apologetically, "We could move faster because we didn't need to identify a medical expert. We're still trying to narrow down an expert for the medical cases. We don't want to charge those until we've done that, but we didn't need that for this woman."

I shook my head. "There is no need to apologize for moving faster with this case. I am so, so glad you did. She deserves it, and the faster he's away from kids, the better. You guys charge whatever cases have the best chance of succeeding, and fast. It doesn't need to be mine." I paused. "Can I ask . . . I know you can't probably say, but . . . Andrea . . . his kids? What about his daughters?"

Larry had brought his firstborn in for me to hold on my last visit when she was only a few weeks old. He knew I loved children, and he used even *that* against me. The memory of the dark-haired baby girl with the button nose and dimpled fist curled up by her soft cheek had followed me ever since. *Is she safe?*

The detective sighed. "We've done everything we can do there. We just . . . we don't know." She hesitated a moment before going on. "You'll hear this in the press conference, but this young woman babysat for them. Even called CPS on him a few times to try to protect them. Larry started abusing this girl when she was only six years old."

I gripped the bathroom counter. *Six. Six!* The youngest reported survivor I'd heard of so far was thirteen when Larry began to abuse her, and I'd held out hope that thirteen was the bottom of his "desired" age range. The little girl I'd tried to keep from being sent to Larry was young—between seven and eight. My hope for the past sixteen years had been that she was younger than the girls he chose to prey upon. But this told me everything I needed to know. Larry essentially had no boundaries. He would abuse anyone, any-where. College students *and* very little children. I could not wrap my mind around this depth of depravity.

"She's doing well, Rachael." Andrea's voice came over the phone again. "She really is. She's doing well. She's an incredibly strong young woman."

I didn't doubt that. She'd have to be to come forward after all she'd been through. *And I can't even know her name.* I cried for her, but I couldn't know her name. That was one of the darkest days.

The next one came just a few weeks later, when the federal prosecutors announced criminal charges against Larry for the possession of child porn—thousands upon thousands of images of child porn. I knew that the MSU PD had executed search warrants on Larry's house and work computers just days after the *IndyStar* story was published, but until that day, I didn't know what they'd found—or the serendipitous timing that provided a huge break in the case.

On the day they searched Larry's home, an officer named Erin Held noticed garbage pickup had been late, so Detective Munford instructed her team to put the cans and bags in the back of the vehicle. They'd sort it later. When they did, they found hard drives in the bags. Hard drives with Larry's name on them, and thousands upon thousands of videos and pictures of child porn. He'd tried to erase much of it, but detectives were able to recover more than 37,000 files of little girls being abused—often sadistically.

A journalist I was in contact with forwarded me the court documents—affidavits and warrants of probable cause. To this day, I cannot describe what I felt when I read them. Some of the files included the ages and names of the children—or at least the names their abusers had given them. When Jacob came into the kitchen that night, he found me standing at the counter, leaning onto it for support and holding back furious, deep sobs. I could not find words to explain the anger and grief I felt—or the kind of evil this represented.

"Do you know how many little girls it takes to create 37,000 images of child porn?" I whispered. "*How many little girls?*" I knew the reality of how these images were produced—many victims likely had been trafficked. Virtually all of them were being abused by someone close to them—someone with constant access. "Who is going to find these little girls?"

The depth of the damage from abuse, especially ongoing abuse like this . . . it follows you. It changes you forever. I had dear friends—many dear friends—who'd suffered varying levels of abuse, and I knew only too well how long the pain lasted, how much it changed everything, and how hard they had to fight for every bit of progress.

I was struggling too. I watched my children every day, and I felt as if I was face-to-face constantly with what *should have been* for all those precious children. The innocence. The trust. The genuine love they had for people. The delight and joy they expressed in the smallest of things. The way their eyes lit up or how they relaxed against Jacob and me as we read them a story.

At night as I worked on my case or picked up phone calls from a number of friends who were survivors, I was constantly aware that I had far less to fight through than the vast majority of survivors. Yet in the throes of fighting to heal, I also felt stuck between what *should have been* and what *now was*.

Despite having the most stable, secure, loving home possible, despite a supportive family and being believed and cared for right away by my parents, I lived with the scars too, and I was wrestling with the reality that full healing doesn't ever come. I was still damaged, and I didn't want to be. I wanted there to be a quick fix, and I felt like I was drowning in the reality that, despite all the healing, the nightmares and flashbacks still came.

Every once in a while, I'd reflexively push away the hand that was always and only ever safe. I didn't want that to be me. I didn't want that to be the reality for those I loved. And I didn't want that to be the reality for every little girl whose name and face I didn't know but for whom I cried in my kitchen over and over again.

21

AS DECEMBER BEGAN, I struggled to fit our family's new normal into the Christmas season. I read Dickens's original *A Christmas Carol* to my tiny people at lunchtime and took immense delight in the two-year-old who had few words but added an emphatic "Bah humbug!" to her repertoire.

I continued spending part of nearly every day fielding calls and emails from reporters. Internationally, the Nassar story was picking up steam. Locally, reporters were tenacious, but the national media were no longer showing much interest. Our case involved girls and didn't involve football, so the outrage generated by other scandals just didn't emerge.

We'd been told it was possible that charges would come sometime in December, but while journalists frequently provided me with breaking news, case updates from the investigators were few and far between. As an attorney, I truly understood why. As a survivor, I wished there were a better way. One night I wrote to Keith, pouring out my exasperation:

> I am finding myself increasingly frustrated by the lack of communication.

More than once I'd gotten calls from reporters letting me know of a press release that had been sent out, but I was never notified by the officials behind them.

> I do understand there are practical and legal reasons to not keep all of us well informed, but frankly, it is beyond frustrating. . . . The fact that the AG office can take the time to send a press release to local media and can't take the time to update the victims who are living this . . . it makes it feel like our voices ultimately still don't matter. When I have to get updates on the investigation from newspapers, it frankly feels very dehumanizing.
>
> The investigation <u>is</u> me and these other women. It's <u>our</u> lives, <u>our</u> medical records, <u>our</u> witnesses, and the decision has massive impact on <u>our</u> futures, and when the press is more important to talk to than the victims, it frankly makes it feel like it's about a notch in a prosecutor's belt instead of justice. Being entirely left out of the process and communication, while other people (reporters), who are, on a personal level, entirely unconnected to the case, are prioritized for communication and updates, makes it feel very much like I'm not much more than another means to an end. This time, hopefully a good end, but just a means to an end nonetheless.

I knew by now that Andrea didn't share that mind-set. I also knew that she thought very highly of the prosecutor assigned to the case, and I reminded myself daily of the realities that drove this investigation. Knowing how poorly these cases were often handled helped me be thankful in the tough moments. I knew we had an amazing team working on this case.

I wished people understood the realities of what life was like for a survivor. What it was like to try to bring justice. What it felt like whenever someone asked—or even insinuated—"Why didn't you report?" I knew that the details of some of our most intimate and horrifying experiences had been entrusted into the hands of others, yet we were not part of the discussions and decisions about the groundwork being laid in our cases. By and large, we as survivors were *told* what was happening to us; we weren't consulted first. We had little to no voice in the process. And after losing my voice once, losing it again was traumatic and painful. But I never said this, because I had no idea what kind of prosecutor we had, and the last thing I wanted to do was to upset a relationship that had to work, likely for the next several years.

> The loss of control and a voice is one of the worst parts of abuse and something victims typically go to great lengths to avoid experiencing again. Going through this process in many ways puts me right back in that place. Not simply from the standpoint of having to relive it all, but because for now, everything I do and say is ultimately still controlled by what Nassar does.

I lived daily with the reality that my life truly was at the beck and call of this case, and every decision I made related to it was made with Larry in mind.

> The role I have to play, what I can and can't say, who I can and can't talk to, I am constantly weighing everything I do, even what I post on Facebook, in light of how it could be used in the future if this goes to trial. How he responds will dictate how I have to respond, what I have to disclose, what I have to say, what I have to be willing to do.

After sixteen years of wading through who I was and where my value lay, I felt I was right back at square one, fighting to hold on to what I knew was true.

> If this goes to court, he gets to be introduced to everyone on the basis of his credentials, his reputation, all the things he has done that arguably make it impossible for him to be a predator. I walk into court entirely defined by something done to me, without any regard to anything I've done. My status and role revolve around nothing I've accomplished and nothing that would normally explain or define who I am. While I realize that in the ultimate, intrinsic, philosophical sense it doesn't change "me," the reality for now is that he's still in control of what I can and can't do, and what I'm forced to do, for the sake of pursuing justice, and I don't get to "define myself." What he did defines me.

Every time I felt the weight that survivors carry, I thought of all those who had little to no support. Whose stories didn't even merit attention. Who didn't have journalists who'd taken pity on them and would pass along updates. Who didn't have an investigative team actually pursuing the truth. It was awful for me, but I knew it was so much worse for those other survivors.

Over and over again, I had to remind myself of the truth of who I was and the reality that success wasn't defined by a result but by faithfulness. I had to remember that my identity and healing weren't dependent on the voices that surrounded me and that the truth wasn't dependent on popular opinion or cultural responses. I had to focus on what was real and true. The straight line instead of the crooked. Jacob constantly had to point out that it was okay to grieve, that it was okay not to be okay, and that it was okay to let others help me—to let him help me. What we were dealing with, he reminded me, was truly hard.

Every day was a fight just to do the next thing and focus on the day's tasks, holding any semblance of routine loosely, knowing that any moment a phone call could derail the best-laid plans.

● ● ●

During Christmas week I got one such phone call—this time from John Manly, the civil attorney who occasionally passed along updates. This conversation started us down a path we hadn't intended to take. Someone else was going to speak publicly—to reveal her name and face.

"She warned MSU in 2000, Rach," he said. "And there's another survivor, a runner, who warned them in 1999. I've done this long enough to know there is much more here. We just don't know it yet."

After putting the kids to bed that evening, I pulled up the press articles for the day. That was the first time I was introduced to the name and story of Tiffany Thomas Lopez, who had gone to see Larry for chronic back pain when she was a student athlete at Michigan State. After he penetrated her with his fingers, she reported him to several MSU trainers. They dismissed her, telling her he was performing standard "inter-vaginal adjustments."[16] It was the first time my name wasn't the only one out there. I was filled with deep gratitude and grief for her. Everything was so tenuous still, the public response so mixed. Whether we would get a conviction, or even charges, really wasn't known yet. Even so, Tiffany took that leap, and what I learned about the cultural dynamics at MSU shattered me. *They knew. They knew before I even walked in the door.* By the time Larry began abusing me, at least two other women had already warned athletic trainers and a track coach that he was digitally penetrating his patients routinely. Both survivors had been assured it was normal medical treatment and—over their protestations and tears—were forced to go back for continued abuse.

I was hit by a fresh wave of discouragement and exhaustion. The institutions that had kept Larry in power showed no signs of being the least bit motivated to examine how a prolific pedophile had flourished on their campus and in their organization for decades. And to a large degree, this was because pressure wasn't being put in the right places.

Larry could have and *should* have been stopped. But no one did the right thing. No one even asked the right questions. Everyone assumed these women were confused—too uneducated to know what real medical treatment was. Their judgment wasn't trusted, not even enough to ask a question.

Tiffany wasn't likely going to do any more interviews, at least not for a while, John told me. But she'd come forward, and that meant the world to me. For the first time that night, Jacob and I started talking seriously about joining the civil suit. The civil process is usually the only way to hold institutions and individual people accountable for enabling abuse. Through this process, we could seek financial restitution for injuries and ask the court to order other steps be taken too, like changing the way abuse is reported or submitting to outside accountability and monitoring. Far too often, the people who run institutions are motivated by money and reputation. In such cases, the only way to make them change is to force consequences that are significant enough that they want to do better the next time. For five months, I'd held out hope that MSU and USAG would take the right steps because they *wanted* to do the right thing—that they would investigate to see what went wrong, admit it, and take specific steps to learn and change in the future. But instead, they'd denied over and over that anything had gone awry and explicitly refused to investigate. That left only one option to try to force change—the civil process.

I'd never intended to join—my abuse had happened so long before that the court was likely to throw my case out. Michigan law gave sexual assault survivors only a few years to file a civil case—time long since past. I already knew the law wasn't in my favor. But I also knew that someone had to fight the culture in both organizations that had allowed this to happen. If I joined the civil suit, I could speak publicly to all these things, even if my case was unlikely to go anywhere.

"Someone has to speak to these dynamics," I said to Jacob that night. "I've already given up all the details, my identity, my privacy . . . There's nothing left to protect."

He nodded. "Yeah, it does have to be dealt with. Is anyone else going to speak publicly?"

I shrugged. "Maybe at some point. Hopefully the more I'm out there the safer others will feel to come forward. But right now, no. And I want everyone else to have that choice."

We talked long into the night and revisited the topic in between Christmas festivities. I knew the attacks that would immediately be levied if I joined the civil suit. I was in it for money. For fame. But I also knew that the criminal process in this country goes only so far. It can stop a predator, but it can't change the culture around him. It rarely deals with enablers. To address those problems, you have to engage the civil process.

"I'll be a target very quickly," I acknowledged to Jacob one night. "They will probably try to get my claim separated and dismissed, but that will take a while. In the meantime, I will be able to speak to the cultural dynamics, since that's the point of the civil suit.

"And if we get really lucky," I added, "it might push this far enough that at least a few survivors will receive some level of justice. It would be worth it if we could do that for them."

Jacob nodded. "What's happened here is wrong, and it did terrible damage. It's got to be dealt with. And I do think you're right—joining the civil process is the only way to do that."

I bit my lip. "So to be very clear," I asked him, "you realize this means that we may carry all the weight and walk away with no justice in our case?"

"Yeah, I do. But if it educates people and enables you to deal with the underlying issues—and hopefully even helps some of the younger survivors get justice—I think it will be worth it." He paused. "I think you should do it."

I needed to check with one more person first, though.

The next day, I called Andrea and broached the issue with her. "I think I need to let you know that I am growing concerned with what I'm hearing about the institutional dynamics at MSU," I said.

She responded immediately, picking up on what I hadn't explicitly said. "Rachael, my loyalty isn't to the school. My loyalty is to what is right. That's my job, and it's unconnected to any civil cases that may or may not arise. If you feel there are institutional things that you need to speak to and that leads you to pursue a civil case, you do that."

Well. That was a clearer response than I expected to get, I thought with relief.

"You know if we make it to trial, the defense will attack you for filing a civil suit," she confirmed. "But I think you are perfectly able to handle those criticisms and explain your reasoning and need to do so. You do what you believe you need to do."

I was so grateful, both to hear that assurance and for an investigator who was really committed to the truth and what was right. So few survivors had someone like Andrea in their court. I hung up with her and called John Manly. I'd vetted his past work thoroughly when we started talking, and if I was going to work with anyone, I wanted it to be him.

"Yeah, I can take your case," he said. "Why don't you lie low and just see where we get, okay?"

I appreciated that. He knew the realities too. But it wasn't about lying low; it was about fighting as hard as possible while we had the platform. I also spoke with the firm in Michigan that John was partnering with. Was there anything I could do to help? I heard back from them quickly. I assured them they could use my name when they filed the claims. About eighteen of us would be filing at this point. They asked if I could make it up to Grand Rapids for the press conference where the suit would be announced. I talked with Jacob. The point was the message and pushing for change, so, yes, we would make that work.

Three days later, on January 10, 2017, I stepped into the law office of Drew Cooper & Anding, the Michigan-based firm that was working with John Manly. The office was calm and quiet, and I was relieved by the level of visible professionalism. The last thing I wanted or needed was a sexual assault case handled sensationally or raucously.

After a few moments, a tall, older man came out of an office and introduced himself as Stephen Drew, a founding partner of the firm. His demeanor reminded me very much of Keith's, the prosecutor who had been helping me for so long. Both men are gentle and full of compassion, but absolutely firm in their convictions and advocacy. Usually, this combination also translates into highly skilled, and if my initial sense was correct, Stephen would be wonderful to work with.

We were ushered into a meeting room and introduced to other members of the team, including Adam, one of the partners, and Robika, an attorney from Ohio who was the legal analyst for Adam and Mr. Drew. And for the first time, I met some of John Manly's team, though John himself didn't make it in.

We sat down at the table and discussed the upcoming press conference. Turnout was good. The room was already filling up. It would definitely be the largest audience I'd interviewed with so far.

"Where do things stand right now, in your professional opinion?" I asked.

"Well," Mr. Drew said with a slight smile, "they may try to target you right away, being that you are out front so much."

I nodded. *Well, we're both on the same page with that potential risk, anyway.* Next we discussed the layout of the press conference and how to handle questions and answers. After that, we walked into the room, which was already packed with journalists and cameras. I experienced the familiar internal conflict—gratitude for the significant crowd but frustration at being left in a position I never wanted to be in, forced to keep speaking because no one who bore responsibility was willing to actually take it. *It's never a choice. Not really. When it's the only way to make things stop, it's not really a choice.*

"We have filed a complaint this morning . . . ," Mr. Drew began. I took a deep breath. Not long afterward, I was able to make a statement laying out my story and explaining my motivation for speaking publicly and pursuing a civil suit:

> I think often of what I tell my own young children as I walk them through the process of making decisions. I tell them daily that there are only two motivations for doing the right thing—they can first

be motivated by love. They can choose what is right because they do not want the people around them to suffer the consequences of their wrong choices. Or they can be motivated by self-interest—because they themselves do not want to live with the consequences for their bad decisions. And I tell my children that love is the motivation that will give them joy and peace when doing the right thing is hard and hurts.

I paused. Love was what we needed. It was also what we lacked.

My greatest hope is that we reach a place in our culture where institutions and those in authority do what is right because they love. Because they care more about the people under their authority or influence. Because they prioritize the bodies and souls of children more than they prioritize their own self-interest. But we are not there yet. And until we reach that place, it is imperative that this civil process mandating necessary reforms be prioritized. For these reasons, I and so many other women who have been deeply wounded through Larry Nassar's sexual abuse, *and* through complacency and complicity of MSU and USAG, have filed a civil suit against these organizations.

For these reasons. In my memory, I saw every word of the complaint I'd reviewed earlier. Eighteen stories. Eighteen survivors. Eighteen people wounded who never needed to be. It was legitimate and right and good to fight for justice for them. Their wounds mattered. What they had been through mattered. And every blind eye turned, leading to the destruction of these women and little girls, mattered. I knew what I'd signed up for and how quickly the arrows would start to fly. I knew that even friends would begin to question both my character and my motivation. I knew there would be little to nothing I could do to defend against it. But I'd told the truth.

Love is the motivation that will give joy and peace when doing the right thing is hard and hurts.

22

THE MORE I LEARNED, the more my intuition was confirmed—stopping Larry had to be done publicly. Anonymous voices were too easily drowned out by his persona and the institutions that had so many reasons to look the other way. He had to be met without flinching where he was most confident—in the public eye.

But I didn't want to be right about this. I would have rather discovered that safety was there all along, if I had only reached for it when I was fifteen. I wanted to be able to say, "I was wrong. Someone would have listened." It wasn't just Larry I had trusted to do the right thing; it was everyone in the gymnastics and medical communities who knew Larry and had heard about his techniques. Knowing for sure that I wouldn't have been protected back then made the pain that much worse now. Coaches and athletic trainers in at least three different MSU sports departments were now known to have received explicit warnings and descriptions of Larry's abuse before or during the time I was seeing him. Each time, these coaches and trainers had sent the victims back for more abuse, assuring them that it was legitimate medical treatment. It *had* to be. After all, it was *Larry*.

I felt some vindication when, toward the end of January, Larry's medical license was finally suspended—though only temporarily.

The pressure on Larry increased just a few days later when a flurry of court motions revealed that new plaintiffs were seeking to join the existing lawsuit. Multiple former gymnasts anonymously alleged having told MSU gymnastics coach Kathie Klages exactly what Larry was doing, dating all the way back to 1997.[17] I felt anger burning in the pit of my stomach as I read the filed complaint. Kathie had waved a report form in front of one of them and said, "I could file this, but if I do . . . there will be serious consequences for you and Dr. Nassar."[18]

Apparently, ensuring the safety of a little girl wasn't worth it if it meant questioning a friend. Many officials implied that Larry's patients must have misunderstood what Larry was doing; we must have been confused. One of Larry's coworkers even told police: "I work with a lot of kids. They think everything between their legs is a vagina."[19] I did understand one thing: His colleagues knew it would have been much easier for everybody if we had simply been confused.

* * *

On February 7, 2017, Larry was charged with attempting to destroy the hard drive and external drives where he'd stored child pornography. A few days later, I got an email from Andrea. "Is there a time next week we can set up a time for you, me, and the assistant attorney general to have a conference call about upcoming steps?" she wrote. I swallowed my disappointment and frustration. I needed an in-person meeting.

When Jacob came home that evening, I told him hesitatingly, "We're going to have to make a trip to Michigan on really short notice." We'd been there only a few weeks before to begin the civil suit, and I knew it was going to be difficult for both of us to take more time off work and for him to miss more classes.

He sighed. "Do you think it's important? A phone call won't work?"

I shook my head emphatically. "No. I don't know anything about this attorney. If she doesn't understand the evidence or have the correct theory of the case, I'm going to have to push back on it. I can't wait until I'm testifying in court to find this stuff out!" I took a deep breath and tried to speak slower. "I have to start my relationship with her on the right foot. I can't do that over the phone."

Jacob knew how much this had weighed on me, and the rigidity in my voice wasn't hiding the stress terribly well. He came over and pulled me close.

"Okay," he said. "We'll make it work. Whatever we need to do, we'll make it work."

I contacted Andrea and asked if we could meet in person in Michigan. Much to my relief, she agreed. The next day, Angela Povilaitis, the assistant attorney general assigned to the case, emailed to tell me she could meet on either Wednesday or Thursday of that week. I blinked. It was already mid-afternoon on Monday. Trying to get everything organized to be able to leave with our three kids for Michigan so quickly was no small task. I called Jacob first and then my mom. "I think we're coming up tonight or tomorrow. Is that okay?" *And I guess I'd better get going on laundry.*

At midnight that night I replied to the assistant AG. We'd have to do Wednesday; Jacob couldn't cancel work to make Thursday an option. We began the six-hour drive to Michigan after Jacob got off work the next day. About five hours into our drive, Jonathan had a major meltdown when we stopped for gas. A few years before, he'd been hospitalized with severe neuro-logic symptoms, the cause of which had never been determined. Even so, he continued to have neurologic follow-up exams every six months. As I soothed him now, I remembered we'd had to postpone his last appointment so that I could go file my police report. My priority when we got back home would be to reschedule that appointment.

When we finally arrived at my parents' home after midnight, they wel-comed us with open arms, a snack for the kids, and an action plan for the next day. They'd rearranged their schedules to ensure they could care for the kids while we traveled to and from Detroit. We dropped into bed, exhausted, and then woke up, not enough hours later, for our meeting with Angela Povilaitis.

As Jacob drove us for nearly three hours, I scheduled press calls and reviewed the applicable case law for what I presumed would be my charges. Kathie Klages had resigned hours earlier, following reports that she'd asked the MSU gym-nastics team to sign a card for Larry after he was arrested. Apparently, she'd told concerned parents that the pornography had likely been planted on his hard drives. *Planted?* I sighed in frustration when a reporter called and asked for my perspective. At the time Larry's hard drive had been seized, only Jamie Dantzscher and I had spoken publicly, and Jamie had been and still was anonymous. I had three kids and precisely no time to somehow plant 37,000 images of child porn on Larry's hard drives all the way from Louisville. *I'm pretty confident Jamie didn't fly out from California to bury hard drives in Larry's trash either,* I thought. Many things seemed obvious to me by now, and one of them was that the problems at MSU ran a lot deeper than one rogue doctor.

When Jacob and I arrived for our meeting with Angela, we approached the large desk in the building's entrance to check in with security.

"Who are you heading up to see?" the security guard asked.

I paused. I realized I had no idea how to pronounce "Povilaitis."

"I have an appointment with an assistant prosecuting attorney in the AG's office," I offered.

"Can you give me the name?" he asked again, pen poised. *Yeah . . . no. I definitely can't spell it either.* I quickly pulled up the email with Angela's last name on my phone, and soon Jacob and I found ourselves sitting in a basic office, waiting patiently to meet the prosecutor whose name I couldn't pronounce. A few minutes later, the door opened, and a woman in a smart blue suit came forward, extending her hand.

"Hi, Rachael," she said with a warm smile. "I'm Angela Povilaitis." *So that's how you say it,* I noted. "You can just call me Angie. Pleasure to meet you."

She shook hands with Jacob and gestured for us to follow her, explaining as we walked that Andrea wasn't feeling well and hadn't been able to make it. On the way back to our meeting room, Angie introduced us to Robyn, the other attorney assigned to this case. She seemed competent and caring but wouldn't be able to join our meeting that morning. Once we had sat down in the conference room, Angie placed the thick case file on the table, rested her forearms on its smooth surface, and leaned over a bit.

"Rachael, it is just so good to finally meet you!"

I smiled back. She was definitely warmer than I'd envisioned.

"I'd like to start by explaining to you the approach our office takes to these cases," she began. "We call it 'victim-centered, offender-focused.'"

I smiled a bit more. The approach was good. Very good. A trauma-informed approach focused on caring for the survivors and listening to their voices, while ensuring that the pressure of the law and court process was placed as much as possible on the perpetrator.

"So a bit of background on me personally . . . ," she continued. I listened as she described her work history. Her credentials were solid. She'd prosecuted some significant cases. "I'll be honest, though," she confessed, "this is definitely the largest case I've done, and the highest profile. There are unique challenges associated with this case that we're really having to work through."

I appreciated her honesty. Candor was far more preferable to false bravado.

"As we've focused on survivors in these past cases, we've been able to do some really meaningful things—things I hope to be able to do with Nassar survivor cases too," Angie said intently. She then began explaining one of her former cases, when she'd held a first-time meeting of survivors who had all come forward against the same abuser but who had never met one another. I looked at her in surprise as I noticed tears in her eyes. "I still get emotional thinking about those cases," she said in a softer tone.

I felt the weight begin to lift off my shoulders. *The more you love, the harder you fight.* Angie's work experience, coupled with her passion and textbook-perfect approach, would make her a formidable opponent for Larry. She truly cared, and that was the strongest guarantee that she would fight for justice in the courts and not back down just because the case wasn't convenient or easy.

Angie laughed as she dabbed one eye. "My nickname around the office is The Hammer," she said, "but I get pretty emotional over this stuff.

"So let's talk about your case," she said, shifting gears again. She then began to walk through the elements of first-degree assault, the prongs we could argue, and the case law (or lack thereof) for each prong. Her analysis perfectly mirrored what Keith and I had already discussed.

"We've got some decisions to make here," she began, "and your voice in this is what we're going to follow, okay?"

I nodded. I appreciated that.

"So there are two ways we can charge your case." She laid out what I already knew. First-degree sexual assault could be proven by showing either that Larry was an authority figure who used his position to abuse or that he had caused severe emotional distress. "The good thing about arguing both is that it gives us two shots at proving it. The difficult thing . . ." She paused.

"It will require a lot of specific testimony," I filled in. "It has to be pled with specificity, so I'll have to testify extensively about the impact on me."

Angie nodded. "Yeah," she said sympathetically.

"And Jacob will likely need to be a witness, too, and will have to be sequestered," I continued. "So he won't be able to be with me in court."

Angie nodded again.

"I'd have to testify about my journal." I sighed. I'd have to read it in open court. Larry would read it. It would get scrutinized and dissected and disseminated for the world to see. I paused, then added calmly, "I think you need to argue both prongs. I appreciate you respecting my choices, but I don't want to look back and regret not giving it everything. I don't want anything left on the table. We only get one shot at this." I paused again. "Did you happen to see the memo I put with my file way back when I first reported?"

She shook her head.

"It's written more like a letter since I wasn't sure who would get it, but it puts a basic outline to the evidence I have and what I can testify to. I do believe there is ample evidence for proving severe emotional distress."

Angie nodded eagerly. "Yeah, why don't you resend that to me when you get home? And if you are good with it, we'll argue both in your case."

I nodded back, squeezing my hands together under the table. "I think it has to be done that way. I was planning on it from the beginning, and I understand what that means."

"Okay, then," she said, "let's talk about overall strategy."

Yes! the attorney in me whispered. Horrific as the subject matter was, I still loved the deductive logic of law. Putting evidence into the right spaces and crafting a smooth legal argument was like putting an intricate puzzle together. It was eminently satisfying. And after so many months of Jacob patiently listening to my musings, it was a relief to *finally* be freely discussing the law and strategy.

Angie explained that Larry's abuse crossed county lines, since it was alleged to have occurred in both Ingham County at Michigan State and in Eaton

County at Twistars USA Gymnastics Club. A few survivors had cases that could be charged in multiple jurisdictions.

"What's so interesting to me is that he keeps denying using any penetrative techniques!" she said in a tone of genuine surprise.

I responded immediately. "So you *do* realize he's not arguing that he does internal pelvic work?" I said eagerly. This had been such a point of confusion for so many people, and it drastically affected the way in which the case should be argued.

"Oh, clearly!" Angie said animatedly. "He's denied it repeatedly." She listed the places where he specifically denied internal work. "That statement by his attorney was just an attempt to confuse things. You don't do 'technical' penetration if you are doing internal pelvic floor work!"

I felt like throwing my hands up and yelling "Thank you!" but opted to stay calm and reasonable.

"It completely changes how we argue the case," Angie said, launching into a discussion of expert testimony and the different role it would have played if Larry had responded by claiming to do internal work.

A flood of relief swept over me, almost pushing me to tears of thankfulness. Angie understood. She really, truly understood. She knew the case. She knew the law. She knew the medical dynamics. She understood the theories to argue. For the first time, I didn't have to teach all of it. She already knew.

My greatest fear for sixteen years had been the possibility of having to rely on a weak investigator and prosecutor or, worse, ones who didn't care. I'd approached coming forward fully anticipating having battles to wage or, at a minimum, having to push for what I knew needed to happen. But instead, I got Andrea and Angie. I could trust them. And they were exceptionally skilled in their fields.

For the first time, the survivors of Larry's abuse weren't fighting to be heard. We finally had someone fighting for us.

23

WE RETURNED HOME TO LOUISVILLE and waited on edge for news about the upcoming charges. "Hopefully next week" was all we'd been told. But the first big hurdle in stopping Larry came that Friday, when the survivor whose abuse he'd already been charged with took the stand in a preliminary examination. She was the sole known survivor of abuse in a nonmedical context.

In Michigan, criminal cases typically require a preliminary examination, which is essentially a shortened trial overseen by a judge. The purpose is to determine whether the prosecution has enough evidence to warrant a full trial in the future.

For the first time, Larry's abuse would be challenged in a legal setting. Angie and Andrea both said this survivor was strong. She had to be, given everything she'd been through. But I ached for her too. Testifying meant digging up memories, remembering painful details, and putting them into words. She'd opted to remain anonymous for now, but she'd grown up in Michigan, where her family still lived, so it was possible people would recognize her anyway.

The press was intensely interested in this hearing, and Larry and his team seemed determined to wield that to his advantage. The prosecution had requested a closed courtroom—no media or public allowed—and Larry's defense attorneys had initially indicated they would not push back on that request. But that morning, Larry and his attorneys walked into court and demanded the courtroom be as open as possible. Cameras. Reporters. Recordings. Only the survivor's face and name should be protected, they argued. Everything else was fair game. Angie presented a number of options that could have protected the survivor while ensuring freedom of information, but the judge made the decision to allow the media in. The survivor's request, and the protections she could have legally been offered, didn't matter. Larry got what Larry wanted. Because the court gave it to him.

Larry may have walked into court with a victory that morning, but he didn't walk out with one. The survivor was strong, and her testimony was compelling. But seeing what unfolded also cemented a decision for me.

When the kids were in bed that night, I wrote to Angie:

> This absolutely solidifies my resolve (if it was possible to solidify it any further) that I want to make the request for the courtroom to be 100 percent open for my testimony, including allowing video, name, everything.
>
> I do NOT want him to go into the courtroom having won any victory, no matter how small. [It] puts him in the position of power starting the hearing, and I do not want that to be the case.
>
> I do NOT want any suggestion whatsoever that I will be intimidated, unnerved, upset, or embarrassed by my testimony. I want him to know that won't work, and that he isn't in control, and I am confident there is nothing to fear.

The more Larry's team felt they could not win, the better the chance they would want to avoid a trial. And I knew that a defense attorney who doesn't want to be embarrassed publicly is motivated to help a guilty client see when a plea deal is the better option.

> I do think this is an excellent opportunity for victims to potentially see inside the courtroom and know they are able to confront their

abuser and do not need to feel shame at testifying, because the shame only belongs on one person—their abuser.

I was trained as an attorney, and this process was intimidating and exhausting to *me*. How much more would that be true for survivors who had no background in the legal system and who had never even seen the inside of a courtroom?

The idea of offering graphic descriptions and depictions of what had happened to me while testifying in an open court and the thought of providing horrific mental pictures of things I never wanted anyone to think about made me want to throw up. But I also knew there was nothing left to protect. My identity as Victim C would be immediately revealed by the charges. There was much to gain simply by allowing the courtroom to be open. Maybe another survivor would see what the process looked like and think, *I can do this too*. And maybe if my court hearing was fully open, the judge would be willing to close it off for the survivors who would testify after me.

Meanwhile, charges were still set to come out on Wednesday, February 22. I'd hoped they would come out before a major news report on USAG and Larry's abuse was scheduled to air, but the segment ran the week before. Former Team USA gymnasts Jamie Dantzscher, Jeanette Antolin, and Jessica Howard all came forward publicly on the program, and I was thankful that this report would publicize the story further. But it was a sharp reminder of how easily Larry was able to confuse people when the report emphasized that the interpelvic work *could* be legitimate but failed to mention that Larry wasn't trained in those procedures and that he had repeatedly and emphatically denied doing internal pelvic floor work. That point was key. It was *the most* critical piece of the story—the one demonstrating that there was no medical cover for what Larry had done.

Angie and Andrea know, I reminded myself with a sigh. But it was discouraging. The report had been an opportunity to publicize this crucial detail to a huge audience, and it had been missed. Instead, a veneer, however thin, that Larry might have been doing legitimate treatment remained. The segment reminded me that even professional journalists who want to report fairly and accurately can become mired in the medical and legal complexities of a case.

That report was fresh on my mind that Wednesday when the attorney general announced twenty-two new charges of sexual assault against Larry, including three counts for his crimes against me. Because I would be called as a witness in the upcoming preliminary hearing, Jacob and I were encouraged not to schedule vacations for a while. With much sorrow, I canceled my plans to teach at my beloved summer camp. I had taught there every summer but one for the past decade. "I need one week to be something other than Victim C," I pled with Jacob. "I want to be *me* for just one week." I felt as if my identity had been swallowed up by the public designation "victim." I loved using my legal training to teach; I didn't want to use it to be a victim. But like so many other things, I didn't get a choice.

• • •

By this point, Jacob and I had finally changed churches.

For months, we had often talked into the early morning hours about our grief over our situation there. How many conversations with elders should we try to initiate? How often had we asked for meetings that just didn't seem to materialize? We both felt completely drained of the energy to keep fighting to be understood.

One night Jacob and I stood in the kitchen after sending yet another email trying to explain our position to the church's leaders. He wrapped his arms around me and I dropped my head against his chest, exhausted.

"This would be so much easier if the place that should be the safest wasn't adding to the pain," I whispered.

He held me tighter. "It always hurts the worst when it's closest to home."

So now at long last we were tentatively testing the waters at a small church twenty minutes from our home.

"Do you want me to give the pastors a heads-up before we visit?" Jacob had asked.

I didn't. I would have preferred to be invisible. And I knew all too well that saying anything at all sometimes made people assume I wanted attention or "credit," and I had no energy left to keep fighting those misperceptions.

Jacob asked me what I thought about the church after that first week, but I was too worn out to even know. A few weeks later, though, the main teaching pastor emailed Jacob. He'd searched for our social media profiles to make a friend request, and the Google results weren't what he'd expected. He said he was so sorry. He was praying for us and was ready to help. I was thankful that he knew our situation and I didn't have to explain it. Very tentatively, we began to try to settle in.

One month after the AG filed charges in my case, the Title IX office finally released their findings. Larry had violated their sexual harassment policies. He'd sexually touched me without consent. For the first time ever, someone had called it like it was, and Larry hadn't been able to twist his way out of it. It was still a long road to a guilty verdict and a just sentence, but it created a huge public shift. Most important, Larry's explicit denials of using penetrative techniques were contained in that report. I reviewed the Title IX report and my police file and found, much to my disgust and relief, that Nassar's colleagues—including the ones who had vouched for him in 2014—also explicitly denied that Larry did any internal pelvic floor work.

MSU chose not to release the full Title IX report publicly, but I could, and did, immediately. Because it contained so many personal details, I hated to do so, but Larry's denials needed to be out there, on record.

"This is really critical information," I explained to journalists over and over. "Check out the statements here . . ." I sent them page numbers, highlights, and quotes. "If possible, can you link to the full report?" I also passed the report on to my civil attorneys, redacting specific information to keep the identities of another survivor and witness protected, and then asked them to release it to their entire media list. It would likely hurt my civil claim, but it helped with the overall goal of holding Larry accountable, so I wanted it out there.

When journalists contacted me to ask for clarification or my response, I knew they were on deadline and always tried to respond immediately. While picking out sweet potatoes in the grocery store and at the same time trying to keep the baby from snatching my phone and the two older ones from tickling each other as they sat in the cart, I would tell a reporter, "No, this isn't a shift; he isn't changing his story." Now that I had Larry's denials in writing, I was going to do everything I could to make it count.

For days after the Title IX report was released, I would feed the kids breakfast, check my email for updates, and thank each reporter who had run my statement. *You will need good working relationships with these journalists in the months to come*, I would tell myself. Then I would take a deep breath as I looked around my messy kitchen. *Okay, we are now hours behind our routine.* Then I'd try to regroup—and follow the pattern that wasn't really a pattern, every day.

●　●　●

On March 29, we received a stunning blow. The first case—the one that had already been through a preliminary hearing—had been sent to the judge who would preside over all our cases in Ingham County. And at the defense's request, that judge had issued a gag order. A *sweeping* gag order, essentially giving Larry everything he and his attorneys had asked for while binding me, and anyone else who might speak publicly, to silence. *Surely*, I had thought, *the voices of victims so long silenced will be seen as a priority. Surely the court will realize the importance of survivors being able to speak—considering the fact that Larry has gotten away with sexually assaulting children for decades—precisely because he's always controlled the narrative.*

The decision to challenge the gag order had to come from the attorney general's office, so I waited impatiently to hear from Angie, who was still in court. Finally, hours later, she called with the answer I was dreading.

"I was given clear direction from my office as to our position on this issue," she said.

I sensed frustration in her voice. I pulled up the PDF of the order she emailed me and read it in dismay. It was broad and sweeping. No disseminating information or releasing documents publicly. No discussing Larry Nassar's guilt. No comments on the strengths or weaknesses of the case. No comments about the reliability of any witnesses, including Larry or other survivors. Binding on all parties. All current *and potential* witnesses, and attorneys for current or potential witnesses. That wasn't just me. That meant Jacob and my mom. It meant anyone who had any connection to survivors or to Larry. I stared in shock at the handwritten notes across the typed page where the judge had added to or tweaked Larry's request.

For thirty years Larry had had complete control of the narrative surrounding his practices with patients. The one and only thing I had to challenge his account—my voice—had now been taken from me again. Even worse, the order would stay in place until proceedings were finished. Arguably, even appeals. If this stood, I would be silenced *for years*. And so would everyone else. I called John Manly immediately.

"This has to be challenged," I insisted. "It's unbelievably overbroad and vague."

John responded quickly and firmly. We agreed that there was no way this should hold up to a constitutional challenge. "We're filing a suit. Are you okay being the named plaintiff challenging the order?"

I laughed. Okay? Yeah. It was okay. I was *asking* for it. There was no way I was going to let survivors' voices be shut down without a fight.

Until now, I hadn't been able to fight directly for any of the other one-hundred-plus survivors who had filed suit or called the police by this point. But now I could. Five days later, the suit was filed. Jamie Dantzscher, Lindsey Lemke, and I were the named plaintiffs suing Judge Rosemarie Aquilina, who would be presiding over my trial—*if* we got that far.

Days later, I picked up a call from John Manly. "Congrats! You just won your first federal motion." A temporary restraining order had been granted, putting a hold on the gag order until a full hearing could be held.

The law of unintended consequences finally bit back against Larry and his attorneys. Rather than making survivors cower further, the gag order galvanized them to speak up. Several took advantage of the momentary freedom produced by the temporary restraining order and came forward publicly on their social media profiles or to the local press, determined never to be silenced again.

The day after the temporary restraining order took effect, I was scrolling through Facebook after putting the kids to bed when I stopped suddenly.

"I'm so proud of my teammate," a friend of mine had posted. Her teammate had come forward as a Nassar survivor. But that teammate . . . had also been my younger sister's teammate.

"No, no, no!" I cried out as I clicked the link. Sterling had been at the gym when I talked to Jackie, but I never knew she had seen Larry. She hadn't been on my team, but she'd been a child athlete when I was a coach in training. I'd occasionally coached her team when a temporary fill-in was needed. I hadn't seen her in years. She'd since grown up and gotten married, but all I could see as I watched her interview was the little girl I'd met so long ago. The one who used to wear a ponytail on the top of her head. I remembered when she stuck her first back walkover on the beam. As a coach, I'd occasionally taped her injury but hadn't known Larry was the one treating it. She'd somehow escaped then without being abused but had gone back years later for a sports-related injury she suffered in college. She had no reason not to. Larry was, after all, the best.

Jacob poked his head out of the office. "Are you okay?"

"I didn't know" was all I could say through the tears. "I didn't know she was seeing Larry, or I would have told her mom right away."

That was one of the worst nights for me.

● ● ●

The next week we waited to find out the date for the hearing to fight the gag order. It meant making a trip to Michigan right before I'd have to testify in the preliminary examination, but Jacob and I had agreed we needed to be there for both. As soon as the date was announced, we quickly made the necessary schedule and travel arrangements—only to be told the day before the scheduled hearing that it had been canceled because Judge Aquilina had opted to vacate the first gag order and rewrite it. If we wanted to challenge this one, we'd have to file yet another challenge.

The new order was still ridiculously overbroad. Larry's attorneys announced that they intended to name every victim and every civil attorney as a potential witness so that none of us could speak until any potential appeals were final. Possibly decades from now. It was beyond frustrating. It was also relatively pointless, because in an effort to maintain constitutionality, the new order specifically exempted discussion or information that related to civil claims. This essentially meant I could say anything I wanted so long as I framed it as a discussion about my civil suit for sexual abuse rather than the criminal one. This revised order wouldn't go into effect until witness lists were officially filed with the court, which most likely wouldn't be for a few months. So for now I could speak and prepare to challenge the order when it went into effect.

May 12—the date of the preliminary exam where I would take the stand for the first time—still loomed before us. The judge had once again refused to close the court, determining that only survivors' names and faces could be protected. I was doubly glad I hadn't even asked for it to be closed in my case. The importance of the press having access and getting information made public became patently obvious just a few days later, when journalists uncovered a series of emails from Larry's boss at MSU, Dean William Strampel, the head of the college of osteopathy. I felt sick as I read the email chain, which had been sent right after I'd filed my police report and come forward publicly. Dean Strampel had assured staff that Larry would be off for just a short time, signing a personal email to Larry with "Good luck. I'm on your side."

The day the *IndyStar* released my video testimony—the one detailing the graphic things no one was ever supposed to know—Dean Strampel had forwarded it to others at MSU. "Cherry on the Cake of my day!" he wrote.[20]

Later that night, I penned an open letter to Dean Strampel:

> I wonder, as you forwarded my video interview around and made light of what this would do to <u>your</u> day, did you once think about what my day was like when my image and details about my body—which no one was ever supposed to know—became national headlines?

There was vindication for me in the emails too. Because only a few days later, Dean Strampel's tone had changed. Things were moving "outside of my control," he wrote to Larry. Because of the press reports, victims had come forward, and it became obvious that Larry hadn't followed the agreed-upon protocol after he was investigated in 2014. He couldn't save Larry anymore.

I also penned an open letter to MSU president Lou Anna Simon, who had recently instructed leaders at the school that predators like Larry were "virtually impossible to stop."

> "Virtually impossible to stop"? . . . President Simon, if this is what you have been told, you need new advisors.
> Are predators highly skilled? Many are.
> Do they sometimes get away with predatory behavior for years? Unfortunately, yes.

Is it because they are "virtually impossible" to catch? Emphatically no.

Instead, predators are left to prey on children for years because the adults in authority either miss or refuse to see the many clear warning signs. . . .

"Virtually impossible to stop"? . . .

That's not true.

It has never been true.

But it does shift the blame. That makes it feel better, doesn't it? Better, at least, for those who failed to protect the children. For those of us who were victims of this man, it's a bitter reminder that our voices counted for nothing. . . .

Children don't need more authority figures who absolve themselves by claiming that it is "virtually impossible" to prevent child abuse. They need leaders who have integrity and passion to defend them—no matter who the abuser, and no matter who the enabler.

Few survivors have leaders who are willing to fight for them. But now it was different. Now the situation was outside of Larry's control—or that of anyone else who would prefer to cover it up.

24

ON THE MORNING OF MAY 12, 2017, I carefully donned my new blue business suit. I hadn't bought a new suit or heels in years, but Jacob had taken me on a shopping date a few weeks before, insisting the outfit would get plenty of use. I wore it for the first time to the preliminary hearing in Ingham County.

"Do you want coffee?" he asked as we drove in the dusky morning. I shook my head. I felt far too sick.

A few minutes later, I asked more sharply than I intended, "Can we just . . . not have music, please?" Jacob quickly turned off the radio.

When we got to the courthouse, we were led to a small room reserved for us. I glanced at other conference rooms as we passed, doors tightly closed. I knew other survivors were behind them, waiting to see if they would testify that day. I wanted more than anything to give them hugs or squeeze their hands. But I couldn't even see them or know their names. *Legally*, we were doing it together, but *practically*, we each had to do it alone. We were literally feet apart, but everything was carefully orchestrated to ensure we never saw one another. Even before I could go to the restroom, someone had to be sure the halls were cleared.

Shortly after we arrived, my dad, brother, sister-in-law, and a family friend showed up to offer their support. My mom had stayed home to care for our kids. My dad and brother would sit with Jacob while he waited. Neither he nor my mom could be in court with me because they were potential witnesses. My sister-in-law and our friend had offered to be in the courtroom. I knew I'd be far too focused to have any idea of who was in the room, but the fact that they cared meant a great deal.

The morning felt as if it dragged on forever. I was scheduled to testify first, but there were plenty of procedural issues to handle before that. Finally Andrea came back to get me. "You ready?"

Never. And always. I straightened my suit coat and tucked a stray wisp of hair behind my ear. "Ready."

• • •

I felt light-headed as Andrea opened the courtroom door and we stepped inside. I made a point not even to glance toward Larry. I hadn't seen him since I was sixteen. I wanted him to know that he had no control anymore. *What he thinks, says, and does is irrelevant to the truth.*

Angie pointed me quickly to Judge Donald Allen, and I stepped into the witness box. I refused to dwell on the reality that every word I spoke would be recorded, transmitted, and out there forever.

I raised my right hand, swore to tell the truth, and sat down. *Calm. Relaxed. Nonthreatening.* "So sweet and innocent . . . but when you get hold of something . . . you just won't let go!" I'd heard it so many times. *Just be that pit bull once more*, I told myself.

I noted everything as I began answering Angie's foundational questions. The gallery and press box were full. I knew Larry had family there, though many of the survivors did not because their family members might be called as witnesses. The press box was directly across from me. The room was tighter than I thought it would be, and Larry was closer than I'd expected, but I continued to avoid so much as a glance in his direction.

Angie began by asking me general questions to establish my background and allow me to find my footing in the courtroom. How long had I been married? How many children did I have? Where did I grow up?

Eventually, Angie began to transition. Did I ever have an injury that led to me seeing a doctor? Which doctor? What did I know about him?

Through her questions, she wove the narrative establishing Larry's reputation and the trust he engendered at the time I'd consulted with him.

"I want to make sure we're talking about the same person," she continued. "Can you just . . . can you point to the person you know as Dr. Nassar? Describe for me what he's wearing."

For the first time, I looked in Larry's direction. He raised his head to look back and meet my eyes. I pointed toward him and intentionally held the gesture longer than necessary.

"He is wearing a striped suit," I responded crisply, still matching his gaze. *Make him look away first.* Larry had spent decades mastering the art of silent control and dominance. I wanted him to know that I saw the subtle manipulation and the hidden power plays—I saw them, and it was over. I continued to meet his gaze until his eyes shifted away and turned back to his papers.

I turned my attention back to Angie. We were discussing what had happened during my first appointment. "And the other hand . . . please tell me again where that went." I remembered everything Larry had said and all the videos and files he'd produced to quell concerns for years. It felt disgusting to be forced to sit and describe what Larry had done right in front of him, knowing he shared the same memories. Knowing he relished them.

The questions continued. How much did I know about my own anatomy? Had I experimented sexually at that point? Did I use tampons? Was there any hesitation in my memory? Detail after clarifying detail. "Describe for me" became the worst—and most useful—question. What *exactly* was he doing? How did it feel? What was my emotional response? What did I think?

"It was clear to me this was a normal method of treatment. There was no pause, no hesitation. His movements were very practiced, very rehearsed." *He is calculated, manipulative, intentional, and skilled. See it,* I willed the judge.

"Describe for me . . . ," Angie asked again as we moved into my second appointment with Larry. What kind of motion was it? I bit my tongue momentarily and then demonstrated with my own hand. I heard the camera shutters clicking, and I felt sick but pushed the feeling down.

As I had learned more about the practices of predators, I'd concluded that Larry was a very victim-centered offender. He derived pleasure from our emotional response and physical pain. He *wanted* to know what his victims thought and felt. And I'd guarded my responses so carefully that he never would. Now I had to sit in open court for hours and give him exactly what he'd always wanted. Intensely private information, things that would never be casually mentioned even in a gathering of close friends, were being livestreamed and recorded.

Angie was able to weave all the pieces of the case together in a way I knew would communicate clearly to the jury. I felt at peace knowing I didn't need to carry the legal analysis; she knew the right questions to ask and how to hit every element, laying out the relevant facts, elements of the statute, and the definitions to help the jury understand the legal elements and how the facts fit into her legal argument.

As the lead plaintiff, I had to use the technical, legal, and medical terms so the judge would have context for what was being described. I worked specific detail into each of my answers, knowing that the witnesses who came after me might not have the same level of clarity, or even the same vocabulary, that I now had. I wanted my descriptions to be crystal clear, so that if those witnesses could not reach that level of specificity, the words they had would be enough to jog the judge's memory of my descriptions. I wanted to lay the foundation for them as cleanly and precisely as possible.

We were laying the cultural foundation too. Why hadn't I realized it was abuse? Where was my mom? Why did I not question anything? Once I did realize that at least one action had been assault, why didn't I speak up? I explained the freezing response. *This is normal.* I wanted every person who heard me to understand. *Don't blame the survivor for not fighting back. They wish so much more than you do that they could have.*

And why did I not tell my mom? "I didn't know how to reconcile who he was supposed to be with what he had done. And I didn't want to give it words. Words make it real." We laid the foundation to show grooming, habit, predatory behavior.

How had his actions affected my life? My marriage? Childbirth? Work? Everything? Why did I finally speak up? And why did I choose to do so publicly?

We both knew this attack would be coming during cross-examination. Angie was giving me the chance to lay the groundwork first.

"Larry Nassar was in such a position of authority, and he was surrounded by such powerful institutions that I was confident an anonymous voice would not be enough." I looked over at Larry as I spoke and met his glance. "Somebody had to meet him where he was most comfortable and do it publicly and in a way that left no doubt." I thought of the survivors sequestered away in separate rooms, behind doors I couldn't open. "I also thought it was very important to give other victims hope and to give them a voice. I am a victim, and I know that you don't talk unless you think you are safe. And I felt that they would need a name and a face to know that they were safe to come forward.

"Doing this publicly . . . has greatly compounded the effects of the sexual assault. It is not a move someone takes because they want healing. . . . This is not me finding my voice. This is me trying to protect the women I couldn't protect for sixteen years. . . . There are things that are more important than what I want and more important than the cost to me. . . .

"I can stop him, but I can't stop the person who rises to take his place if I don't talk about why he was able to continue abusing."

Finally, more than an hour and a half after we'd started, Angie said, "I have no further questions at this time."

The judge glanced at the clock. It was past eleven. "How are you doing?" the judge asked, glancing my way.

"I'm fine," I answered honestly. After a moment the judge consulted with one of Larry's defense attorneys, Shannon Smith. Would she prefer a quick break or an early lunch before resuming? She opted for an early lunch. No one asked me. Like with so many other things, I didn't get a choice, or even a chance to give input. I'd been waiting sixteen years; I'd rather get it done. It didn't seem like asking too much to suggest that Larry and his team didn't get priority when I was the one having to testify.

The bailiff called a recess, and I stepped out of the box near the door where Andrea stood, waiting for it to be unlocked. Without ceremony, she tersely, though not unkindly, moved me to the other side of the walkway. I could sense the heightened tension in her and briefly wondered why, but

I was too exhausted to think more about it. I didn't realize then how closely Larry, who was supposed to allow me to exit the courtroom before even standing, had been walking behind me as I left the room. I was too worn out and stressed to be aware of my surroundings, though I didn't even realize it at the time. Andrea had noticed, however, and sought to shield me. It was another reminder of how much survivors must rely on the court to protect them.

We then took what was—in my opinion—a completely unnecessary break for just over an hour. I picked at a salad and waited. Finally, at 12:34, I was called back in for cross-examination. From what I'd heard, Matt Newburg, Larry's other attorney, intended to handle cross-examination for the rest of the survivors who would testify, but Shannon was going to handle mine. I'd researched her work and her methods as soon as Larry had hired her. Her firm, of which she was a founding partner, was dedicated to defending those charged with sexual crimes. As a lawyer, I agreed that everyone was entitled to a good defense, but *how* an attorney did that defense said a lot. I had reviewed her cases, tone, and interactions—I had seen how lawyers like her operated and sensed how this was going to go.

Shannon began questioning me in a friendly tone, as if trying to establish a favorable rapport. "Your medical records show you were also experiencing . . . some scary symptoms that needed to be *really* investigated," she remarked earnestly.

Then she moved on to the appointments themselves. "You did not ask Dr. Nassar, 'Hey, can you explain to me what you're doing?' . . . correct?" I had never told my mom or asked her to clarify or expressed any concern whatsoever, had I?

I sensed where she was going. She was attempting to lay the groundwork to show I'd only convinced myself I'd been abused later—or worse, made up the story as grounds for a civil suit.

I responded immediately. It hadn't seemed necessary to clarify what he was doing because I knew at the time that interpelvic procedures could be used and I'd presumed that's what Larry was doing.

Then she began asking questions as if gathering basic facts. Had the contact I believed was abuse happened at every single appointment? No? Hmmm

. . . well, was it fair to say then, that at the appointments where it happened, Larry was treating a different part of my body?

"He was treating you for issues that included problems with your hip, problems with your back, problems really with what I guess I would term the 'core of your body.' Do you agree with that? And also he was treating areas that are closely connected . . . all right in this core area." She gestured around, pointing to various areas on her body, and laughed. "[I'm] trying really hard here!" she chirped at the judge. I knew exactly where she was going—attempting to argue that the "sexual" contact wasn't sexual at all but was necessitated by the areas Larry was treating.

I wasn't about to give that ground. I picked the most glaring and obvious deviation Larry had made from treating the core and responded calmly and pleasantly.

"I don't think the clitoris is connected to that, so I would take exception with that."

She rushed in. "That's not what I asked, though."

I smiled inwardly. Actually, yes, it was.

"Glutes and back," I responded, clarifying her attempts again. "I was not seeking treatment for any abdominal or frontal pelvic pain." That exchange was all it took for her tone to rapidly change.

She tried again. "Is it fair to say that one of the things that really concerned you was that you did not see these techniques explicitly in your medical records?"

"No," I answered calmly. "What really concerned me was knowing that I had been sexually assaulted when he massaged my breast, and that caused me to question the external genitalia contact. . . . Finding out that they were not charted was further concern, but that was not my initial concern."

She tried once more, asking whether there was ever a moment in time when I could pinpoint knowing I'd been abused.

I tried to keep the surprise off my face. Had she really asked such an open-ended question? She was giving me the opportunity to push back and rebut the defense I saw she was trying to build. So I graphically described Larry's erection, visible arousal, and abuse. "That is the moment in time I knew I had been sexually assaulted."

Shannon glanced down at her notes. Didn't Larry have to treat my ribs?

"No," I responded clearly.

"Okay." She paused. "At the same time, though, Dr. Nassar—we've already established—is the gold standard. He has his own way of doing things."

I felt an odd sense of relief. This was seriously all they had. As if Larry had invented some bizarre, unknown medical technique that somehow required him to put his fingers inside little girls anytime they had an injury. This actually *was* the best defense they had. And it was absurd.

Shannon pressed on. "So your experiences, we can agree, with other physical therapists, other doctors, other people, was never the same as what you experienced with Dr. Nassar."

"Thank God, no!" I responded with emphasis. The glance she shot let me know it wasn't the answer she'd hoped for.

She circled around the same line of questioning a few more times before transitioning to my friendship with Ashley, the teammate I'd been with at a joint medical appointment where we'd both been abused. I hadn't provided her name to anyone, even investigators, out of respect for her privacy.

After I'd confirmed the basic details about that appointment and my conversation with Ashley on our drive home, Shannon looked back at me, pen poised. "Can I please have her name?"

I felt anger rising in me for the first time. *Did you really just ask me to give you the name of a sexual assault survivor in an open courtroom with the cameras running?*

"You may not," I responded firmly. It was one thing to target me. I'd made myself a target, and I'd done it on purpose, because someone had to. But I couldn't believe she was going after the privacy of a survivor who was legally entitled to privacy—a survivor I'd come forward ultimately to protect.

"You have actually had a fight with this friend about coming forward in this case; is that correct?"

"No, I would not characterize it that way. She has asked me to keep her out of it, and to the best of my ability I intend to," I said firmly.

"If, at some point, the court orders that you release the name, will you provide the name to the attorney general's office?" she asked.

I kept my tone even and calm. "If the court so orders, I will do so."

She began circling once again around how I could possibly know that Larry's treatments weren't medical. I wasn't, after all, an osteopathic physician myself.

"*You* did not see any reason to have any kind of treatment that may have resembled pelvic floor treatment; is that a fair statement?" she pressed.

"I did not see any reason," I responded.

Soon she pressed further. "It's possible still that he knows something you didn't know, with his training and expertise in this field?"

"No, ma'am." I was completely confident at this point that Larry knew absolutely nothing about pelvic floor treatment that I didn't know. In fact, I suspected he actually knew less than I knew, given the way he'd gotten away with it for so long.

"Are you suggesting that the stretches and exercises he gave you to do helped, but not the physical manual treatments he did on you?" she asked.

Once again I graphically explained every action Larry had taken, repeating the details that I knew would ring true in each survivor's story. The details Larry explicitly denied. The details that were clearly and overtly sexual. Those "did not help my symptoms."

Shannon pressed on. It wasn't in my "wealth of knowledge" to know what helped and what didn't, was it? she asked.

At that point, I'd had it.

"I think it is fair to say that sexual contact does not treat a back injury. I have sex with my husband, and my pinched nerve is still there when I'm done." *Shoot. I just said that out loud. With cameras running*, I thought. I sighed inwardly. *I mean, we have three kids, so it's not like that's a secret, but I never intended to literally tell the world either.* Back in the waiting room, where Jacob was streaming the hearing, he'd laughed and remarked, "She's going to be so mad she said that out loud." He knew me very well.

It appeared to be enough to make her shift the line of questioning, at least. I'd prepared a lot before coming forward, hadn't I? she asked. I'd written a letter? Brought a character witness? Reviewed statutes and case law?

"And you put together essentially a package of what would need to be shown and what you believe your facts indicated to show them this was a legitimate crime; is that correct?"

Yes, it was.

"Letters where you literally put headlines on them about what these letters prove? . . .

"You also took the time to sit down and explain to [investigators] why you believed it was relevant and helpful and essential to building your case, correct?"

I'd known this would be a line of attack. She was arguing that I'd used my legal training to fabricate rather than to prove a case.

I answered bluntly. "I'm an attorney. I knew what you would ask."

"You did spend a wealth of time putting together these things and documenting what you believed would make the case stronger, correct?"

"I think when it comes to stopping a child predator, every effort should be put in. So, yes, I did spend a lot of time."

Shannon surprised me again when she began asking me about two osteopathic terms: the "thrust" technique and "Thiele stripping." I was pretty sure Shannon knew about them only because, in anticipation that Larry would claim to have been using those techniques, I had explained in my past research why those didn't match what he had done. Her question provided me with an opening to explain my research directly to the judge, who was unfamiliar with the terms and asked me to explain them.

That was just my interpretation, though, right? Shannon asked me. But it wasn't; it was the definition that osteopaths themselves gave to those terms. Around and around we went, until the judge put an end to it.

A little later she said, "You testified that the only thing worse than being sexually assaulted is having an audience. . . . It's fair to say, though, that when you've been given the option in this case, *you* are the one who has requested an audience, correct?"

"No, that is not correct."

She raised her eyebrows. "*You* are the one who *wanted* all of the cameras in the courtroom and the print papers . . . correct?"

"I would be happy to speak to that. . . . I did not want Larry Nassar to walk in here thinking he had won a victory." I paused and looked directly at Larry. "I want him and I want the public to know that I know where the shame and the guilt for this lies. It lies on him. It does not lie on me, and I am not afraid of the truth."

"And that is what you have said in your interviews to *Dateline*, to *60 Minutes*, to *People* magazine, to numerous other news agencies; is that correct?"

"I have never done interviews with *Dateline* or *60 Minutes*," I responded calmly.

"Okay . . . I apologize." She then suggested I had released statements because I wanted them disseminated to the public and because I wanted everyone to know what I was saying. Was that fair to say? she asked.

"I think there are things that are more important than what I want, and stopping a child predator is one of them."

Shannon switched gears. I wanted money, didn't I? I chose my words carefully, working in every single disclosure I'd made since I had been abused. *Was she really going to argue I had a sixteen-year strategy to file a civil suit?*

By the time Shannon finished, she'd used every single line of attack I'd expected from the first day I began to realize what had happened. She'd checked every box. Every cultural myth. Every knee-jerk attack. Every character assumption.

Angie got back up and did a brilliant redirect, skillfully unwinding every thread Shannon had sought to weave. When all was said and done, I'd been on the stand for close to three hours, and I was exhausted.

● ● ●

My parents secured a hotel room for us that night. At Jacob's insistence, we went there to sleep, taking the nursing baby with us and leaving the older two in my parents' care. I felt numb but was too hurt and worn out to fall asleep. I dreaded the nightmares, and I refused to read the news reports that came out that night.

Once we had settled into our room, I told Jacob, "I want to watch *Spotlight*."

"Are you sure?"

Jacob knew that, before now, I'd refused to watch this movie about the *Boston Globe*'s investigation into sexual abuse in the Catholic Church, but I wanted to see it after my day of testimony. I wanted to see someone else fighting abuse. To feel less alone and isolated in the fight.

As we watched, I wanted to cry. The story was so perfectly told. The devastation portrayed so accurately. The fear that members of the *Boston Globe* team felt when they realized it could have been them or their children. The anger when they began to uncover the evil. And the grief as each member of the team had to reckon with the reality that they'd been warned. Everyone had been warned. The signs had been there for the public to see, but no one cared. And so the abuse had continued.

The weight of how we fail our children pressed on me as an attorney for victims who'd been abused by priests told a *Globe* investigative reporter: "Mark my words, Mr. Rezendes. If it takes a village to raise a child, it takes a village to abuse one."[21]

And it does. It always has. But the film showed that it takes a village to stop the abuse too. One rogue attorney unwilling to let it go. One survivor who stood up first and said, "You can use my name." One newspaper editor who said, "This matters," and a team who poured their hearts and minds into it. A village had cast a light where only darkness had been allowed to reign before.

Now we had that village too. A detective insistent on finding the truth. A prosecutor who wasn't going to let it go. Journalists who saw that this case mattered and who told the story about corrupt institutions and abusers in their own hometown. And now survivors who were beginning to find their voices. Slowly but surely, the village needed to take down a predator and demand change from the institutions that harbored him was taking shape.

"It's time, Robby! It's time!" reporter Mike Rezendes had yelled when his editor questioned whether the timing was right to print an article exposing a cover-up by the Boston cardinal. "They knew and they let it happen! To *kids*! Okay? It could have been you, it could have been me, it could have been any of us. We gotta nail these scumbags! We gotta show people that nobody can get away with this, not a priest or a cardinal or a freaking pope!"[22]

And not an Olympic team doctor. Or the Olympic governing body. Or a Big Ten university, I thought as we turned out the light and tried to sleep. *It's time to show people that nobody can get away with this.*

25

BEFORE WE LEFT THE HOTEL to rejoin the kids the next morning, I scanned the news articles to glean what I could about the rest of the hearing. Someone had already posted my full testimony on YouTube, and it had been viewed hundreds of times. The most intimate, graphic details about my abuse—things I'd never wanted people to know—were now available to anyone. But it was the testimony of the two survivors who followed me that affected me most. I felt deep gratitude wash over me as I read a news report that explained,

> It was only in the past year that Victim G and another friend began reflecting on whether "something was wrong" about those treatments. . . . When Denhollander's story came out in the news, that gave them "the courage" to report their experiences.
>
> "It made it less embarrassing and less scary to come forward," Victim G says of Denhollander's public story. "We didn't want to do this on our own."[23]

I'd wanted to do anything possible to help survivors feel less shame and fear and to recognize they weren't alone in their pain. For the first time, I had heard directly from a survivor that she had felt empowered when I came forward. That meant the world to me. The strength it took to do what she had done was incredible, and I knew that testifying to the abuse would have left her feeling raw, exposed, and reviolated. I hoped she felt the power of what she had done.

I hoped the same for the other young woman who began her testimony after I had finished.

One . . . who testified Friday was a minor, so young and inexperienced that she had to be gently walked through terminology for where she was allegedly touched. "You know when you pee, where you wipe? Did he touch you in that area?" the prosecutor asked.[24]

She was the age I had been when I first realized Larry had abused me. I wished I could have told her how much courage she'd shown and how much she mattered, but I wasn't even allowed to know her name. I felt frustration rising when I read that this survivor hadn't been able to finish her testimony before the workday ended. In a few weeks, she would have to rearrange her schedule once again and make the several-hour drive back to court just so she could provide one more hour of cross-examination testimony. Many of us had waited years to stop Larry, yet the court couldn't be extended a single hour so a young survivor could finish her testimony rather than living with the stress of another court hearing for the next several weeks.

I seethed when I read that, after I'd left, a news crew had inadvertently livestreamed part of an anonymous survivor's testimony, revealing her identity. The judge kicked the crew out of the court, but it was too late. Right there on the stand, while testifying about the most private abuses, she had to find out that her identity had been leaked and then somehow muster up the strength to go on, with the rest of the cameras still in the room.

"Judge Allen could have prevented it!" I cried to Jacob. "The judge in Eaton County closed the court; he could have, too, but he didn't. Because they didn't matter enough." Even after that error, the judge refused to close the court for the remainder of the hearing. He'd reevaluate if it became obvious on the stand that the witnesses were traumatized, he said.

Over and over again, Larry was handed the weapons to try to manipulate, shame, and control. Over and over again, survivors were forced to bear the cost, not just of their abuse, but of every agonizing effort to make it stop. They were offered no protection, no consideration, no voice. They were just pawns in a process that might or might not ever stop a pedophile. Angie had fought as hard as she could, but her articulate and skilled petitions didn't matter when the court system didn't seem to care.

I couldn't help but think of the question I hear over and over: "Why don't victims report?" I wished every person who asked would put themselves in the victims' place. Into the witness seat where they had to relive their horror in front of an abuser who reveled in the details. Into the police station where they had to tell anyone who asked exactly what happened. Into the stirrups for a rape kit exam where the violation they suffered and the parts they wanted to hide were on full display, touched and photographed. And then, much of the time, the kit ended up buried in the back of a police station. Victims also had to face officers who asked what they'd been wearing. Or a prosecutor who just couldn't be bothered. Or a judge who wouldn't take the simplest steps to protect them.

Why don't victims report? Because most of the time, the only thing reporting accomplishes is heightening the trauma to almost unbearable levels. It invites an audience to view your sexual assault. It's choosing to have no voice in the process after having it stolen from you. That's why victims don't report.

•   •   •

We headed back to Louisville a few days later, since the preliminary hearing wouldn't resume until the end of May. As we pulled back onto the highway after making a pit stop just outside of Anderson, Indiana, our van simply . . . died. Right there on the highway. Jacob barely managed to pull off to the side of the road safely.

Then he put his head down on the steering wheel. "It couldn't just work, could it?" He sighed. "Okay," he said. "One step at a time. I'll call a tow truck, and we'll figure it out from there." We were quickly getting hot inside the van and knew we might be in for a long wait. I looked outside and noticed that we'd broken down next to a huge construction site.

"Okay, guys!" I called cheerfully. "It's going to be an adventure. Let's go watch the construction!" I carefully led the kids away from traffic and down a hill, pointing as I went. "Look! The cement mixer is getting ready to pour!" As we sat down on the dry grass, construction workers waved. A couple of them walked over to offer us water, reminding me how much a small act of kindness could mean.

Jacob worked on getting a tow truck while I texted family members and asked for help finding hotel options, and then we switched places. Jacob sat with the kids and sifted through the hotel list my mom sent over while I pulled the luggage from the back of the van and repacked the essentials into an overnight bag. By the time the tow truck arrived, we had reserved a room at a nearby hotel and begun walking there. I'd strapped the girls to my front and back, so they giggled and played peek-a-boo around my shoulders, while I grasped Jonathan's hand and Jacob carried our luggage.

Jacob commemorated the event by posting a photo of our poor van on social media, so by the time we reached the hotel, several people in the area had reached out offering to help, including *IndyStar* reporter Mark Alesia and his wife. Their simple act of reaching out meant so much to us.

Determined to make the day count, we took another "adventure walk" to find swimsuits for the kids and lunch from a Subway near our hotel. To our three kids, a rare visit to a restaurant, swimming, and the chance to watch *Toy Story 3* while curled up in shared beds made for a vacation.

When Jacob and I looked at each other from across the room that night, he shook his head. "How did we get here? And *what* are we doing?" he asked.

"I have no idea," I answered. And I half-meant it too. It felt as if we were figuring every day out the way a young child has to make sense of the new world they've been pushed into.

Once the van was fixed late the next afternoon, we drove home. When we arrived, we discovered that my sister-in-law had cleaned the house and my sister had brought us dinner. We unpacked, exhausted and full of emotions— everything from deep grief to overwhelming gratitude that we weren't doing this alone.

• • •

As the preliminary hearing continued, one day blurred into the next. After my testimony, the Ingham County hearing went so long that it extended into late June. But eventually our cases were bound over for trial and put into Judge Aquilina's courtroom. A week later, the Eaton County court also determined there was enough evidence to warrant a trial there. Judge Janice Cunningham would preside over those criminal cases.

In the midst of these long legal proceedings there were bright spots, including a supportive new church family. I didn't know what to think the first time a member we didn't even know approached us and said, "I've been praying for you continually. How did the hearing go?" Members of our church actually knew what was going on *and* cared enough to ask.

Our pastors had asked us how we were most comfortable keeping everyone up to date, and they had done what we requested. But honestly, I hadn't really expected anyone to pay attention—or to reach out with tangible offers of support.

"Can we bring you a meal?"

"Can I come watch your kids for a few hours so you and Jacob can get a bit of time away?"

Our church family in Michigan was no less involved, offering places to stay, childcare, and prayer support.

The things that might seem the smallest meant everything—like the reporter who wrote to say she was reading the resources I'd listed in my open letter to MSU's president Simon in preparation for a story to help people understand how predators get away with abuse.

"I have this quote above my desk," she added. "'Our job is to move a case towards justice. . . . We aren't the court of justice, but we can be part of reaching for justice.'[25] . . . How do you use this coverage to talk about how predators operate? If we don't do that, we failed. Anybody can take notes in court or tweet or point a camera."

As we waited, we tried to figure out how to plan. Trials were set for the fall but were likely to be moved back. We also had the civil process to go through. Jacob would need to take a semester off—whatever semester the trial fell in—but his school didn't allow for much time away without getting dropped from the program. Should we appeal to the administration now for extra time, or wait to see if we got lucky and trials fell in between semesters? My work contract would be up for renewal in the fall, and I was still behind on the hours for my current contract. But the grant-based project wasn't likely to be available in six months, so foregoing the job opportunity now likely meant permanently abandoning it, and we needed to shore up our finances after all the missed work, travel, and vehicle repairs. For the first time in our entire lives, we had a credit card balance. But was it fair to sign a contract knowing I'd possibly be in court and take much longer to complete the hours? My sister was likely to be engaged soon, to a medical student, no less. (I found it ironic to be adding a doctor to the family in the midst of this particular trial.) But how precisely does one plan a wedding that accommodates the schedule of a medical student and steers clear of, say, being in the middle of a trial you can't plan for?

•　•　•

Jacob called from work one day in early July. "Reporters are saying Larry is going to get a plea deal for the child porn."

I was shocked and frustrated. *What motivated this deal?* I wondered.

I got a call not much later from an attorney who knew. The plea deal, federal investigators had informed several elite gymnasts, was being offered in exchange for not pressing charges in their case for abuse that took place overseas.

I was livid. "Did those gymnasts *want* the plea deal, or were they *told* about it?"

As I'd feared, they'd been told. Not asked. Not given a voice. Pressured into accepting rather than supported in their quest for justice.

Larry pled guilty on July 11, but sentencing wasn't set for five more months—December 7, the day before my birthday. We got word our criminal trial had been pushed back too—our cases had been joined to Kyle's, the first charged victim, but that meant backing the trial date up until at least January. Our civil suits went to mediation a few days later, but MSU refused to accept responsibility for what had happened on their campus.

The university claimed that the trainers and coaches to whom patients had reported Larry's abuse hadn't believed it was abuse, so they weren't at fault either. Even as the criminal case was winding its way through the courts, survivors were having to face MSU's attempts to deflect responsibility.

In August, I flew to California on a whirlwind trip to do a press conference with Jamie Dantzscher during one of the biggest gymnastics meets of the year. As I always did before such events, I shot Angie a quick text to let her know what was going on. Just twenty minutes before the press briefing was to begin, Angie wrote back to advise me that I was under a gag order. Nassar's attorneys had named me as a witness, triggering the order to go into effect, but in the chaos of everything, I'd never been notified that the witness list had actually been filed.

At the time, Angie was prosecuting another high-profile case in my Michigan hometown—and it became a reminder of how fast a case could go sideways. A trucker connected to numerous rape allegations across the country had been charged in connection with a violent assault in Kalamazoo. It wasn't the first time he'd been accused. Victims from across the nation had reported him right after being assaulted, but the judge in Michigan refused to let most of the evidence showing that pattern into the trial. The legislature could have passed a law years earlier that would have made this evidence easily admissible, but that bill had languished in committee. So when Angie argued the case that autumn, jurors weren't allowed to hear most of the evidence. Despite the fact that the women had similar injuries and had each reported right away and endured degrading rape exams, the accused walked free after the defense made the simple assertion that these women were prostitutes who were just angry because they hadn't been paid. The jury came to their conclusion despite the lack of evidence that the women were sex workers and plenty of evidence that they'd sustained significant physical injuries and defensive wounds.

It was the first jury trial Angie hadn't won in ten years. And I knew that could happen to us. It *had* happened to us. Each person who had reported Larry's abuse for nearly thirty years had been told something similar: "You're wrong." "You're confused." "He wouldn't do that."

In the aftermath of the case in Kalamazoo, Shawana Hall, the lead survivor, died of a drug overdose. And I cried for her. She had fled across four lanes of traffic and pounded on the window of a police car nearby, crying that she'd been raped.[26] She had done everything right. And it hadn't been enough. She was worth so much, but the court system that should have protected her implied that she wasn't. *I* was barely surviving the system—and I was from an intact, supportive family. What happened to survivors from minority communities? Survivors with no access to the press? No family support? No investigator and prosecutor passionate to do it right? It was a bitter reminder—even as we were preparing to go to trial and advocating for change—that real people pay the price when society gets it wrong. It can literally be a matter of life and death.

26

AROUND THE TIME of the one-year anniversary of my coming forward, a journalist inadvertently published the age of Larry's oldest daughter—the one I'd held as a baby—before quickly amending and redacting it. But not before I realized that something didn't line up.

Larry had only charted my back treatment through April 2000, and my medical records barely extended into 2001. But his daughter—if her age had been reported accurately—had to have been born near the end of 2001. *How is that possible?* My mind reached for answers. Neither Angie nor Andrea could disclose his family's information, but they did confirm that she wasn't born early in 2001. I felt the ground slip out from under me again as I realized with icy shock that I'd still given Larry the benefit of the doubt.

I remembered abuse that seemed to span two years, but when my medical records showed only five appointments for my back, and no record of visits after January 2001, I thought I must have been mistaken and remembered incorrectly. When there had been a choice between what I remembered and what he charted, I'd trusted him and hadn't even realized it. It shook me to the core.

That fall I was asked to deliver a keynote address at a fund-raiser for an organization working to advance victims' rights. It was the first request I'd received to speak as an advocate. "What do I do with this?" I asked Jacob, feeling confused. "What do I do when I'm being given a platform *I never wanted* to talk about an issue *I don't want to talk about?*" Of all the things I'd taught on or advocated for, never once had I entertained the idea of becoming an advocate for victims of sexual assault. It was too personal. Too private. Too painful. *How do you even explain to people why you agree to talk about something that you don't want to talk about?* I thought in frustration. "Someone has to talk about these issues," I said, trying to express the conflict I felt. "And I can. So if I *can*, do I have a responsibility to?" I finally agreed, but once again I struggled with what my identity had become.

I was also relearning the very painful lesson that full healing never really comes. I wanted healing to mean that I would go back to being who I was before I was abused—like it hadn't happened. But the scars from Larry's abuse were visible to the whole world. They would never *not* be part of my public identity now.

I had to let myself grieve again because grief was the outlet that allowed unhealthy anger to be washed away. And I had to remind myself that longing for what is straight is good. *The straight line is there*, I told myself. *And you can see the evil, because you know the good. Let the grief at what is so crooked turn you to what is straight.* I remembered that diagram I had drawn so many years ago. Good and right do exist. Truth does exist.

And that *was* a good thing, because near the end of October, Larry filed the motion I'd been waiting for—a sweeping request for sensitive and personal medical records, and a motion to compel me to testify at any level of detail about my sexual assault at church.[27] Larry's attorneys argued that I was deeply psychologically troubled because of prior abuse and that I had projected that onto Larry. I should be compelled to testify about that abuse, and the jury should be allowed to see all my journal entries, including everything related to my first assault, so they could be aware of the root causes of my "troubled psychology." That stung more than anything because it meant Larry had read my journals. Every word.

"I wanted you to get this from me and not the media, in the event they obtain copies," Angie wrote, trying to give me a heads-up before my first sexual assault became a news story too. The motions were reported later that day, though journalists gave me the cover they could, not linking my name to the victim identity in the court briefs.

However, I felt as if I'd been broadsided by a prominent publication in my hometown when the day before those motions were argued in court, it published a profile of Shannon, with a picture of her next to Larry. Her representation of sex offenders was characterized as "completely honest"—heroic, even—caring for them like "a loved one," doing the job no one else wanted to do, representing abusers who felt bullied by a powerful government with "unlimited funds."[28] I shook my head in disgust. Advocates had a name for this tactic: DARVO—Deny, Attack, Reverse Victim and Offender. Make the perpetrators out to be the ones picked on and harassed.

Whereas every statement I had made to the press was carefully presented as an "allegation" and run by Larry's team for their response before publication, everything Shannon had said was presented as the unvarnished truth—no qualifiers needed.

And of course, there was *no* corresponding story about Angie or Andrea, who *also* took on the cases no one else wanted to take. Nor was there a follow-up piece on the many survivors who had willingly laid out the most horrific thing they'd ever endured, just to keep other children safe.

It was yet another example of rape culture at work. The day before the court was to decide whether to pierce the rape shield protection and compel me to testify about my former abuse, this attorney—whose client had already pled guilty to possessing the most horrific child pornography collection the federal judge had ever seen—received one-sided press coverage that portrayed her as a super lawyer who spoke the truth and defended the innocent, no "allegedly" in sight.

· · ·

My weariness mounted as the legal proceedings dragged on, but I discovered an additional source of my exhaustion on the morning of my sister's bridal shower in early November, when I saw two pink lines on four different pregnancy tests. I was already pretty sure that another tiny person had taken up residence in my body, but having it confirmed it was a whole other story. The only thing I could think of that would be worse than testifying about sexual assault was doing so while visibly pregnant.

Jacob was so stressed trying to finish his final papers for his PhD courses that I determined not to tell him until his semester finished the following week. But Angie should probably know right away because any complications could affect my appearance at court hearings. I texted her quickly. She responded almost immediately—and very enthusiastically. I'd totally made her day, she said. I stared at the phone in disbelief.

I guess if she's excited, this means I can be excited too? I wasn't quite sure what to feel. It wasn't the timing I would have picked, but in all the darkness, there was new life. And life was a gift. And I was secretly excited, despite being entirely unsure how it would all work out.

I did manage to keep it quiet from Jacob right then, though I blurted the news out to my mom, who had to keep the secret with me. Jacob's response when I informed him a week later was more akin to shocked silence. But not long after, I found myself in a tiny ultrasound room with three very excited children squirming in their chairs, waiting to see the baby. As they giggled in delight at the little heart we could see and hear beating on the screen, tears of joy pressed in.

"I saw my baby!" two-year-old Ellianna joyfully giggled into the phone when we called Jacob and my mom to tell them all was well. It wasn't "good timing," most would say, but that little baby was there, and its tiny heart was beating strong, and that little life had value. And we could rejoice in that.

●   ●   ●

Later that week as I was loading groceries into the van and attempting to keep three energetic children corralled, my cell phone rang. It was Angie.

"Hey!" I said cheerfully as I picked up the phone. Hefting a few gallons of milk into the trunk, I whispered to the kids, "You guys can play in the car. Take turns!" Pretending to drive was an all-time favorite activity, and since I had the keys, it was a relatively safe way for the kids to occupy themselves while Angie and I talked.

"We don't know yet what will happen," she began. "But I want to talk about the possibilities with you and see how you feel about things, okay?"

I motioned to Jonathan to give one of his sisters a turn pretending to drive.

"Yeah, go for it," I answered, pulling a few more bags out of the cart.

"We got a call from Shannon and Matt. They've asked about a plea deal."

I stopped, bags suspended in midair. "Are you serious?" I never expected this. I was convinced that Larry was such a narcissist and consummate manipulator that he would still be certain he could talk his way out of it. He'd actually tried to go on the stand at the preliminary exam, certain his persona alone would carry the day. I was sure there was no way he was going to plead guilty. I hadn't even let myself hope for it. When the sentencing hearing for the child porn was pushed out until December 7, three days after jury selection was set to start in our trial, we thought we'd lost any chance of his offering to take a plea deal. The only reason to plead guilty before our trial started would be if the sentence for the porn charges was so long that he'd be put away for life anyway. There would then be no benefit to fighting the rest of the charges.

"The *only* way we will do this is if the survivors all support it, and if *all* of you have a voice," Angie said. "I would require that all the survivors be allowed to speak as part of the plea, so that everyone's voice is heard, and everyone has access to the courts. Everyone who wants to can be part of putting him away. I won't offer a plea on any other terms."

I nodded. That was vital to me, too. "Will the judge agree to that?" I asked.

"I don't know," Angie said honestly, "but it will be in the agreement. It's nonnegotiable in my opinion."

"Okay," I said, taking a deep breath and collecting my thoughts. "Can we talk through the risks and benefits, and the statutory scheme for sentencing?"

We ran through them together. The pros and cons. The effect a trial could have on Larry's sentence as compared to only a sentencing hearing. The risks and benefits. More information would come out in a trial than in a sentencing hearing—that extra information could lead the judge to see the importance of a lengthy sentence. But it also opened us up to the risk that a jury could get confused, or that someone would make an error that would lead to an appeal. We went over the statutory guidelines in Michigan for sentencing and parole—how could a deal be crafted to give the strongest chance that Larry would be put away for life?

"What do the other survivors want?" I asked. "Are there survivors who feel that they won't have justice if their case isn't charged, or if we don't go to trial?" That, along with what would put Larry away forever, was the vital question.

"I don't know yet," she answered honestly. "You were my first call. But we'll be asking those questions of everyone. Everyone's voice matters. And top priority, along with putting Larry away forever, is making sure you all know your voices are heard and that you've gotten justice."

I quietly closed the trunk, hoping to soften the exuberant race car noises coming from the front seat.

"Okay," I said decisively. "This is where I come down. You make whatever decision is needed for the other women." I paused, searching for words. "I didn't do this for me, you know," I said, glancing through the windows at the very active three-year-old gleefully climbing over car seats. "I don't need anything myself. If there are others who feel they must have their cases charged, or that we have to go to trial, I'm willing to go to trial." I knew that likely meant I'd be a witness at every trial—a commitment for a long time forward. "But if the other survivors would like to avoid trial and feel they will have received justice and been heard with just a sentencing hearing, then do that." I paused and reemphasized. "Do what the other survivors need. I'll be there regardless."

One week later, the newspapers caught wind of the discussion. I was tense, hoping that added publicity wouldn't derail the process. Finally I received the call I'd been waiting for. "November 22," Angie told me. "And when he pleads, we think everyone will agree to lift the gag orders as well."

I called Jacob and then texted the family: "Ummm . . . I think we'll be back in MI for Thanksgiving after all?"

We'd switched locations of our family Thanksgiving celebration twice already, first *to* Michigan, because Larry was initially supposed to be sentenced in federal criminal court for his child porn plea that week, and then back to Louisville when the hearing was changed to December 7. And now back to Michigan.

"I'm bringing a super cookie," I said wryly to Jacob. The allergen-free Louisville bakery Annie May's Sweet Café made this wonderful creation— a cookie sandwich made with two fluffy chocolate chip cookies and chocolate buttercream in the middle, all dipped in chocolate ganache.

"If he actually goes through with the plea, I'm celebrating with that cookie," I declared. "And if he backs out at the last minute, I'm drowning my sorrows in it."

●   ●   ●

The next week, we traveled back to Michigan. Right around the day of the hearing, MSU announced they would not be releasing anything their so-called investigation had uncovered about why Larry had been able to abuse for so long.[29] It struck me as an unbelievably tone-deaf announcement to make just as we were preparing to head back to court.

That night, as Mom and I headed out to shop for groceries, I got an email from Angie with a copy of the plea agreement. She asked me what I thought of it.

I pulled it up on my phone as we walked through the parking lot to the store and then glanced over it while Mom grabbed a cart.

The terms themselves were perfect, exactly what we'd talked about. Angie had pointedly secured the right for every victim to speak, among the other technical provisions. The problem was the language Larry had to admit to in court: "Defendant put his ungloved finger into the vagina of Victim —." That wasn't enough. What Larry had done was sexual. Not for any medical purpose. For his own gratification. It's not as if he'd done a legitimate exam, but without consent. He had done it for sexual reasons. The problem was, the plea statements had to mirror the language in the statutes, and the statute itself didn't include any phrase like "not for medical purposes." *This isn't enough*, I thought in frustration. The confusion in the media, the pushback we still sometimes got, was "What's the big deal? Doctors sometimes have to do pelvic exams!" But this wasn't an exam. It was done for his own sexual gratification, and I wanted him to have to say it.

As Mom and I breezed through our shopping list, I pulled up the Michigan criminal code on my phone, searching through the definitions and provisions for a way to force Larry to admit that what he'd done was sexual. None of the statutes Larry had been charged under had an element of "sexual intent," and *sexual* wasn't a defined term in the penal code either.

There, I thought with a jolt. *Right there*. "A person is guilty of criminal sexual conduct in the first degree if he or she engages in sexual penetration." *Sexual* penetration. I scanned the statutes related to the other survivors. All of them referenced "sexual penetration."

I texted Angie. Could we not simply require him to say that his act was "sexual penetration"? It was right there in the code.

She wrote back immediately to tell me she was making "the 'sexual penetration' addition now."

I felt like crying as I read that email, walking through the dark parking lot to our car, groceries in hand. Angie had asked what I'd needed. She'd *listened*. She'd given me a voice. It meant everything.

Before the sun was up the following morning, I pulled the chocolate-covered sandwich cookie I'd brought from Louisville out of the freezer and left for Lansing with Jacob. I felt well enough to grab a mocha at Starbucks this time, and I squeezed Jacob's hand as we drove, trying to quell the nervous excitement and stay prepared for the very real possibility that Larry could back out at the very last minute.

"We are lifting you up in prayer today," our pastor had reminded us in an email early that morning.

Upon arrival, we went through security and stepped into a large courtroom.

I glanced around. *Surely the other charged victims are here, right?* I recognized civil attorneys and a few survivors I'd seen speak publicly recently, but the victims who had been at the preliminary hearings were all still anonymous.

My emotions ran deep after finally meeting a few of these women, like Larissa, the gymnast who'd told MSU's gymnastics coach way back in 1997. I turned around as the door opened and saw Sterling, the former teammate of my sister, walk in with her mom. We hugged, grateful to see each other but feeling the weight and awkwardness of reconnecting after so many years, bound together by experiences we never should have shared.

After what seemed like hours but was really only a few minutes, court was called to order. Larry was led in by a female officer and flanked by three male officers, and we began.

The judge ran over the procedural requirements. Larry was called to the podium, accompanied by his attorneys, and Angie stood and read the plea agreement requirements: Mandatory HIV testing. Registry on the sex offender list. The statutory basis for the charges.

"For count 5, criminal sexual conduct first degree . . . this is related to Victim C," she continued. "The defendant did engage in sexual penetration . . . with a child . . . and the defendant was in a position of authority over the victim and used this authority to coerce the victim to submit."

She repeated the statement for all seven of us—every statutory basis. Then it was Larry's turn.

The judge turned to Larry and asked him to step up to the microphone. "Count 5, criminal sexual conduct, first degree, relationship, Victim C. How do you plead?"

"Guilty."

Larry's voice actually said "guilty."

She repeated the request for all seven of us. "How do you plead?"

"Guilty."

"Guilty."

"Guilty."

The same response each time.

"Did anyone force, threaten, or coerce your plea?"

"No, Your Honor."

"You are doing this of your own accord?"

"Yes."

Then Judge Aquilina said, "At this time, I'm going to allow your attorneys to inquire of you in regards to the counts that you've pled to."

Shannon began asking Larry to confirm his intention to enter a guilty plea for the charges related to each victim.

"With respect to count 5, Victim C, do you agree that between February 1, 2000, and April 30, 2000, that you sexually penetrated Victim C?"

"Yes."

"At that time, was Victim C between the age of fifteen and thirteen?"

"Yes."

"And do you acknowledge that as her doctor, you were in a position of authority over her and used your position of authority to constructively coerce her to submit to the penetration?"

"Yes."

Yes. Yes. Yes. For all of us. Yes.

"You are waiving any defenses that your actions were for a legitimate medical purpose?"

"Yes."

Then Judge Aquilina stepped in with some clarifying questions to Larry for the record.

When he had penetrated his victims, he was ungloved, correct?

"Yes, Your Honor."

"And it was not for any medical purpose; is that correct?"

"What?" Larry blurted out in confusion and frustration. He had refused to put that in his statements and couldn't be forced to, because it wasn't in the statute. I gasped slightly as I realized what the judge was doing. She had the power to ask clarifying questions, and she was requiring him to admit what he did not want to acknowledge.

"It was for your *own* purpose; is that correct?"

Larry closed his eyes. "Yes."

"And in fact, it was against medical protocol; is that correct?"

"Yes."

I was not prepared for the flood of relief that washed over me in that moment. I remembered every night I had pounded my pillow in the basement, wanting nothing more than answers. I remembered when I realized my healing couldn't be dependent on courtroom justice or an admission from Larry. *You will never get that*, I thought. And for sixteen years, I had believed that. I hadn't even hoped for it. Now I had received what I never thought I would. I was overwhelmed with the gift that it really was—a gift few survivors ever receive.

My feelings shifted to disbelief and incredulity, however, when Shannon spoke again.

"Your Honor, while I know this is an unusual request, may Dr. Nassar please make a statement at this time?"

Jacob and I glanced at each other, and I glanced at Sterling, my sister's teammate. *This is going to be interesting.*

Larry stepped up to the mic, looking worn.

"*Mr.* Nassar," Judge Aquilina said patiently, pointedly dropping the *Dr.* from his title. "What would you like us to know?"

"I think this is important," he began, "that—what I've done today to help move a community forward." My eyebrows reached the highest they could go. "That's—a couple of things that I could do to stop the hurting is this . . .

"For all those involved . . . I'm so horribly sorry," he said, shaking his head. "This was like a match that turned into a forest fire out of control."

I wasn't sure if he meant his own perversions, or the "media frenzy" that took things "out of his control" as he'd referenced in emails before.

"I have no animosity towards anyone," he said earnestly.

"Well, that's a relief," Jacob whispered in a voice choked with suppressed laughter.

"I just want healing," Larry explained. "It's time. . . . We need to move forward in a sense of growth and healing, and I pray that."

If anyone wanted a case study on self-deception and narcissistic behavior, I thought, *there it is.*

We waited for court to conclude and be dismissed, and Jacob and I turned to each other in shock and—at this point—actual amusement.

"Did he just say he bears no animosity?" Jacob asked.

I nodded. "Well, I'm glad I stopped basing my healing on Larry's repentance a long time ago."

Afterward, I did a press conference with a few survivors, including Kaylee, one of the young women who'd been behind a conference-room door back in Ingham County. It was the first Michigan press conference I didn't have to do alone. And sitting there with them, so thankful they'd spoken up, that Kaylee felt ready to speak publicly, made it almost impossible for me to hold back the tears. As we headed to my parents' home after a long, exhausting day, I remembered that the next day would be Thanksgiving. And there was so, so much to be thankful for.

27

THANKSGIVING MORNING I was up at 5:30—way earlier than I'd have chosen. But CNN's *New Day* had asked if I would come on, and it was a prime opportunity to address the cultural issues around this case.

Unfortunately, no broadcast studios were available on Thanksgiving, so they asked me to Skype in. Only later did I consider the logistical hurdles. My parents' house was small, and my brother and sister-in-law had come in for Thanksgiving too. Just about every room in the house, including the basement, would be filled with sleeping people. The living room and the downstairs bathroom were the only two rooms available, but if I taped in the living room, CNN viewers across the country would almost certainly be privy to the hysterical, loud crying of a two-year-old who had gone searching for her mother.

I pulled my brother aside the night before and asked the very unusual question, "So, is it okay with you if I sneak downstairs while you guys are asleep and do an interview in the bathroom tomorrow morning?"

He raised one eyebrow. "You can do whatever you want at 6 a.m. I'm going to be *sleeping*."

So, early the next morning, I slipped into a blouse, keeping on my pajama pants (which wouldn't be on camera anyway), put on makeup, and crept downstairs to the bathroom.

The only wall big enough to provide a plain backdrop was between the sink and the *commode*, so I dragged in a rolling desk chair and propped my computer there. *Ewwww.* I grimaced. It was not flattering, to put it mildly. I also noticed that the slightest twist of the chair was enough to put the toilet into the viewing screen. *I'm going to wind up flashing a toilet on national television*, I thought with consternation. *That's gonna go viral for all the wrong reasons.* I searched for options. The best I could come up with was draping a teal bath towel over the toilet, in hopes that if I did make the error of bumping the computer enough to flash something into view, it wouldn't be instantly recognizable as a toilet. Jacob slipped into the room to make sure the technology was working properly. (He knew I wouldn't know how to check on that, which is why he showed up before I even asked.)

I breathed a sincere sigh of relief when the interview ended without my accidentally showing my parents' toilet on national television. Even better, I'd had the opportunity to highlight how detrimental a cavalier attitude toward sexual assault within institutions can be.

"Great interview!" my attorneys shot me in an email later, and I smothered a laugh. *If only people knew how much "real life" was going on when I talked to the press.*

We headed home to Louisville that weekend. I had desperately wanted to stay for the guilty plea Larry would make in Eaton County, but we just couldn't afford more time off work, especially since we had to return for Larry's federal sentencing hearing on December 7 and then in January for his sentencing in our *own* hearing.

"We'll stay for Eaton County in January," Jacob promised as we drove. "It's important for you to see it end and be able to meet any survivors who are comfortable meeting with you." As we waited over the next six weeks, I continued to do as many as six press interviews a day and compile information for upcoming hearings. I also began to work on legislative reform with a Michigan state senator whom I'd met years before through SSI.

• • •

Just a few short weeks later, we were heading back to Michigan again. During Larry's federal sentencing for child porn, certain victims were supposed to get the chance to speak publicly, including the elite gymnasts who'd agreed to the plea deal with assurances from the federal prosecutors that they would be given that right. Unfortunately, the prosecutors had failed to put those terms into the plea deal, and the judge had ruled that we could submit letters only. I was angry on behalf of the gymnasts who had been promised the right to speak in exchange for the plea, and I also felt grief over the child porn charges—none of those victims were there. It was a "silent" crime. No one would see their faces or hear what had been done to them. More than anything, I wanted someone to speak for those precious girls.

I'd agonized over that letter for days, reading every court document I could find. The descriptions of what was on Larry's hard drive haunted me, but I couldn't choose to ignore them. Someone had to bear witness to the evil. Looking away didn't change what was there. It only made it impossible to stop.

Judge Neff, I am writing to urge you today to impose the maximum available sentence against Larry Nassar for each count of his possession of child pornography.

I went over it all. How what Larry had done to me demonstrated the elements she must consider in sentencing and how these things pointed to the necessity of imposing the maximum sentence.

But even greater than my own experience and pain, and above the statistics for re-offense, is a question that must be answered when Larry's sentence is determined: "How much is a little girl worth?"

It was the first chance I'd had to ask that question. I wept as I continued typing.

How much is the little girl being assaulted in Larry's video "Kelly 13 young girl" worth? How much does the precious child in the film "vicky_10_year_old_orgasm" matter? Are they valuable enough to protect with the fullest weight of the law? Does the destruction of these precious children matter enough to provide every measure of justice the law can offer? The sentence you hand down will answer these questions.

Tell these little girls who have been used as Larry's tools for masturbation, and tell everyone, "These children are worth everything the law can offer." For the sake of justice for every little girl whose violation and destruction Larry found pleasure in, and for the sake of the children Larry can victimize if he is released, I plead with you to impose every measure the law can offer. Because "everything" is what these children are worth.

I cried in my kitchen again that night, the names of those precious girls in Larry's file still in my mind. I prayed Judge Neff would hear my heart. She was the only judge who held the power to impose consecutive sentences, meaning sentence two wouldn't start counting down until sentence one was complete—a key provision because Larry could be sentenced to a maximum of only twenty years per count on the porn charges. If they ran concurrently, he might be released with years left to continue abusing. And while it was a lot to hope for, the judge could even require that the federal sentences be completed before the state sentences started, ensuring that Larry would never go free.

●　　●　　●

On December 7, the day before my thirty-third birthday, we were in court. Once again, Jacob held my hand tight as the attorneys ran through the procedural requirements and we waited. There was one more chance for each side to make what was essentially a closing argument, and I wondered what might proceed from Larry's mouth this time. His attorneys, arguing on his behalf, showcased his purported desire for redemption. He'd helped other inmates earn their diplomas. He was writing a book. He attended Bible studies. He'd even helped an inmate fix his ankle pain.

Then Larry spoke. His work was stressful, he justified. He'd turned to the wrong thing for stress relief. Like being an alcoholic, he explained. He hoped his experiences would help educate others.

Judge Neff listened patiently, and then the microphone was yielded to the federal prosecution team. The prosecutor spoke passionately about the horror of what Larry had done and the justice owed to each little girl represented in those files.

Tears flooded my eyes as the prosecutor read a line from my letter in open court on behalf of the precious children in those images. "How much is a little girl worth?" The chance to speak for them meant everything to me.

I waited, rigid with anticipation as the judge began collecting her thoughts and speaking. She laid out the sentencing guidelines and the factors she was to consider. Then she handed down her sentence in a clear, unflinching, and immovable voice. She minced no words, though her tone remained calm and even. Larry should never be allowed to be around children again, she said firmly.

She imposed the maximum sentence of twenty years for each count of possession of child pornography. I took a deep breath. Without a pause she added that the sentences would run consecutively. And consecutive with whatever state sentences would be imposed for the crimes for which he would be sentenced in state court.

I squeezed Jacob's hand as hard as I could and exhaled, fighting tears. It was everything we'd asked for but had barely dared to hope for—the best "birthday gift" I could have received.

Following the hearing, there was a meeting with survivors so the prosecutors could answer any questions about what had transpired. Tiffany, the first survivor to speak publicly after I did, had come in from across the country, and I could finally thank her in person for what she had done. Some of the former elite gymnast survivors were also there, along with many of the survivors who still lived in the area. As I looked around, I realized that, slowly and steadily, an army was building.

And it was an army USAG feared. On that very day, as Larry was being sentenced, USAG sent notification that they were filing a motion with the court, asking them to dismiss all claims against them.[30] They stated they owed us—dues-paying members of their program at the time when we were abused by their team physician—no duty of care. Not even the little girls and women who were abused after USAG knew full well what Larry was doing—and reported him to law enforcement in 2015.

•　•　•

We zipped back to Louisville shortly thereafter for my sister's wedding. It was a beautiful respite from the exhaustion.

In the midst of it all—the wedding festivities and the holiday season—I continued accepting press interviews, keeping up to date with the legal pleadings, writing sponsors and board members privately to urge them to take specific action toward real reform, and interfacing on a legislative package being put together in Lansing. Details on the January sentencing hearing in Ingham County continued to filter in . . . the date was pushed out a week . . . Larry would be required to sit in the witness box. I was actually relieved at that; it would make it easier to address him, and I didn't like the idea of him being behind me. He'd always stood behind me. And it felt right that the focus should be on him and what he'd done.

Life became more complicated again around Christmas when my dearly loved aunt died after a brief, fierce battle with cancer. Just a few days later, Ellianna was hospitalized on Christmas Eve with a severe asthma attack. Mercifully, she was released only twenty-four hours later, but our Christmas "break" was spent in the hospital—and we now had more financial pressures due to the hospital bills. Once Ellianna came home, we prepared for our extended stay in Michigan for the hearings in both Ingham and Eaton Counties. One of the prices we paid for seeing the court process through was missing the memorial for my aunt in Colorado. While the rest of my family was gathered there, Twistars owner John Geddert filed a motion seeking to dismiss all his gymnasts' claims against him,[31] arguing in a footnote that I should be suing my own mom. She was as responsible as he was, he claimed.

"It's getting to me again," I wrote to Angie, "and I keep wondering if it ever *won't*. I feel like I ought to be 'used to it' after having to do so much publicly already. I keep sitting down to write my impact statement and . . . I've got nothing."

"I'm not going to be able to hold it together much longer," I kept saying to Jacob. The weight of the last year and a half, the grief too deep for words, the names of the little girls on Larry's comhuter, and the Jane Doe designations of now over a hundred women, their stories filling the legal briefs I read . . . I felt like I would go crazy some days.

"If I don't get a chance to cry, I'm going to lose it at some point and not be able to stop." Maintaining a calm, rational, firm demeanor had been necessary in order to advocate, but I also needed to be able to express the grief somehow.

But that chance didn't come before January 15, when we were back in Lansing for a private meeting Angie had arranged for any survivors who could attend. It was a chance to meet one another and gain support before beginning the week of testimony during the sentencing hearing. Well over one hundred women had come forward, almost all anonymously, either to police or civil attorneys. Approximately ninety-two were scheduled to give impact statements, many of them planning to attend the private meeting the night before.

I wasn't sure what to feel or do. Everyone knew who I was, but I didn't know who most of them were, save for the dozen or so survivors I'd met at the federal sentencing and plea hearings. And yet I knew many of their stories.

How do you explain to someone you've never met how much you have cried for them? What a gift it was to finally hear their names and see their faces and thank them for coming forward? These were the women who had filled my mind and heart for sixteen years. I wanted them to know we'd done this together. One police report would never have forced a guilty plea. Whatever was to come this week, it was because of all of us.

Jacob, my mom, and I arrived at the large community building where the group would meet. As we walked toward the "Povilaitis meeting," I paused. The hall was filled with a line of women, some accompanied by husbands or parents, waiting to check in at the door. I glanced inside. It was full. It was full of survivors who never had to be there. Full of women and young girls who never should have met. Families disrupted and torn apart. Parents grasping for ways to support the daughters whose violations they had witnessed and did not know to stop. It was one thing to know the numbers. It was another to witness the reality. I almost turned around and left, certain I would not make it in the door as I started to shake with suppressed sobs. But I also knew this was the only chance we'd have to meet like this, and I would regret it forever if I did not find a way to make it through the night. So one more time, I fought for control and tried to smile.

As I approached a table filled with smooth black stones, our victim advocate encouraged me to pick one out. "We spent hours painting them for you all!" she said. The surfaces were filled with simple designs and single words. *Hope. Faith. Beauty.* I smiled and looked at the various expressions on each one.

Truth. I picked that stone up. *This is the one.*

"I thought of you when I painted that," the victim advocate said, smiling. "It fits."

We meandered our way to a table near the back, where Sterling and her mom were seated. I smiled and hugged the few survivors I'd met before, meeting others for the first time, greeting spouses and parents in the process. Each handshake and knowing smile was a gift—silent understanding of all we'd been through.

Later Angie and Robyn gave us a rundown of what the week would be like and the support systems available to us as we gave our statements. Survivors spoke up, suggesting tips for preparing—things they'd found helpful or planned to talk about. We heard one another's voices for the first time. And by the end of the night, the check-in sheet, where each survivor was to confirm whether she was speaking publicly or staying anonymous, had been revised more than once, several shifting their choice from "Jane Doe" to "speaking publicly."

When the rented time for our room had expired, and the remaining bits of pizza the police chief himself had sprung for had grown cold, we separated for the night. No one really knew what the week would bring. But after that night, we did know we'd be doing it together. No one was alone anymore.

28

EARLY THE NEXT MORNING, Jacob and I drove from Kalamazoo to Lansing for the first day of the sentencing hearing. By the time we arrived at the courthouse in Ingham County, news trucks were already parked outside, and reporters and survivors stood on the sidewalk in a long line winding up to the courtroom, waiting to make it through security. Anxious survivors and family members smiled tentatively at one another. No one had the emotional energy for words. I chatted briefly with various reporters I'd come to know over the past year and a half, trying not to dwell on the grief sitting heavy inside me.

Andrea joined us in the elevator, and I got a much-needed laugh as we joked about the Diet Coke already in her hand. We became silent once we neared the courtroom. A therapy dog sat outside, and quiet spaces had been set up for anyone who might need a break from the hearing. Inside the courtroom, it was silent and tense. Kleenex boxes were sprinkled throughout the seating area.

By the time the bailiff called, "All rise," the courtroom had filled. Larry was led to the witness box by a female officer, where he would sit with his attorney Shannon Smith.

More than twenty survivors were expected to speak that day. Each would be introduced just before she spoke. Kyle, the young woman whom Larry had begun abusing in his home when she was only six, was first. As she stepped to the podium, her mom and Angie standing nearby for support, photos of a little girl came up on the screen. She spoke on record, with her identity being fully made known for the first time.

"I'm addressing you publicly today as a final step and statement to myself that I have nothing to be ashamed of." She began powerfully and graphically, laying out exactly what Larry had done. She had been six years old. "Let me remind you of the interests of a six-year-old girl," she said. "My favorite TV show was *Clifford the Big Red Dog*. . . . I could not do a multiplication problem and still had not lost all my baby teeth. . . . Without my knowledge or consent, I had engaged in my first sexual experience by kindergarten."

I could not hold back the tears. I was a mom to a child that age. I'd read *Clifford* to my daughters just yesterday. My son had just lost his two front teeth. The beautiful, precious little girl that Kyle was, and the depth of what had been done to her, flooded the courtroom. And so did her strength. She had paid for her counseling by babysitting for the Nassars' children, and she stayed in their lives to try to keep them safe. With incredible courage she laid out the horrific damage caused by sexual abuse. Even with cameras trained on her, she did not flinch, forcing the world to come face-to-face with the devastation of assault and the incredible manipulation of a pedophile.

"I've been coming for you for a long time," she told Larry, her voice tinged with anger and power. "I've told counselors your name in hopes that they would report you. *I've* reported you to Child Protective Services *twice*. I gave a testament to get your medical license revoked.

"Perhaps you have figured it out by now," she said, without flinching. "Little girls don't stay little forever. They grow into strong women that return to destroy your world." I smiled as she said it. Immediately after the preliminary examinations where Kyle, and then I and others, testified, Jacob had tweeted an almost identical phrase, but I never expected to see it lived out as powerfully as Kyle had just done.

When Kyle finished, the emotion and power in the room was palpable.

Survivor after survivor came forward, nearly all speaking publicly, *all* demonstrating incredible strength. I posted the name of each survivor who spoke publicly on my Facebook feed. These women deserved to be heard.

An older woman came forward to tell the story of her daughter, Chelsey. I heard audible sobs when she revealed—partway through her story—that she spoke on behalf of her daughter only because her daughter was no longer here. Chelsey had committed suicide, never having recovered from the damage of what Larry had done.

Each time a survivor spoke, a picture would go up on the screen. Almost always of a little girl. Or a very young woman. "I was nine." "I was eleven." "I was only eight." Grieving parents stood behind daughters who had been forced to grow up long before their time but who now boldly stood and confronted their abuser.

And then Angie would say the words she said over and over again. "This survivor has just decided to speak publicly for the first time."

The floodgates had opened. We didn't know, as we sat in the courtroom with tears streaming down our faces, that the world had begun to take notice. But as each woman stood to face her abuser and speak the truth, the world was coming face-to-face with the damage of sexual assault in a way it never had before. Jane Doe had a name. She had a story. She had a voice. And she couldn't be swept aside anymore.

By lunchtime, the energy in the room was shifting. The grief was still palpable. The effects of abuse—shaking knees, ragged breathing—were still visible. But now there was *more than* the grief. There was beginning to be strength. Press requests came thick and fast during breaks, as everyone began to slowly awaken to the reality of what was happening. It wasn't until that night, though, after we'd gone home—emotionally exhausted—that we really started to understand.

Angie texted me. Her email in-box and voice mail were filled with messages from survivors. They were ready to speak. Was there still a chance? By the next morning, we knew that the four days initially reserved for the hearing wouldn't be enough. We were concerned that the press might leave, having gotten a story from the first day of the hearing. That would minimize the reach of each woman's voice. But by lunchtime on the second day, journalists began to tell me, "I've called my editor. . . . We're asking for permission to stay until it's done. . . . We have to be here." And they were.

Each morning we showed up at the courthouse in the bitter cold, clutching coffee or tea, waiting in the blowing wind in a long line to make it through security. Each morning the camera crews and reporters dragged in equipment or set up tents and trucks outside the courthouse to broadcast the statements. Every day I sat with Jacob, or my mom or sister, to do what I had longed to do for sixteen years—bear witness to the survivors who came before and after me. Nearly all of them came after Larissa made the first known report of abuse in 1997. Each story was a testament to their courage and bore witness to the cost of failing to listen and believe when a survivor speaks. Most of us should never have had to be there.

Just when I thought nothing could surprise me, we learned that Larry had written a six-page, single-spaced diatribe about how difficult his life was. The judge read pieces of it aloud.

"I am very concerned about my ability to face witnesses these next four days mentally," he wrote, referring to his sentencing hearing as a "four-day sentencing media circus."

Channeling the sentiments the judge knew the survivors felt, she turned to Larry. She took aim at his complaints about the media. They'd followed this case from the beginning, so it was not surprising that they were there to follow the case that day, was it? She waited for him to answer.

"No." Larry sighed.

Had his counselors noted a need for courtroom accommodations for his health during sentencing?

No . . . no, they hadn't.

And then she became pointedly direct. "I didn't orchestrate this; you did, by your actions. . . . Nothing is as harsh as what your victims endured for thousands of hours at your hands."

There were bright spots too, like the day Coach Tom Brennan accompanied one of his athletes to the witness stand, and the world got to see what it looked like when an adult responded properly to allegations of abuse.[32] I wanted to cry as I heard Tom explain that he'd been a longtime friend of Larry's—a colleague, even. Larry was his advisor after graduate school. When

I came forward, Tom heard the reports. And he listened. Even though he was Larry's friend and colleague, he went back to the athletes he was close to and asked them if they had been abused. When they denied it, Tom went a step further, asking the questions that had to be asked so survivors could verbalize and face what had been done to them. Had Larry done the "procedure" I'd described? Had he worn gloves? Did he get consent? And as the horrific reality dawned on Tom, he helped his gymnasts accept and face it too. He helped them report to the police—coming to court with them, standing behind them as they spoke, steely anger burning in his eyes. Tom had done what no other authority figure had done for more than twenty years—believed and acted.

Another bright spot came the morning Jacob entered the courtroom first, only to quickly walk back toward me.

"Melody is here!" he said, his eyes brimming with tears. I made a beeline to where Jacob pointed, and Melody and I hugged and cried together. She had been the very first survivor to call me after the *IndyStar* report but had requested that her case be dropped early on. Yet she had played a vital role in stopping Larry. She was one of the first survivors willing to allow the *IndyStar* to use her story and the first to link Larry's abuse to his home, which made it possible for the child porn to be found. Now she had found her strength and had come to court to confront Larry.

Fellow survivor Brianne, the other woman I'd spoken to right after my story went out and who'd filed the first police report in 2004, sent me a text message to let me know she was flying in to give a statement as well.

There was Amanda, the survivor who'd filed the police report in 2014, the one whose case was closed just months before I came forward. Investigators had told her she was just confused. Now the world finally heard her speak and knew she'd told the truth back then.

Early one morning while walking from the parking garage to the courthouse, I heard someone call my name. I turned around as 1996 gold medalist Dominique Moceanu and her husband, Mike, stepped forward to meet me. Dominique knew what it is like to speak up and be berated or ignored, and she and Mike wanted to give us the support she had never received. Several other Olympians and elite gymnasts who had spoken up either submitted statements or came to the sentencing as well. Jamie Dantzscher, Jeanette Antolin, Mattie Larson, Jordyn Wieber, and Aly Raisman all flew in, lending their voices and platforms to take down their abuser and confront the institutions that had, for so long, enabled him.

• • •

Each night, Jacob and I would go back to my parents' home, exhausted. And each night, around 11:00, Angie would text me. "Not tomorrow." When the hearing started, I had an estimate of when I would give the final statement, but by the second night, the unprecedented and continual flow of survivors made it impossible to estimate any longer. We just had no idea what each day would bring. And still, unexpectedly, the world continued to watch. And as they did, the truth began to come out. John Geddert was unmasked for his explosive anger and gamut of abuse, from dropping gymnasts off the high bar to throwing them into equipment, or equipment into them.[33] Key leaders within MSU and USAG began to resign. Journalists published stories on how victims had been silenced over and over for years. A tidal wave was growing.

We recessed over the weekend. Sleep and time with the children were a welcome relief. I'd given up working on my impact statement.

"I've already said it all," I said to Jacob. I didn't need to describe what Larry had done. I'd been discussing my abuse and everything that surrounded it, almost daily, for a year and a half. I didn't need to tell Larry about the effect it had had on me. I'd already said it all under oath, and he had read my journal. Every word. What was left?

Finally, Angie texted me on Sunday evening. She was pretty sure we'd wrap up Wednesday, the twenty-fourth of January. Sterling and I—along with Kaylee—were scheduled to end the hearing, and then the judge would pass her sentence. Realizing I couldn't put off writing my statement any longer, I curled up with a blanket in my old bedroom that night, the room dark and silent as Ellianna slept in the crib next to me.

I began to type. And when I did, it was as if a dam inside me had been opened.

29

ON WEDNESDAY MORNING, January 24, 2018, we arrived at the court-house in the bitter cold for the last time. Once more we waited in line with survivors, parents, and news crews. The air was still tense, the grief ever-present. But the strength that had flowed from the moment Kyle began to speak had only grown. There was anticipation—a hope that it would be over—and that Larry would be given a sentence that ensured we would never have to do this again.

Sterling began that morning, her strong voice ringing out clearly and powerfully. How far we'd come from our days in the gym, now reconnected by an experience we should never have shared, but a beautiful friendship and alliance was growing out of the darkness.

When Kaylee rose to speak, she was already weeping. There was so much behind those tears, so much that she had already fought for. That day, as she spoke, her voice grew strong, unwavering.

"Ultimately, Larry, you made a critical mistake," she told him. "You underestimated the mind, power, and will of your victims. . . . We were ultimately strong enough to take you down. Not one by one but [as] an army of survivors."

I hugged Kaylee on her way back to her seat, so proud of the warrior she was, and had been, for so long. She was right; we had all done it together.

Then it was my turn. Angie introduced me to the judge, and I was filled with memories of everything she and Andrea had done. They had been the first people outside my family to cry with me. The first to say, "They deserve a voice," when our charges were going to be dropped. The first to pick up our reports and say, "I will fight for all of them." And because of them, because of the journalists in the courtroom who had tenaciously fought for the truth and told it for a year and a half, and because of the strength of every survivor who'd spoken up, we'd gotten here.

Jacob whispered, "I love you," and I felt the weight of what he meant, and everything that represented, and how faithfully he *had* loved me, more than anyone could ever know.

I approached the mic and began.

Thank you, first, Judge Aquilina, for giving all of us the chance to reclaim our voices. Our voices were taken from us for so long. . . .

There are two major purposes in our criminal justice system, Your Honor—the pursuit of justice and the protection of the innocent. . . .

The sentence rendered today will send a message across this country. A message to every victim and a message to every perpetrator. . . .

I submit to you that the preeminent question in this case as you reach a decision about how best to satisfy the dual aims of this court is the same question that I asked Judge Neff to consider in Larry's federal sentencing: How much is a little girl worth? How much is a young woman worth?

As I began, the words of the abolitionist William Wilberforce ran through my mind: "You may choose to look the other way but you can never again say you did not know."[34] In 1789, filled with passion over the evil of slavery and an unflinching commitment to see it end, he had risen in the British Parliament and described in unwavering graphic detail the evil of racism and the slave trade. He stood for hours, his words in stark contrast to the ornate building and sterile, haughty procedure that normally filled those chambers. He forced the comfortable elite to come face-to-face with the price of their apathy. My heart's cry as I spoke was the same—to remove the excuse of ignorance. To never again let the world say, "We did not know."

Next I turned to answering the question so many had asked in confusion. "How could this happen?" I could feel the anger rising as I spoke. For seventeen months I had asked the questions I would now ask again.

Was this the *right way* to respond to an allegation of sexual assault on MSU's campus? I asked over and over, laying out each and every known institutional failure. Each and every silencing, blaming, minimizing response. Was it right? I named the survivors known to have reported, their courage a model for everyone.

> I did not know that at the same time Larry was penetrating me, USAG was systematically burying reports of sexual assault against member coaches in a file cabinet instead of reporting them, creating a culture where predators like Larry and so many others in the organization, up to the highest-level coaches, were able to sexually abuse children, including our Olympians, without any fear of being caught.

This story was about so much more than Larry. And the voices that started the tidal wave were so much more than mine. One of those voices belonged to Becca. She sat quietly in the courtroom that day, but her presence meant so much to me. She was a survivor of a serial predator too—a USAG coach who had been allowed to move from gym to gym, abusing little girls. She had been one of the first to speak up to the *IndyStar*,[35] allowing them to put together the news story that prompted me to come forward too.

And then I began explaining to the courtroom the impact Larry's abuse had had on my life. How it had followed me. I'd been instructed to express everything the abuse had cost, and so I did.

My advocacy for sexual assault victims, something I cherished, cost
me my church and our closest friends three weeks before I filed my
police report. I was left alone and isolated. . . . When I came out,
my sexual assault was wielded like a weapon against me.

For more than a decade, I had refused to allow my abuse to define me.
But others didn't extend me that same courtesy. Once people knew about
my abuse, they no longer saw me first as a congregant, attorney, or any of
my other positions. They saw me as a sexual assault survivor. If I offered a
reasoned opinion on abuse, I was immediately categorized, maliciously or
not, by my own history as "emotional," "wounded," or "projecting her own
experiences." Knowing that this was the predominant way people—even the
most well-intentioned—thought about me was one of the most painful parts
of this experience.

I was subjected to lies and attacks on my character, including very
publicly by attorney Shannon Smith, when I testified under oath.
I was being attacked for wanting fame and attention, for making
a story up to try to get money.
    Your Honor, since these attacks were made on my character
very publicly, on public record, I would like to take an opportunity
briefly now to correct them.

Originally, I had no intention of referencing Shannon, who had stopped
coming to court after the first few days of impact statements. But when
Bailey, another survivor, gave her statement, she expressed her disagreement
with how Shannon had handled the case. One of Larry's attorneys interrupted
her. Apparently Shannon was following the proceedings from afar. I learned
later that she had instructed that lawyer to object to Bailey's statement and to
insist that Angie instruct the rest of us not to discuss defense counsel again.
The judge had allowed Bailey to continue, but I decided right then that my
fellow survivor wouldn't be left alone. I'd back her, if it was one of the only
things I put in my statement.
    I kept my remarks factual. I drew no conclusions and made no attacks.

Instead, I recited publicly available facts from the preliminary hearings, pointed and calculated to respond to the exact attacks Shannon had levied against me.

> Out of the two women in question that day—Ms. Smith and I,
> who were attempting to communicate through either questions
> or answers—I would like to note that only one of us was taking
> pictures of the courtroom on her cell phone. Only one of us posed
> for the press and said, quote, "I feel like I should say cheese!" And
> out of the two of us, only one of us was making money off her
> court appearance that day.

I saw Shannon's colleague rise up and begin to object. "I don't feel the need to say anything else," I cut her off. "I think I've communicated clearly." I then turned to Larry, to speak to him directly.

> The cost, emotional and physical, to see this through has been
> greater than many will ever know. . . .
> But I want you to understand why I made this choice, knowing
> full well what it was going to cost to get here and with very little
> hope of ever succeeding. I did it because *it was right*. No matter the
> cost, it was right. And the farthest I can run from what you have
> become is to daily choose what is *right* instead of what I *want*.

So many nights I had sat alone, the grief pressing in hard. Sometimes I'd ask myself, *Why can't I get over this?* But I came to realize my sorrow was a reminder that what Larry had done was the opposite of all that is beautiful in life. My grief was a normal response to what he had stolen from me, yet it was also a reminder that I could still choose the good and the true, as difficult as that often felt. It wasn't easy, but it was right.

> You have become a man ruled by selfish and perverted desires,
> a man defined by his daily choices, over and over again, to
> feed that selfishness and perversion. You chose to pursue your

wickedness, no matter what it cost others. And the opposite of what you have done is for me to choose to love sacrificially, no matter what it costs me.

So many nights, Jacob and I had sat up in the dark, wondering, "How does one get to be Larry? What makes a person become what Larry is?" Some people had theories, but really, no one knows the answer. What I did know was this: Larry did not wake up one morning and suddenly find himself to be a serial predator and pedophile. Whatever happened, happened in increments. One small choice after another. One refusal to turn away from evil. One decision to feed perverted curiosity. One attempt to see how far he could go. I was certain of this much—the very first time Larry saw child porn, or chose to abuse, he did not anticipate finding himself here, one of the worst pedophiles in recorded history. He made the choice, convincing himself it wasn't as bad as it really was. Not knowing what he would become as one choice followed another choice, action followed action, perverted thought followed perverted thought.

I wasn't Larry, but I had choices too. And like Larry's, those choices didn't stand in isolation. They set a trajectory. They forged a path. Thought by thought, action by action, my choices changed and guided who I was and who I would become. The choice had to be what was right. And it had to be motivated by love.

That sacrificial love does not exist in the abstract. It has a basis, a foundation, far beyond my human opinion or perception. I continued:

In our early hearings, you brought your Bible into the courtroom, and you have spoken of praying for forgiveness. And so it is on that basis that I appeal to you. If you have read the Bible you carry, you know that the definition of sacrificial love portrayed is of God Himself loving so sacrificially that He gave up everything to pay a penalty for the sin He did not commit. By His grace, I, too, choose to love this way.

And then I said the one thing that I still needed to tell Larry. The one thing related to him that I still prayed for.

You spoke of praying for forgiveness. But, Larry, if you have read the Bible you carry, you know forgiveness does not come by doing good things, as if good deeds can erase what you have done. It comes from repentance, which requires facing and acknowledging the truth about what you have done in all of its utter depravity and horror. Without mitigation. Without excuse. Without acting as if good deeds can erase what you have seen in this courtroom today. The Bible you carry says it is better for a millstone to be thrown around your neck and you thrown into a lake than for you to make even one child stumble.

Tears welled in my eyes as the face of each child from the past seven days flashed through my mind.

And you have damaged *hundreds*. The Bible you carry speaks of a final judgment where all of God's wrath, in its eternal terror, is poured out on men like you. Should you ever reach the point of truly facing what you have done, the guilt will be crushing.

So often in previous court hearings, I had watched Larry sit in the witness chair and bow his head. I watched tears fall. I saw the visible weight on his face as the evil he had done was paraded not just before him, but before the entire world. And I saw the battle. The hardness that would come and go as he warred with himself. The letter sent to the judge, full of self-pity and self-deception. The power of lying to *himself* about who he really was. The need he had to pretend what he'd done wasn't so bad, was justified, or was mitigated.

And so often I wondered, *What if that were me?* I wasn't Larry. Not by a long shot. But *what if* I had sat in that witness chair and every person I'd ever wounded with a thoughtless word, a wrong choice, or a lie stood before me? What if every broken thought I'd ever had were paraded before the world? What if I were fully honest with myself about every wrong choice I'd ever made, without minimizing, without mitigating, without turning my attention to nice things I'd done to cover over any guilt I felt? The power of self-deception and the need we all have to find a way to absolve our guilt was magnified tenfold in the broken man sitting in front of me. But the *pattern* of seeking ways to minimize or obscure our own wrong choices—that is in all of us. The danger of lying to ourselves about who we really are or things we've really done, no matter how "small" they seem in comparison to what others have done, is real.

> That is what makes the gospel of Christ so sweet. Because it extends grace and hope and mercy where none should be found.

I took a deep breath and continued:

> I pray you experience the soul-crushing weight of guilt so that you may someday experience true repentance and true forgiveness from God, which you need far more than forgiveness from me, though I extend that to you as well.

I remembered every night I cried in my basement. The circle diagram I'd drawn. The daily choice to let the darkness point me to the light. For wherever goodness exists, there is hope.

> Throughout this process, I have clung to a quote by C. S. Lewis, where he says, "My argument against God was that the universe seems so cruel and unjust. But how had I got this idea of unjust and just? A man does not call a line crooked unless he first has some idea of straight. What was I comparing the universe to when I called it unjust?"
>
> Larry, I can call what you did evil and wicked because it was. And I *know* it was evil and wicked because the straight line exists. The straight line is not measured based on your perception or anyone else's perception, and this means I can speak the truth about my abuse, without minimization or mitigation, and I can call it evil, because I know what goodness is.
>
> And this is why I pity you. Because when a person loses the ability to define good and evil, . . . they can no longer define and enjoy what is truly good. . . . You have shut yourself off from every

truly beautiful and good thing in this world that could have and should have brought you joy and fulfillment. And I pity you for it.

So many days during the last two years, as the depth of Larry's evil pressed in on me, I found refuge and rest in what was beautiful and good. The trustworthy, sacrificial love of my husband. The sacredness of true intimacy. The safety of my own father and mother. As I wept for the children in the videos found on Larry's computer, I wrapped my own children in my arms and breathed in the unspeakable joy of being their refuge. I felt them relax in my arms and knew the gift of *being safe*. I remembered the days I coached and how perfect and sweet it was to help a child find confidence and delight and see her own strength and growth.

In the very first *IndyStar* interview, I had listed everything Larry was capable of, and the trust and love he had engendered, and I'd said, "What a waste," trying to express the grief I'd felt. Because it was. *He could have been everything he pretended to be.* He could have *had* everything we all thought he had. The prestige, the reputation, the genuine love and gratitude of so many. A good marriage. The love of his children. *He could have had it all.* But over and over again, he'd listened to the lie that it wouldn't satisfy. Over and over again, he'd chosen to believe that he needed something else. The fact that he needed it—or simply wanted it—was enough to make that thing excusable. With the ability to delight in what was right and good gone, he was left with perversions that could never satiate. He had turned away from the good and beautiful things that could fulfill and was left with nothing.

In losing the ability to call evil what it is, without mitigation, without minimization, you have lost the ability to define and enjoy love and goodness. You have fashioned for yourself a prison that is far, far worse than any I could ever put you in.

As I considered what Larry had forfeited, I felt deep sadness well up inside me.

And I pity you for that.

Yet love was also what made the process so painful.

> In many ways, Your Honor, the worst part of this process was each
> name, each number, who came forward to the police. With each
> Jane Doe, I saw my little girls, and the little girls that were. The little
> girls who walked into Larry's office that I could not save because no
> one wanted to listen. . . .

I could barely hold back the tears. The courtroom was filled with these
women. The ones I had cried for in my kitchen over and over. The ones I
wondered if I would ever meet.

> I cried for them, and with every tear that fell, I wondered, who is
> going to find these little girls? Who is going to tell them how much
> they are worth? How valuable they are, how deserving of justice and
> protection? Who is going to tell these little girls that what was done
> to them *matters*? That they are seen and valued? That they are not
> alone and they are not unprotected? . . .
>   To everyone who is watching, I ask that same question. How
> much is a little girl worth? . . . Look around the courtroom.
> Remember what you have witnessed these past seven days.

Do not forget, I pled with everyone. Do not look away. Remember this
moment the next time you are faced with choices that are right, but hard.

> *This is what it looks like* when someone chooses to put their selfish
> desires above the safety and love for those around them. And let it
> be a warning to us all. . . .

> *This is what it looks like* when the adults in authority do not respond
> properly to disclosures of sexual assault.

> *This is what it looks like* when institutions create a culture where a
> predator can flourish unafraid and unabated.

This is what it looks like when people in authority refuse to listen, put friendships in front of the truth, fail to create or enforce proper policy, and fail to hold enablers accountable.

This is what it looks like.

I felt every tear that had been cried over the past week, by every sister survivor. Every broken parent. Every bit of anger and despair. And every bit of strength.

It looks like a courtroom full of survivors who carry deep wounds. Women and girls who have banded together to fight for themselves because no one else would do it. Women and girls who carry scars that will never fully heal, but who have made the choice to place the guilt and the shame on the only person to whom it belongs—the abuser.

With each word, the survivors and their families had picked themselves up and done what no one else wanted to do. And with each word, they reclaimed who they were.

But may the horror expressed in this courtroom over the last seven days be motivation for anyone and everyone, no matter the context, to take responsibility if they have erred in protecting a child. To understand the incredible failures that led to this week, and to *do it better the next time.*

Nearly forty minutes after I approached the podium, I made my final request.

Judge Aquilina, I plead with you, as you deliberate the sentence to give Larry, send a message that these victims are worth everything. In order to meet both the goals of this court, I plead with you to impose the maximum sentence under the plea agreement. Because everything is what these survivors are worth.

I stood as the judge spoke gracious words of encouragement, and then I gathered my notes, turning one final time to look at Larry. As I turned back toward the courtroom, I was overwhelmed at the gift we had all been given. The strength we had found together. What I had hoped to accomplish had grown so far beyond what I could have even imagined, because of every voice that was raised.

I hugged the fierce women who had brought us here, the first ones to fight for me—for all of us—Angie, Andrea, Robyn. And then I reached Jacob. He wrapped me in his arms and I relaxed for what felt like the first time since August 12, 2016. Deep sobs shook his body, and I whispered, "Done. It is done." I had finished what I'd started.

•   •   •

I listened as Larry stood to make his final statement, speaking words of sorrow and apology, turning repeatedly to face the survivor army as he did so. He said all the right things. He slumped in just the right posture of brokenness.

I watched as Judge Aquilina skillfully unmasked, once again, a predator's incredible power to manipulate. "I know there are still some who ask, are you broken because you got caught?" she said calmly. Then she pulled out the letter Larry had written to her, telling the court she wanted to read more of it aloud:

> The federal judge went ballistic at sentencing since I pled guilty
> to the state cases. . . . I was sentenced to 60 years. Not proper,
> appropriate, fair. . . . I tried to avoid a trial to save the stress to this
> community, my family, the victims, yet look what is happening.
> . . . I was a good doctor because my treatments worked, and those
> patients that are now speaking out were the same ones that praised
> and came back over and over. . . . The media convinced them that
> everything I did was wrong and bad. They feel I broke their trust.
> Hell hath no fury like a woman scorned.

A murmur of disgust rose in the gallery. Survivors who had sobbed at Larry's apology lifted their heads, seeing through the carefully crafted words and artfully expressed emotional facade from just moments earlier.

Judge Aquilina turned to Larry. "You have not owned what you did," she told him. And she sentenced him to a minimum of 40 years in prison, up to 175. He would never harm a woman or child again.

Over the coming days, I thought often of what I had whispered to Jacob. "It is done." Deep inside, I knew when I said it, that it wasn't really over. Nothing ever is.

When the other survivors and I exited the courtroom after raising our voices—many for the very first time—the hard road of healing began. Finding ourselves—discovering who we now were in the changed world we'd created—would be a journey. The cultures and institutions that had enabled our predator still remained. The societal and legislative changes we needed to see would be slow in coming.

But "it is done" was also true. What I had set out to do—stop a predator and give survivors a voice—had been accomplished. No, the work wasn't done. But that chapter was. And in many ways, that chapter was less about finishing and more about *starting*. Starting the healing for so many. Starting a new day where Larry had no more power. Starting the change. Starting to find our voices.

And together, we had.

Epilogue

AS I'D KNOWN, the work really wasn't done. This was a "now or never" moment for change, and we had to seize it. Immediately after I spoke, I was swept into a flood of media interviews and private meetings that had been arranged days before, not knowing what would transpire in the Ingham County courtroom. That very night, I sat in the president's mansion at MSU with Lou Anna Simon and Lt. Governor Brian Calley, who had been helping survivors behind the scenes long before anyone knew of his support. When we'd set up the meeting, we'd planned to discuss a way forward, but President Simon tendered her resignation that evening.

By 11:00 that night, I was on a plane to New York City for more media interviews, arriving back in Michigan the next day for another late-night meeting with the MSU board chair and another trustee. They shed tears as I pled with them to take steps toward accountability and transparency, to stop treating survivors as adversaries, and to realize the damage their response to this crisis was causing young women. However, after I left that meeting, I never heard from either one again.

John Engler, the former governor of Michigan, was appointed MSU's interim president just one week later over the objections of faculty and staff who'd urged the board not to hire a former politician. The board received a vote of "no confidence" from the faculty shortly thereafter. Engler rejected repeated requests by Lt. Governor Calley and other lawmakers to meet with me.

Under intense pressure, MSU eventually requested that the Michigan attorney general review the situation for potential crimes related to the handling of the Nassar scandal. MSU then withheld critical information, claiming attorney-client privilege; intentionally copied attorneys on internal communications so they could invoke attorney-client privilege; and responded to many of the AG's document requests either with silence or by sending a deluge of irrelevant documents, such as their policies for dealing with bed bugs in dorm rooms.[36]

At the time of this writing, three high-ranking officials at MSU have been criminally charged. Kathie Klages and Lou Anna Simon were indicted for allegedly lying to investigators about prior warnings of Larry's behavior. Larry's boss, Dean William Strampel, was charged with criminal negligence in his supervision of Larry, as well as criminal sexual conduct with medical students. Reporters and investigators eventually discovered that Dean Strampel's MSU personnel file contained accounts of his own abusive and harassing behavior, while his work computer contained photos of nude MSU students and their genitalia, images prosecutors say he solicited from students. His response to allegations against Larry, and his failure to supervise him, made a lot more sense when these details became public.[37]

Other high-ranking officials at MSU resigned without acknowledging any failures, but many of the employees who were involved remained employed without sanctions. Among these were the athletic trainers who were told of Larry's abuse; the Title IX coordinators who first cleared him; and the MSU police detective who did not interview any outside medical expert during the 2014 investigation of Larry, despite a request from the county prosecutor.[38] Several employees received promotions. MSU has yet to answer the questions I posed in my impact statement, or admit even one misstep. At the time of this writing, they have still refused to allow investigators to evaluate any failures beyond criminal failures, though most of what allowed Larry to abuse for decades wasn't illegal.

Survivors, particularly Kaylee and I, endured repeated attacks by MSU and USAG leadership. A reporter told me that, behind closed doors, MSU spokesman Jason Cody had said I was in this for the money. Reporters also found private emails between John Engler and leaders at MSU, speculating that I'd "manipulated" survivors for monetary kickbacks.[39] At about the same time, I received a message from Kaylee and her mom: Had I met with John Engler? During a private meeting, Engler asked Kaylee to tell him how much money she wanted. Would $250,000 be enough? When Kaylee told him she was looking for accountability and reform, not a payout, he told her she should tell him how much she wanted because *I'd* met with him and demanded a specific dollar amount.[40] I was shocked as I read Kaylee's account of their conversation, and I told her the truth: I had never met with him and certainly never demanded money. Publicly Engler said simply that his "interpretation and memories" of the meeting differed from theirs.[41] Yet MSU suggested in internal emails that Kaylee had been spreading "false news," and implied that survivors were willing to say anything for money.[42] But when we entered mediation a short time later, MSU's first offer matched the exact number Kaylee publicly reported Engler had offered her in their meeting.

We discovered that, while MSU was refusing to meet with survivors, they'd paid hundreds of thousands of dollars to PR firms to monitor survivors' social media accounts.[43] Survivors told me that both MSU and USAG hired private investigators—not to find out what allowed Larry to abuse for decades, but rather to track and discredit his victims. One woman told me her past boyfriends had been contacted, another that her identity as a survivor had been disclosed to her boss by a private investigator, and a third told me that an investigator had threatened her with a subpoena if she refused to disclose the names of other victims. (A private investigator has no such power.)

In the midst of what seemed like a constant onslaught, Sterling and I continued to work with Michigan senator Margaret O'Brien, a passionate and skilled lawmaker whom I'd met more than a decade before, on a series of ten bills designed to strengthen Michigan's protections for sexual-crime victims, which were some of the weakest in the country. Our efforts began in the Senate in the early spring. Our package passed in the Senate, despite MSU's publicly opposing it and John Engler personally visiting the Senate Majority leader's office.[44] Multiple witnesses told me that the discussion became so heated that

Engler began swearing and yelling, demanding that the reforms be stopped. I expressed concerns about MSU's and Engler's stand against survivors and was told by Engler's spokesman that it was "inappropriate" for us to speak up.[45]

Our Senate package was sent to the Michigan House of Representatives. During testimony in support of the bills in the House, survivors begged lawmakers to stand with them, but the responses of several representatives were so vitriolic during questioning that at least one witness left in tears. On the day we reached a settlement with MSU, we discovered that the most important provisions in the package would never make it out of the House committee, effectively killing our legislation. People who thought we were in it for money said we should be celebrating the settlement, but instead I hugged weeping survivors who wanted to know how children could matter so little to their elected officials. Our settlement was reached without MSU agreeing to any measures of reform or admitting any wrongdoing.[46]

The survivors and our supporters realized, over and over, how close we had come to losing the opportunity to stop Larry and how pervasive institutional corruption is. Journalists who had been trying to discover what happened to the first report USAG made to the FBI in 2015 told me things weren't lining up. In 2018, emails came to light that revealed how Steve Penny, when he was president of USAG, met for drinks with Jay Abbott, the special agent in charge of the FBI's Indianapolis field office, who was supposed to be investigating Larry. There was a job opening at the United States Olympic Committee (USOC), Penny told Abbott, and Abbott applied for the position. Penny then recommended him for it.[47] Meanwhile, the agency's investigation of Larry stalled for more than a year, during which time he treated and abused more children in Michigan.[48]

When I came forward in 2016 and investigations finally began in earnest, Penny sent a USAG employee to remove all the medical files housed at the Texas facility where many top USAG gymnasts trained. No one knows what happened to those records. Penny was asked to testify before the US Senate during an inquiry, but he pled the Fifth, refusing to answer a single question. At the time of this writing, Penny has been charged with evidence tampering, and the FBI's handling of the Nassar case is under investigation by the US Justice Department.[49]

Penny had also turned to Bruce Smith, his friend and the then-head of the Indianapolis Metropolitan Police Department's child abuse unit, to help quash the first *IndyStar* report—the one that had prompted me to come forward. Penny asked Smith to help him "kill the story," according to correspondence between the two. "We need to body slam the other sources," one of Penny's text messages read.[50] We now know of at least five separate times law enforcement could have, and should have, stopped Larry. But no one did—until Detective Andrea Munford.

In early 2018, I received an offer from USAG to join its board when the USOC forced resignations from past members. I told them I would gladly consider it once they took steps toward accountability, transparency, and caring for the gymnasts who'd been abused by coaches they had allowed to continue unchecked in the program, even after receiving warnings. That was the last time USAG leadership ever contacted me. The organization is now on its fourth president in less than two years and has filed for bankruptcy.

Along with eight other survivors, I was selected to serve on a committee participating in the bankruptcy court process; the nine of us represent all survivors who were abused within USAG. In February 2019, several of us attended a bankruptcy hearing on behalf of the committee, where I had the opportunity to ask questions of USAG. Among other questions, I asked if the organization had reviewed the files that the *IndyStar* reported in its first article—the one that contained reports of abusive coaches—to ensure that alleged abusers were no longer coaching. They hadn't. The USAG leader to whom I addressed my question said he wasn't even aware of the reports. At the time of this writing, bankruptcy proceedings are ongoing.

MSU, USAG, and USOC do not stand alone, however, in their resistance to institutional change. The line in my impact statement about losing my church had an effect I never foresaw. It garnered the attention of national publications that began investigating the missteps churches so often make when handling abuse. Some prominent evangelical groups that had heralded my victim-impact statement for its gospel message cooled when I continued to speak about the scandals and serious allegations made against prominent leaders and religious groups—the community of Christians I call my own. With a heavy heart, I saw again that everyone appreciates advocacy when it's directed to those "outside the camp," but when it demands that we evaluate our own faith communities, political parties, favorite sports team, candidates, or beloved leaders, we scramble for reasons why things are "different" in that space. This is the blind spot that keeps abusers protected and convinces victims that it's never safe to speak up.

Yet in the midst of it all, there have been bright spots too. I've been encouraged by advocates and allies who refuse to give up on what is right. Journalists who won't let go of the truth. Church leaders and pastors who recognize the need for change and growth, taking constructive steps to learn and to address these problems. Jacob and I were contacted by elders from our former church. We met multiple times, engaging in open conversations that were full of grace. Relationships were restored, and the honest and straightforward public statement they issued not long after, with actions that followed, brought healing for us all.[51]

Our fourth child and third daughter burst into the world at the end of July 2018. She shares her middle name, Renee, with Andrea Munford, whose work changed my life and so many others' when she chose to listen and pursue the truth, no matter the cost. Our daughter's first name, Elora, means "to God belongs the victory," a fitting reminder at the end of this journey and our reassurance for whatever comes in the future.

Jacob is gradually working to finish the PhD coursework that was so thoroughly derailed by the Nassar investigation. We are striving to find a new normal as a family of six and to heal from what we've been through over the past three years. We have begun the work of education and advocacy in earnest, speaking to a vast array of organizations, from universities to nonprofits, bar associations to churches.

In December 2018, Elora and I walked the red carpet with Angela, Andrea, Aly Raisman, and Judge Aquilina for the *Glamour* Women of the Year awards. I'd received an email months before informing me that the five of us had been chosen. Fittingly, I opened the invitation just as Elora blew out her diaper, a second child had an accident, and I was facing a mountain of laundry—an ironic and hilarious message to receive in that moment and a tribute to the "real life" going on as we navigated this new path.

A couple of months before the awards presentation, *Glamour* invited a larger group of the survivors to gather for a group photo in Michigan's Supreme Court building, which is fittingly known as the Hall of Justice. I held my three-year-old, Ellianna, in my arms as the photographers began lining us up for the photo. With her head on my shoulder, she gestured with her dimpled hand toward the women and asked in her baby voice, "Who are they, Mommy?"

"They are Mommy's friends, sweetheart, the ones who put a bad man in jail. Now we're helping change things so that it isn't so easy for bad men to do bad things again."

"But Mommy," she replied in confusion, "there are kids in there."

"Yes, baby girl. There are kids in there."

"But Mommy, *why* are there kids in there?"

"Because even kids can be courageous, tell the truth, and stand up for what is right."

And then she paused, taking in the sight of so many women standing shoulder to shoulder, her little mind clearly working to make sense of it all.

"But Mommy, why are there so many?"

I held her tight. I couldn't answer because I knew I wouldn't be able to hold back the tears anymore if I tried. *There are so many, sweet girl, because no one did the job these women and courageous children are doing now. There are so many because no one listened. No one wanted to know the truth. No one did the right thing.*

She looked at me, her eyes wide with innocence. "All of you are doing it together?"

"Yes, honey," I said, hugging her tightly and then relinquishing her to my mom's arms so I could join the photo. "We're doing it together. Like a big team, we're doing it together."

We're doing it together, I mused, taking my place among the sisterhood, *because we can't do it alone.*

So much work remains. So much evil to fight. So much healing to reach for. So many wounded to love. Consider this your invitation to join in that work. To do what is right, no matter the cost. To hold to the straight line in the midst of the battle. To define your success by faithfulness in the choices you make. The darkness is there, and we cannot ignore it. But we can let it point us to the light.

Acknowledgments

Everything that has transpired over the past few years could never have been accomplished without the incredible support we have received from so many.

First, an incredible thank-you to my amazing sister-in-law, the *other* Rachel Denhollander, who loved on our kids, folded endless loads of laundry, and kept me supplied with espresso through this process (a lot of espresso was required). Without her selfless care for all of us, this project wouldn't have been completed until I had grandkids. Any good that this book is able to do was made possible through her sacrificial service. With much thanks also to my sister-in-law Miriam, who likewise sacrificed a great deal so that this project could come to fruition.

To my sister, Bethany, and brother-in-law, Charlie, and to my brother and sister-in-law, Josh and Christa—thank you for the immeasurable ways you have all supported us at significant personal cost. Caring for our kids, bringing meals, cleaning the house while we were away in court, and traveling to be with us. You "did life" with us in intensely personal and practical ways, and we felt your love and support every minute. It made more of a difference than you will ever know.

A heartfelt thank-you to Pastor Jim and Becky, and the other pastors and their wives at RBC Louisville for shepherding us well, caring for us so compassionately, speaking the truth, and being willing to step into the mess with us, providing wisdom, encouragement, and care. Your faithful service and leadership have been a gift to us beyond what we could express. An immense thank-you to Heather for sacrificing so much time, loving our children and us so compassionately, and providing respite and care when we were exhausted and worn. Thank you to Tammy, Michelle, and so many others who provided practical care and deep encouragement when we most needed it. And grateful thanks to our church family at RBC Louisville—your prayers and care, and the time you took simply to listen, have strengthened us so many times over the past two years and brought comfort when we needed it the most.

We are equally grateful for the pastors and church body of RBC Kalamazoo, who likewise poured out care, wisdom, and compassion, supporting us in prayer and never ceasing to offer practical help as we walked this journey. The love you have shown, even though we are so far away, has been an incredible testament to God's love and grace, and has brought rest and healing to our souls.

To the Denhollander family—Mom and Dad, Sarah and Jordan, all our siblings and in-laws—we are so grateful for your support, prayers, and encouragement over the past few years. Love truly does cross the miles, and we felt it through the most painful times.

To my Oak Brook brothers—thank you for bringing healing and setting a positive example of manhood when you could have done so much damage, and for the support and encouragement you provided as we walked this road.

To Keith, who first willingly stepped into this with us and proactively sought to help in the journey—your life of doing justice, loving mercy, and walking humbly has impacted us so much more than you will ever see. Amy, thank you for taking the time to meet regularly with my mom and lift all of us up in prayer. For offering practical support, providing meals when we came into town, and accompanying me to court more than once. Like so many, you did not need to enter this with us, but you chose to, and through your compassionate care, brought encouragement, joy, and hope.

To my entire Tyndale team, especially Sarah, Carol, Kim, and Jan—thank you for the endless hours and incredible effort you have put into this project, and into me. This was the project I never wanted to do because I knew how painful it would be, but your passion for impacting the world through the written word made it worth the struggle. You have cared well for the message, and for me, through every part of this process. Thank you for hearing my heart, using your skills to bring this book into a (somewhat) reasonable size, and keeping me amply supplied with enough super cookies to get over the hard parts! You've given these truths a voice, and poured your expertise and energy into ensuring the heart and message of the story is communicated clearly, accurately, and powerfully.

To my mom and dad, who taught me every lesson that made this possible and have sacrificed so much throughout my entire life, and especially these past few years, to support and care for us—it is impossible to express the depth of gratitude we feel or how much impact you have had. You laid the foundation lovingly and patiently from the day I was born. Mom, you taught me how to heal, and that hope was worth fighting for. I knew from you that the work of healing was hard, but possible. That marriage, children, and joy can come after abuse, and that sacrificially doing what is right is worth it, no matter what the cost. You didn't sugarcoat the realities, but you did not leave me wallowing in them either. Everything that has transpired began in our little home, decades ago, with the faithful, wise, nurturing care of you and Dad.

To my dad and brother—thank you for being the first examples of safe manhood; for affirming me, protecting me, and showing me what integrity and honor look like. I often wonder where I would be had you not impacted my life literally every day.

And to Jacob, who has displayed strength and sacrificial love far beyond what I could ever have asked or imagined. You promised me in the beginning that the hand I held would only ever be used to care for me, and you have kept your word at every point. You have sought my good when it cost you greatly. You have willingly given up desires so you could walk with me every step of the way. You have sacrificed in the greatest and most tedious ways. You have been my safe place, my comfort, my greatest encourager. You have helped me grieve and made me laugh, kept me safe and challenged me to grow, though it felt frightening. You have brought more healing than I thought possible, and your example challenges me every day to love better. We did this together, and it could not have been done any other way.

> *Now to Him who is able to do far more abundantly beyond*
> *all that we ask or think, according to the power that works*
> *within us, to Him be the glory in the church and in Christ*
> *Jesus to all generations forever and ever. Amen.*
>
> EPHESIANS 3:20-21

Notes

1. Marisa Kwiatkowski, Mark Alesia, and Tim Evans, "A Blind Eye to Sex Abuse: How USA Gymnastics Failed to Report Cases," *IndyStar*, August 4, 2016, https://www.indystar.com /story/news/investigations/2016/08/04/usa-gymnastics-sex-abuse-protected-coaches /85829732/.
2. L. M. Montgomery, *Anne of Green Gables* (Boston: L. C. Page, 1908), chap. 2.
3. Matt Mencarini, "John Geddert Investigation Still Open a Year After It Began in the Wake of Nassar Sentencings," *Lansing State Journal*, January 22, 2019, https://www.lansingstate journal.com/story/news/local/2019/01/22/john-geddert-still-under-investigation-year -after-larry-nassar-cases/2605297002/.
4. C. S. Lewis, *Mere Christianity* (New York: HarperCollins, 1952), 38.
5. This expression was popularized by the University of Chicago scholar Richard Weaver in his 1948 book with that title.
6. P. G. Wodehouse, *Piccadilly Jim* (Woodstock, NY: The Overlook Press, 2004), 298–99.
7. Tiffany Stanley, "The Sex-Abuse Scandal That Devastated a Suburban Megachurch," *Washingtonian*, February 14, 2016, https://www.washingtonian.com/2016/02/14/the-sex -abuse-scandal-that-devastated-a-suburban-megachurch-sovereign-grace-ministries/.
8. Kwiatkowski, Alesia, and Evans, "A Blind Eye to Sex Abuse."
9. Mark Alesia, "Why Coaches' Hugs Make Becca Seaborn Cringe," *IndyStar*, August 4, 2016, https://www.indystar.com/story/news/investigations/2016/08/04/usa-gymnastics -why-coaches-hugs-make-becca-seaborn-cringe/87967164/.
10. Here and following, quotes are from videotaped interview with Mark Alesia of the *IndyStar*; see Tim Evans, Mark Alesia, and Marisa Kwiatkowski, "Former USA Gymnastics Doctor Accused of Abuse," *IndyStar*, September 12, 2016, https://www.indystar.com/story/news /2016/09/12/former-usa-gymnastics-doctor-accused-abuse/89995734/.
11. Statistics on rape from "The Criminal Justice System: Statistics," Rape, Abuse & Incest National Network (RAINN), accessed April 16, 2019, https://www.rainn.org/statistics /criminal-justice-system; information on untested rape kits from "What Is the Rape Kit Backlog?" End the Backlog, accessed April 16, 2019, http://www.endthebacklog.org/backlog /what-rape-kit-backlog.
12. Evans, Alesia, and Kwiatkowski, "Former USA Gymnastics Doctor Accused of Abuse."

13. Marisa Kwiatkowski, Tim Evans, and Mark Alesia, "16 More Women Accuse Former USA Gymnastics Doctor of Sexual Abuse," *IndyStar*, September 25, 2016, https://www.indystar.com/story/news/investigations/2016/09/25/16-more-women-accuse-doctor-sexual-abuse/90410436/.

14. John Manly has spoken publicly about his personal story, including a 2018 interview with Gustavo Arellano in *Alta* entitled "The Advocate."

15. Matt Mencarini, "Ex-MSU Doctor Accused of Sex Assault Gets 2,700 School Board Votes," *Detroit Free Press*, November 9, 2016, https://www.freep.com/story/news/local/michigan/2016/11/09/msu-doctor-sexual-assault-election/93546324/.

16. Julie Mack, "MSU Officials Told in 2000 of Sexual Abuse by Dr. Nassar, Lawyer Alleges," MLive Media Group, December 21, 2016, https://www.mlive.com/news/2016/12/msu_athletic_trainers_told_in.html.

17. Matt Mencarini, "Kathie Klages Charges Tied to Two Teens' Complaints of Larry Nassar's Sexual Abuse in 1997," *Lansing State Journal*, August 30, 2018, https://www.lansingstatejournal.com/story/news/local/2018/08/30/kathie-klages-charges-arraignment-larry-nassar/1124034002.

18. Dory Jackson, "Ex-Michigan Coach Kathie Klages Charged with Lying in Larry Nassar Investigation," *Newsweek*, August 23, 2018, https://www.newsweek.com/kathie-klages-charged-lying-larry-nassar-sexual-abuse-1088489.

19. Julie Mack, "MSU Colleagues Initially Defended Nassar, According to Police Investigation," MLive Media Group, April 4, 2018, https://www.mlive.com/news/2018/04/msu_colleagues_initially_defen.html.

20. Will Hobson, "Doctor at Center of USA Gymnastics Scandal Left Warning Signs at Michigan State," *Washington Post*, April 25, 2017. For Rachael's open letters, see Nick Martin, "Gymnast Writes Open Letters To Michigan State Leaders Who Claim Sexual Abuse Couldn't Be Prevented," *Deadspin*, May 2, 2017, https://deadspin.com/gymnast-writes-open-letters-to-michigan-state-leaders-w-1794844898.

21. *Spotlight*, directed by Tom McCarthy (Los Angeles: Open Road Films, 2015; Universal City, CA: Universal Studios Home Entertainment, 2016).

22. *Spotlight*, directed by Tom McCarthy.

23. Kate Wells, "Three Alleged Victims Testify against Nassar in Graphic, Tense Court Hearing," Michigan Radio, May 13, 2017, https://www.michiganradio.org/post/three-alleged-victims-testify-against-nassar-graphic-tense-court-hearing.

24. Wells, "Three Alleged Victims Testify against Nassar."

25. Katharine Quamby, quoted in Shelagh Beckett et al., "Covering Child Sexual Abuse," Dart Center for Journalism & Trauma, https://dartcenter.org/resources/covering-child-sexual-abuse.

26. Matt Mencarini, "11 Rapes, 4 States, 1 Suspect: The 'Extraordinarily Improbable' Defense of Calvin Kelly," *Lansing State Journal*, February 1, 2019, https://www.lansingstatejournal.com/story/news/2019/01/08/calvin-kelly-rape-investigations-memphis-kalamazoo-st-louis/2462538002/.

27. Madison O'Connor, "Motions to Be Discussed in Nassar Court Hearing Friday," *State News*, November 2, 2017, https://statenews.com/article/2017/11/nassar-court-preview.

28. Emily Lawler, "Meet the Attorney Defending Michigan's Most Notorious Sex Cases," MLive Media Group, November 2, 2017, https://www.mlive.com/news/2017/11/attorney_shannon_smith.html.

29. Brian McVicar, "MSU Attorneys Tell AG Schuette That There Is No Nassar Investigative Report," MLive Media Group, December 8, 2017, https://www.mlive.com/news/2017/12/msu_attorneys_tell_ag_schuette.html.

30. Jessica Schladebeck, "USA Gymnastics Argues It's Not 'Liable' to Victims of Larry Nassar's Sexual Abuse," *New York Daily News*, December 12, 2017, https://www.nydailynews.com /news/national/usa-gymnastics-not-liable-victims-larry-nassar-article-1.3694063.

31. Rebecca Kruth, "Gymnastics Club Owner Wants Larry Nassar Lawsuit Dismissed," Michigan Radio, January 15, 2018, https://www.michiganradio.org/post/gymnastics-club-owner-wants -larry-nassar-lawsuit-dismissed.

32. Tracy O'Connor, "Coach Slams Gymnastics Doctor Larry Nassar for Hiding His Face," NBC News, January 17, 2018, https://www.nbcnews.com/news/us-news/coach-slams -gymnastics-doctor-larry-nassar-hiding-his-face-n838396.

33. David Eggert, "Molested Gymnasts Blast Coach Who Sent Them to Larry Nassar," *Chicago Tribune*, February 1, 2018, https://www.chicagotribune.com/sports/international/ct-molested -gymnasts-blast-coach-who-sent-them-to-doctor-20180201-story.html. See also Mila Murray and Kara Keating, "Day 1 of Nassar's Sentencing in Eaton County Begins," *State News*, January 31, 2018, https://statenews.com/article/2018/01/nassar-sentencing-in-eaton-county.

34. From William Wilberforce's 1789 Abolition Speech, quoted in Georgeta Raţă and Patricia-Luciana Runcan, eds., *Social Issues* (Newcastle upon Tyne, England: Cambridge Scholars Publishing, 2014), 42.

35. Alesia, "Why Coaches' Hugs Make Becca Seaborn Cringe."

36. Kim Kozlowski, "State Investigator's Report: MSU 'Stonewalls' Nassar Probe," *Detroit News*, December 21, 2018, https://www.detroitnews.com/story/news/local/michigan/2018/12/21 /investigators-report-says-michigan-state-stonewalls-nassar-probe/2376904002/.

37. Tracy Connor, "Michigan State Admits It Was Warned about Dean William Strampel in 2015," NBC News, May 2, 2018, https://www.nbcnews.com/news/us-news/michigan -state-admits-it-was-warned-about-dean-william-strampel-n870616; Dan Murphy, "William Strampel Charged with Assaulting Students, Storing Nude Photos," ESPN, March 28, 2018, http://www.espn.com/college-sports/story/_/id/22930449/michigan -state-official-william-strampel-charged-criminal-sexual-conduct.

38. Matt Mencarini, "Larry Nassar: 2014 Police Report Sheds Light on How He Avoided Criminal Charges," *Lansing State Journal*, January 26, 2018, https://www.wgrz.com /article/news/nation-now/larry-nassar-2014-police-report-sheds-light-on-how-he-avoided -criminal-charges/465-40c19051-219c-4add-b5ef-9213056b7e7a.

39. David Jesse, "MSU President Engler: Nassar Survivor May Get Kickbacks from Lawyer," *Detroit Free Press*, June 13, 2018, https://www.freep.com/story/news/local/michigan /2018/06/13/msu-larry-nassar-rachael-denhollander/699307002/.

40. Kate Wells, "Nassar Survivor Accuses Engler of 'Secret Payoff' Attempt," Michigan Radio, April 13, 2018, https://www.michiganradio.org/post/nassar-survivor-accuses-engler-secret -payoff-attempt.

41. Ibid.

42. "Michigan State VP Knocks Nassar Victim, Then Apologizes," Associated Press, April 18, 2018, https://apnews.com/040a364850ca4d81a824674a3ce1ce8a.

43. Riley Murdock, "Report: Firm Charged MSU $500K to Monitor Survivor, Journalist Social Media," *State News*, March 29, 2018, https://statenews.com/article/2018/03/msu-pr-firm -500k-monitor-social-media-survivors-journalists-january.

44. Jonathan Oosting and Kim Kozlowski, "Engler: Lawmakers 'Interfered' in Nassar Lawsuit Talks," *Detroit News*, March 15, 2018, https://www.detroitnews.com/story/news/politics /2018/03/15/msu-nassar-lawsuit-talks-divisions/32961185/; Emily Lawler, "MSU Interim President John Engler Privately Worked to Stall Senate Sexual Assault Bills," MLive Media

Group, March 15, 2018, https://www.mlive.com/news/2018/03/msu_interim_president
_john_eng.html.

45. "Michigan Senate Passes Legislation That Gives People Who Are Sexually Abused More
Options," ESPN, March 15, 2018, http://www.espn.com/college-sports/story/_/id
/22766765/michigan-senate-passes-legislation-backed-victims-larry-nassar.

46. Lauren Theisen, "Here's Michigan State's Settlement Agreement with Larry Nassar's Victims,"
Deadspin, July 18, 2018, https://deadspin.com/heres-michigan-states-settlement-agreement
-with-larry-n-1827705229.

47. Serge F. Kovaleski and Juliet Macur, "Steve Penny Asked F.B.I. to Help Protect U.S.A.
Gymnastics' Image during Sex Abuse Case," *New York Times*, October 18, 2018, https://
www.nytimes.com/2018/10/18/sports/steve-penny-usa-gymnastics-fbi.html.

48. Dan Barry, Serge F. Kovaleski, and Juliet Macur, "As F.B.I. Took a Year to Pursue the Nassar
Case, Dozens Say They Were Molested," *New York Times*, February 3, 2018, https://www
.nytimes.com/2018/02/03/sports/nassar-fbi.html.

49. Kovaleski and Macur, "Steve Penny Asked F.B.I. to Help Protect U.S.A. Gymnastics' Image
during Sex Abuse Case."

50. Tony Cook, Tim Evans, and Marisa Kwiatkowski, "New Nassar Report Details USA
Gymnastics Chief's Cozy Ties with IMPD, FBI Officials," *IndyStar*, December 14, 2018,
https://www.indystar.com/story/news/politics/2018/12/14/ropes-gray-larry-nassar-usoc
-report-usa-gymnastics-indianapolis-police-fbi-cozy-details/2275210002/.

51. "Our Pastors' Statement to the *Washington Post*," May 31, 2018, https://immanuelky.org
/articles/we-were-rachaels-church/.

About the Author

RACHAEL DENHOLLANDER is an attorney, advocate, and educator who became known internationally as the first woman to speak publicly after filing a police report against former USA Gymnastics team doctor Larry Nassar, one of the most prolific sexual abusers in recorded history. As a result of her activism, more than 250 women came forward as survivors of Nassar's abuse, leading to his life imprisonment.

For her work as an advocate and educator on sexual assault, Rachael was named one of *Time* magazine's 100 Most Influential People and one of *Glamour* magazine's Women of the Year in 2018. Additionally, she received the Inspiration of the Year award from *Sports Illustrated* and was a joint recipient of ESPN's Arthur Ashe Courage Award, as well as numerous other awards and recognitions.

She has been a guest on CNN, ABC, CBS, NBC, Fox News, the BBC, and NPR. She regularly appears in national and international print media, including the *Washington Post*, the *Wall Street Journal*, and the Associated Press, and is a *New York Times* and *Vox* op-ed contributor.

Rachael has been recognized and honored in both the Kentucky and Michigan legislatures for her advocacy, and she has been active in spearheading legislative reform at the state level. She has lectured and participated in live Q&As on the campuses of numerous universities across the nation, including Harvard University, New York University, and the University of

Southern California. She continues to educate others on issues of abuse by supporting and speaking at organizations that advocate for victims of sexual and domestic abuse, teaching at abuse-prevention conferences, and helping companies and other institutions create safe environments for addressing abuse and harassment.

Prior to beginning her work as an advocate and educator, Rachael worked in public policy, performed research and wrote for human rights organizations, and spoke widely, including testifying before state judiciary committees.

A member of the California Bar Association, Rachael holds a juris doctor from Oak Brook College of Law, based in Fresno, California, and possesses an honorary doctorate from the American University of Paris.

She and her husband, Jacob, live in Louisville, Kentucky, with their four young children.

LET YOUR LITTLE GIRL KNOW SHE IS WORTH MORE THAN SHE CAN IMAGINE.

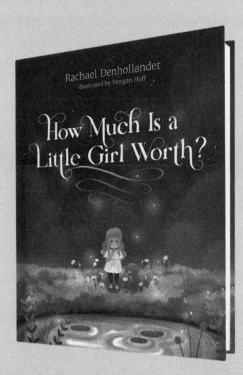

Your value is found not in what you can do

Or the things you accomplish and win.

It is found in how you were made, precious girl—

Created and cherished by Him.

How Much Is a Little Girl Worth?
will inspire young girls to understand
how precious they truly are.